Archibald Alexander

Theories of the Will in the History of Philosophy

Archibald Alexander

Theories of the Will in the History of Philosophy

ISBN/EAN: 9783337078034

Printed in Europe, USA, Canada, Australia, Japan

Cover: Foto ©ninafisch / pixelio.de

More available books at **www.hansebooks.com**

THEORIES OF THE WILL

IN THE

HISTORY OF PHILOSOPHY

BY

ARCHIBALD ALEXANDER

NEW YORK
CHARLES SCRIBNER'S SONS
1898

PREFACE

In the following chapters will be found a concise account of the development of the theory of the will, from the earliest days of Greek thought down to about the middle of the present century. It is not sufficiently comprehensive to be called a history, for it includes only the theories of the more important philosophers, and does not by any means exhaust the literature of the subject. In addition to contributing something to the history of philosophy, it has been my purpose to introduce in this way a constructive explanation of voluntary action. After some years of study in the preparation of such a constructive theory, I am confirmed in the opinion that a historical treatment is indispensable to a proper presentation of the subject; and this essay is the first of a series. The account closes with the theory of Lotze, chiefly as this is contained in his earlier treatise, *Medicinische Psychologie*. This termination is not altogether arbitrary. During the last quarter of a century, as all readers of philosophy are aware, the methods of psychology have been greatly modified, if not revolutionized. It is a change which has been brought about by several causes. Without doubt, the most efficient of these has been the rise and increasing importance of the theory of natural evolution, as presented by Darwin, and as adopted or modified by his successors. Whether we admit the principle, wholly, or in part, or not at all, it will hardly be denied that the effect of the emphasis laid upon evolution has been to regard no psychical states as self-explanatory, but rather as a result of antecedent conditions, possibly as a compound of simpler elements. This has been manifested conservatively in the tendency to seek the germs of psychical states in the adult, in the conscious life of the infant; it has been manifested more radically in the attempts made to find at least analogies, if not connecting links, between the psychoses observed indirectly in the lower animals and those observed directly in man. In the same way, the tendency to seek in the lower species initial stages in that process of which man's body is the present result, has led to the special study of the human brain from the point of view of comparative anatomy and animal physiology. The union of such methods with older methods which had led to the localization of mental functions in the organs of the central nervous system, while beset by many difficulties, is likely to produce important results. It is not unreasonable to expect that the genesis of conscious volition may be explained not only by the more rudimentary processes in the child, but also by the phenomena presented in the lower animals.

In this account of the earlier theories, I have tried to avoid intruding my own opinions as much as possible. But it may appear that speculation and the introspective method of studying the will have almost reached their limits. The state of contemporary psychology makes this equally apparent. I have ventured to express an individual judgment only on matters of doubtful interpretation, and it is hoped that where the interpretations of higher authorities are questioned, there is justification for at least a difference of opinion.

In some cases the chronological order has been disregarded, in order to exhibit more clearly the logical relations of certain doctrines to each other. The doctrines of the will in Christian Theology have been considered in a separate chapter, although they form a part of the development of systematic thought. I have used the term will with and without the definite article; and neither use is to be understood as implying or justifying any particular theory of faculties. I make no apology for the extensive quotations from certain authors, without translating them into English. Especially in the case of the German writers, the advantage of quoting the original is self-evident.

A. A.

CONTENTS

INTRODUCTION

Nemesis follows philosophers in their efforts to use language with precision. A writer may coin words to define his scientific doctrine, or may adopt words from ordinary speech, and give them a special meaning. Like the coinage of money, the coinage of words must represent some recognized standard. The technical terms must be redeemable in language which can be understood, or there will be obscurity and pedantry. Unfortunately ordinary words adapted to philosophical uses carry their popular associations with them, and are often inadequate to convey distinct impressions. Conversely the language of philosophy finds its way very soon into the speech of every day, and its original meaning is lost. In addition to this, language has been used ambiguously by philosophers themselves. An author will often use a word in more than one sense, and two or more authors will often use the same word in different senses. This misfortune has been all the greater, because of the interchange of philosophical conceptions among nations speaking different languages. There was less confusion from this cause when Latin was in general use, although complaints might be made of what Lucretius calls *egestatem linguae.* But philosophy now speaks the languages of all civilized nations, and in the translation of terms there is wide opportunity for error. The philosophy of the Absolute translated literally into English, furnishes an example of such confusion. The word *will* is an example of this unfortunate ambiguity. Among some writers on psychology there is reluctance to use it, and a tendency to resort to various devices in order to escape equivocation. The ambiguity extends to many words often used in connection with the subject; such as, *motive, choice, freedom,* and *necessity.* A definition of will involves a consideration of the history of theories; it involves criticism, and even controversy. Some writers have defined the term, others have thought it indefinable. It has been used in a general psychological sense, to denote the whole character and disposition of man, together with the expression of these in action. It has been used in a special sense to describe the *fiat* of the mind in effecting action, an intellectual affirmation or denial, an impression, a muscular feeling, or a nervous impulse. It has further been used to denote a general metaphysical or moral principle, as in the systems of Kant and Schopenhauer. Moralists have fixed its meaning in conformity to their practical needs; metaphysicians have sometimes discussed it, with very little reference to the facts of consciousness. Above all, the whole subject has been confused by that interminable dispute usually called "the free-will controversy." Probably the most fruitful source of obscurity has been the readiness of both learned and unlearned men to launch themselves upon this debate without determining the nature of the will, before discussing its freedom.

While, at the outset, it seems inadvisable for me to attempt to define the will, a provisional statement may be made in order to point out the general field which is to be traversed. Will is a general term, applicable to certain psychical events, and is primarily an object of psychology. These events are not all of the same kind. They cannot be called conscious states or acts, for some philosophers hold that there is unconscious volition. They cannot be said to be peculiar to man, for theologians treat of the will of God; and there are no good grounds for denying that there is will in the lower animals. They cannot be said to be altogether deliberate, for there is a distinction between impulsive volition, and volition with a purpose. However we may interpret the proposition, *I will*, there is substantial agreement as to that which is to be interpreted. But theories of the will in the history of philosophy vary so widely, that any definition given now would be inadequate to comprehend them all.

The student of philosophy is concerned chiefly with the human will. The will of God, either transcendent or immanent, is more properly an object of theology. The will as an ontological principle, not identified with God, calls for incidental notice, although this conception has not been of frequent occurrence in Western thought. The physiological aspects of subject have not been of importance until the present century. I shall therefore consider principally the psychological and ethical doctrine of the will in the history of philosophy.

Like some other conceptions of psychology and ethics, a doctrine of the will cannot be merely descriptive ; it involves explanatory discussion. It is closely related to problems of ontology, the theory of knowledge, and logic. In successive systems, there have been various methods of interpreting this relation. Some philosophers deduce their theory of the will from general principles; others are satisfied with the results of the empirical method, or an appeal to consciousness; others draw conclusions as to what the will is, by setting out with a moral theory of what the will ought to be.

The historical method of introducing this subject has certain serious disadvantages. It leads the student through chapters of unprofitable controversy. The history of the doctrine has been to a great extent a history of the dispute about freedom and its opposite, which has an unpleasant notoriety. Any one who troubles himself or others with this subject is popularly looked upon as the victim of *une idée fixe*, and consigned to the class of zealots who have hopes about the quadrature of the circle. Few will agree with Milton that discourse upon necessity and free will is to be reckoned among the joys of Paradise. Many will remember with approval that Laud forbade his clergy to preach about predestination. There are legends of those who have been driven to suicide by the mysteries of Calvinism or the Third Kantian Antinomy. But aside from the question of utility, almost every thoughtful man has "views" about the will, which may affect the tenor of his life. In such individual opinions are to be found every kind of conception, from the crudest fatalism to the most extreme doctrine of contrary choice. Still, the disputes of the past have not been fruitless, and there is no good reason why "the problem of the will" should be thought insoluble.

The development of the doctrine of the will is an example of the progress from the homogeneous to the heterogeneous; or, to use an older phrase, the genus will has been differentiated into its species. For at the beginning will was not distinguished from other states of mind. The actions of men were ascribed to sense or feeling or reason. The earliest philosophers made no clear distinction between willing and doing, wherein they were nearer the truth than many modern writers have been. In the system of Aristotle, will was distinguished from other states of the soul, and different species were described. In the theology of the Christian Fathers the term acquired a more general significance, as is fairly represented in the words of Augustine: "We are nothing else than wills." From the time of Descartes, the intension of the term began to decrease; and Spinoza, for example, recognizes no distinction between will and intellectual affirmation or denial. Hume and those who follow him deny the primacy of the will, and apply the term to a species of impression. Theologians have for the most part followed the Patristic usage; and the same may be said of Kant and many German philosophers since his day. The principle, however, upon which the doctrine has developed may be called evolution, or a process of alternate analysis or synthesis, or successive generalizations and specifications. The mind was analyzed into distinct faculties or states; these elements were studied, until the necessity arose for a new synthesis. At the same time, I may be permitted to enter a caveat against any artificial construction of the progress of thought. The growth and decay and revival of doctrines cannot be proved to be an organic process, like the development of a single complex organism. It is analogous rather to the irregular appearance of vegetation over a wide tract of country. All the plants there are not of the same height, or of the same species, and do not bear fruit at the same season. The history of philosophy is still an inductive science, and *schematismus* is here likely to cause dislocation and disorder. For not only are objections present to such an artificial arrangement in the general history of philosophy, but especially in the arrangement and classification of theories of the will. In philosophy generally, there is usually a certain logical and real relation between method and principles, between principles and their application. But particular doctrines of the will are not necessarily implied in the theories of philosophers about other principles. We may not infer that Epicurus was a determinist because of his materialism; nor that, because the Stoics taught a doctrine of self-control, they be-

lieved in free will. The teaching of the Critique
of Pure Reason does not consistently apply to the
Critique of Practical Reason. There is an empirical theory of knowledge, but it does not imply
necessarily any particular theory of the will.
Empirical principles may lead logically to a
certain view of volition, but we shall find no historical justification for saying that they have always
done so. I shall therefore first simply consider the
origin of the doctrine of the will in Western thought,
and then proceed to give an account of a series of
typical examples.

Attention was attracted to some of the phenomena of will at a comparatively early period.
Without repeating the familiar story of the rise of
systematic philosophy out of the primitive mythology and cosmogony of Greece, there are two ideas
which first emerged, and which may be first discussed.

I. The Principle of Fate in relation to human
   action;
II. The Opposition discovered between Reason,
   or Understanding, and Feeling.

In relation to these two ideas a theory of the
will was developed. It need not be asked which
came first in order of time. In the earlier literature they were synchronous. In each of them a
conflict is implied,— in the one case between a
supernatural principle and a natural order; in the
other, between a rational tendency and the feelings. To adjust the conception of man's autonomy

to belief in the irresistible power of Fate was the first problem. In solving it, or attempting to solve it, the science of ethics was born. Thus volition was first distinguished as a principle of ethics.

There should be caution in making psychological inferences from the free and naïve language of the early poets,—such as the terms used in Homer to denote different states of mind. They have little more scientific significance than his well-known localization of psychical functions in organs of the body. Germs of subsequent philosophical opinion are doubtless to be found in his epics; as, for example, where he is cited by Plato as a witness to the difference between the rational and emotional elements in man.[1] The characters of the *Iliad* and of the *Odyssey* are distinctly drawn, while the souls of gods and heroes are portrayed as an arena upon which feelings are contending for the mastery. Where it is not explicitly stated, it is at least implied that the reason can control the passions; but the crude psychology of the poet need not be further noticed. We find in Homer, however, a plain recognition of divine supremacy, particularly the supremacy of Fate. This conception is characteristic of almost all Greek thought and Greek literature, down to the time of the Alexandrian schools. It is a conception which has philosophical importance. The term Fate is used indifferently in the singular and plural. The Greek terms Μοῖρα and Εἱμαρμένη refer

---

[1] See Homer, Od. III. 272, 342, 395.

to that which has been actually allotted or ordained. The Latin equivalent is *Parcae*, used in the plural only. According to Hesiod, the Fates, three in number, have an origin; yet Μοῖρα from the earliest times was looked upon as an independent principle, and sometimes as superior even to Zeus. Aristotle is inclined to identify the fatal principle with God, to whom many names are given. One of these names is Fate, another is Necessity.[1] The Fates are originally the decrees or allotments of the gods, especially of Zeus. In the literature before Aristotle there had been two views taken of the relation between Fate and God. On the one hand, Fate was a decree, dependent for its effectiveness upon the divine will. On the other hand, it was personified, and conceived of as an independent principle controlling the acts of gods and of men. The former view is that of Aristotle also, and he is thus free from the inconsistency of the popular myths which sometimes left the relation of Fate to Zeus undetermined. Du Maistre has said that Greece was born divided. It was natural that the patronage and influence of the gods should be associated with the fortunes of individual men and communities. The defeat of one city by another, the successes and disasters of particular families or persons, was ascribed to the agency of the gods. A god had conferred or withdrawn his favor. The plans of one deity had been thwarted by another. The power of the lesser gods was merely relative. The vicissitudes of Greeks and Trojans in the

---

[1] Aristotle, De Mundo, 401, b. 20 f.

Iliad were ascribed to the alternate successes and failures of protecting divinities. But the intervention of Zeus was always sufficient to decide the conflict. Defeat or victory came at his bidding. He had local temples, but was not a local divinity. He was without fixed prejudices. He had unlimited power. In the council of the gods, the plans of Zeus are law. In the changes of war, the gods appeal to him. He is king of mortals and immortals.[1] He is the god of kings. Even in the tragedies his sovereignty is recognized. None of the gods is eternal. In Hesiod's *Theogony* we are left in doubt as to the beginning of divine existence, unless we regard the eternal universe as the parent of all deities. In the old polytheism, therefore, there is the inconsistency of a Supreme God who has an origin in time. Evidently in allusion to the mystery of their influence, the Fates, like sleep and death, are children of Night.[2] The distinction noticed by Hesiod between the fatal three was adopted by later writers, explicitly by Plato and Aristotle. It is seldom that the decrees of Zeus are considered as subject to the control of Fate. There is a notable exception in the *Iliad*, where Sarpedon's life is in danger. Zeus is summoned to interfere, but refuses on the ground that the hero's death had been ordained by Fate.[3] In the *Prometheus* of Æschylus it is said that Fate is above Zeus, but

---

[1] Homer, Il. I. 525, 554; XII. 241, 242; Od. IV. 78, 237. Æschylus, Suppl. 589 f.; Prom. 550. Sophocles, Electra, 174, 175; Antigone, 604, 610.

[2] Hesiod, Theogon. 217.   [3] Homer, Il. XVI. 433 f.

the surprise and horror of the chorus at the speaker's impiety show that this sentiment was not in harmony with the ordinary belief.[1] The harmony of both views is evident, if it be remembered that the decrees of God were thought to be fixed as soon as uttered. They could not be recalled. This is the interpretation of Seneca, who finds consolation in the inevitable necessity of Fate which governs both gods and men. *Jupiter ipse omnium conditor ac rector* inscribes the Fates, yet follows them.[2] The Latin writers followed the Greek in their conception of the fatal principle. Thus even the conceits of the old mythology have a philosophical meaning. This belief in a mythical principle, which was afterwards to assume an abstract form, was an article of the popular religion. The old creed was deeply fixed in the mind of the people. The frequent comments on the poets in the writings of philosophers, and the respectful attitude of historians, show how firm a hold the earlier epics and stories had acquired. The persistence of this religious faith is further exhibited by the success of Neo-Platonism, in which an abstract and metaphysical polytheism was presented in speculative dress. Negatively it is evident that Augustine, when at a late day he attacked the old Roman religion in his *De Civitate Dei*, was referring to opinions still firmly held by his contemporaries.

The idea of Fate is one of the marks of the transition from the mythical to the philosophical

---

[1] Æschylus, Prom. 513–520. [2] Seneca, De Provid. V.

conception of nature. It shows, at any rate, a tendency to reach a principle of unity higher than the gods. At length the mythical idea of Fate was exchanged for that of fatal necessity as a principle of philosophy. This doctrine of fatal necessity prevailed in a great part of ancient thought. It was rejected, however, by the later Academy, and by the Epicureans; and Cicero declares: *anile sane et plenum superstitionis fato nomen ipsum.*[1]

According to Hegel, Fate was the necessary principle which controlled generally the acts of gods and men. The gods were creatures of the popular imagination. The fatal principle had its own sphere, and interfered when there was a collision of interests.[2] Comte, regarding polytheism as a development from fetichism, and monotheism as a transition to a positive view of nature, shows that polytheism, when fully developed, introduced under the name of Fate or Destiny a general conception to serve as a fundamental principle of invariable natural laws. To the primitive man, nature seemed arbitrary and irregular; experience revealed the uniformity of natural law. To the ancient world, Fate was the principle of unchangeable uniformity, the necessary corrective of polytheism.[3] This view is consistent with that of Aristotle, to which reference has just been made.

The relation of this principle to human action, as well as to the purposes of the gods, was also considered by Greek and Roman writers. How-

---

[1] Cicero, De Divin. II. 7.   [2] Hegel, X_2, 100.
[3] Comte, Phil. Pos. III. 308, 309.

ever genial and attractive the earlier polytheism may have been, a minor note is audible in all classical literature. There is a point at which human effort and human action are in vain. While it is expressed in the earlier epics, and recognized by some of the elegiac and lyric poets, the principle of Fate appears most prominently and significantly in the tragedies. The stories or legends upon which these were founded were well adapted to illustrate the subjection of man to this higher power. There is a difference which is very suggestive, between the view of this taken by Æschylus and Sophocles respectively. The Fate of the former is less blind and arbitrary. The events are inevitable, but they follow each other with some show of justice. The moral questions are less perplexing. The rebellion of Prometheus is the ground of his torture and perdition. It is necessity which makes the retribution inevitable; but there is no intimation that necessity impelled him to steal the heavenly fire, or to defy the power of Zeus. The *Persæ* preaches resignation to the evils sent by the gods.[1] The *Septem* declares that submission is the parent of beneficence;[2] the *Agamemnon*, that justice will be done to the poor and humble; the *Choephori* connects the Furies with retribution,[3] while the *Eumenides* presents an impressive picture of deities pleading in the court of Areopagus. It is chiefly in the *Prometheus* that the moral difficulty of divine omnipotence is raised. We ask

---

[1] Æschylus, Pers. 285.　　　[2] Id., Sept. contr. Theb. 206.
[3] Id., Choeph. 636 f.

whether a man, who has defied God for the benefit of his fellows, should be found guilty. The divine supremacy is vindicated at the expense of justice and mercy. The catastrophes in the other tragedies of Æschylus are of another kind. Clytemnestra, with her guilty love for Ægisthus, is not a very suitable instrument for executing celestial justice, and avenging Iphigenia's death. But Clytemnestra perishes by the hand of Orestes. If the sacrifice of Iphigenia was justifiable, Agamemnon was unjustly slain; but if Agamemnon was justly slain, the vengeance of Orestes was unjust; if the vengeance of Orestes was unjust, he was unjustly acquitted by Athene, but if just, the torments inflicted by the Furies were unjust. Such are some of the alternatives suggested. The moral of these tragedies is that punishment follows crime. Fate makes the punishment inevitable. Justice is allied with Fate, and the Furies are their ministers.[1] The subjective states of the *dramatis personae* are of secondary importance.

The moral issues raised by Sophocles are even more perplexing. The blind and arbitrary work of Fate is vividly set forth in the familiar story of Laius. A series of inevitable catastrophes overwhelm the unconscious agents. Œdipus, for example, leaves the oracle aware of his criminal destiny. He kills his father at the trivium, not because of parricidal feelings, but in ignorance of his parentage. He is a victim of events in which he has been the chief but most unconscious actor. It is repugnant

---

[1] Æschylus, Eumen. 324.

to ordinary conceptions of responsibility. It is quite in accordance with Greek ideas that the consequences of his acts should pursue him. The suicide of his mother, and his own self-inflicted blindness, are the beginnings of the misfortunes which are continued in the *Œdipus Coloneus* and in the *Antigone*. The same relentless Fate appears in the pathetic story of Philoctetes, whose bravery is rewarded by the persistent tortures of his wound, and in the *Ajax*, where the hero has sacrificed his honor in a fit of madness. Of Sophocles one may say with the scholiast: "He would affirm that neither the things done in heaven, nor on earth, nor in the sea happen, except according to Fate."[1] It is this which determines the death of Laius,[2] the crimes of Œdipus, the madness of Ajax, the sorrows of Philoctetes, and the vengeance of Orestes and Electra. There is a collision between the individual purpose and the divine order.

The form of the French classic drama, borrowed from the Greek, illustrates the same kind of ideas. Carlyle has compared this unfavorably with the conceptions of English and German dramatic writers.[3] But in the latter, although the effects are not always attributed to Fate, the principle appears disguised in psychical and ethical forms. Faust may deliberately and freely bind himself to the devil, but after the compact has once been made, there is no retreat. The "Fate

[1] Scholia, Sophocles, Antigone, 951.
[2] Sophocles, Œdip. Rex, 711-714.
[3] Carlyle, VII. 154.

and metaphysical aid "[1] of Macbeth and his consort is unscrupulous ambition, so uncontrolled as to become the "insane root that takes the reason prisoner." Even the irresolution of Hamlet seems to be inevitable and to produce inevitable results. It is the manifestation of a character which he is unable to overcome. He is an example of the Pyrrhonist, who submits to the order of circumstances, rather than resist the course of events and oppose a sea of moral troubles. In the modern drama the determination of actions is ascribed to subjective states. Fatalism holds that certain results will be effected, whatever may be willed to prevent them. The ordinary theory of moderate predestination is kindred to this; the purpose of God will be accomplished, whatever may be willed to the contrary. Logically the fatalist should say that the will is determined by means of motives. There is an obvious difference between the assertion that an end will be attained because men are determined so to will, and the assertion that an end will be attained whatever men will. It was possibly the idea of the fatal order as divine which gave the ancient tragedies their religious importance. If we remember the fear and reverence of the gods in the Greek and Roman world, the recognition of divine supremacy and human dependence, we can understand the significance of the Epicurean revolt against the popular theology, and the substitution of chance for necessity in spite of a materialistic philosophy. We may also understand why Lucre-

___

[1] Shakespeare, Macbeth, I. 5.

tius thought belief in the gods to be one of the two great evils, and preferred to imagine them as remote from all human interests. And yet the fatalism of the Stoics was not altogether in harmony with the ethics of the Greek theatre. The Stoics were impressed by the needless display of passion on the stage. In reacting against emotional tendencies, they taught the wisdom of apathy, of submission to the fatal or natural order, which could not be changed, which should be endured.

Belief in a fixed supernatural order of events is related also to man's curiosity concerning the future. The ancient fatalism, like the modern, was a motive to seek knowledge of what was about to happen. In the absence of a prophetic class, such as was to be found in ancient Israel, the Greeks and Romans consulted oracles at the seats of the gods, examined the entrails of animals, observed omens and prodigies, in order to gain knowledge of the future. Aside from the repeated references by historians to these practices, the treatise of Cicero, *De Divinatione*, presents the arguments employed in their favor, but argues that these practices are unnecessary and useless. Divination was favored even by the Emperor Julian, who himself assumed the functions of an augur. The oracular sayings were usually so ambiguous as to justify the idea that the future was contingent. But it is logical to infer that if coming events can be foretold, their occurrence must have been previously determined. If the prophecy or oracular prediction could be reversed by human agency, the

c

information acquired might be useful, but would prove to be untrue. This contradiction is well represented in the famous dilemma of the crocodile, which so amused the ancient authors.[1]

The crocodile promises to return the child which he has taken, on condition that the parent is able to say truly what the animal has decided to do. If the parent says that the child is about to be returned, when the crocodile has determined to devour him, then the child will be lost; but if the parent says that the child is not about to be returned, when the crocodile has determined to return him, then the child will likewise be lost. The crocodile will adhere to his determination in any event, and it is this which creates the difficulty.

Fatalism and indeterminism have one point in common. Both minimize the importance of *antecedent causes* in relation to *human action*. What Fate accomplishes, irrespective of human volitions, that is effected by *liberum arbitrium*, when the action of the will is undetermined. The problem of the freedom of the will in its philosophical sense was not suggested until the subjective side of man's nature had become an object of inquiry. The philosophical theory of fatal necessity recognized the determination of the will by necessary causes, but did not apprehend the psychological process involved. A merely theological or metaphysical answer is insufficient. The problem is chiefly psychological.

[1] See Lucian, Vit. Auct. 22; Hermot. 81; and Lotze, Logik, 337.

Having thus noticed the antithesis between Fate and human action, as suggesting the questions about the will, I shall turn to the other antithesis, between the emotional and rational elements in man's nature.

The psychology of all the Socratic philosophers was undeveloped, and their moral teaching was independent of their metaphysical and physical theories. Our sources of information show that their view of the will was only rudimentary, if indeed they can be said to have had the subject before them at all. The ethics of the period before Socrates were didactic, and were commonly in the form of maxims. In no instance is there any scientific treatment of human conduct. In the primitive Pythagorean doctrine, attention was directed to the relation of the body to the soul. The soul was said to be imprisoned in the body; its activity is hampered and hindered by this connection.[1] This view was in accordance with the ascetic morality of the order. The object of the Pythagorean discipline was to attain to communion with the gods. To this religious end, all the exercises of soul and body are directed. The limitation of the soul by the body is a conception which does not involve a theory of volition, but its relation to such a theory is obvious. The directions given for the attainment of this end imply a belief that, although the body limits the soul, it is itself subject to voluntary restraint. The Pythagoreans insisted upon the control of the appetites,

---

[1] Plato, Phædo, 62.

the observance of stated periods of silence, and temperance. In their psychology, they are said to have anticipated the Platonic partition of the soul into the rational and irrational,[1] as well as the threefold division of the parts of the soul, and the specification of the different kinds of knowledge. Plato objects to the Pythagorean doctrine that the soul is a harmony, on the ground that by this the body is made the master of the soul. The philosophy of Heraclitus, in which may be discerned germs of Stoic doctrine, lays emphasis upon the worth of the rational, as distinguished from the sensual or emotional life. Virtues such as orderly living and contentment are placed above conformity to the lower appetites.[2] Empedocles notices feelings of pleasure and pain in relation to human action. The object of the will is pleasure, and the will itself is said to be formed of a mingling of elements;[3] but his conception of the faculty is very indefinite. Just as his theory of *similia similibus percipiuntur* maintains a certain likeness between the knowing power and the thing known, so we may here suppose that there is a correlation between appetite and will on the one hand, and the object sought after on the other. The psychology of the early Atomists is likewise imperfect. While the Epicureans, who taught the freedom of the will, derived their physics from Democritus, the early Atomists show no signs of holding any such doctrine. Nothing exists except atoms and empty

---

[1] Cicero, Tusc. IV. 5 ; Theognis. V. 1053.
[2] Zeller, Phil. d. Gr. I. 660.   [3] Plutarch, Plac. V. 28.

space, and the soul is composed of atoms. There is no beginning of motion, and Aristotle says that the philosophers of this school never investigated the origin of motion. Whatever happens, happens of necessity. The soul which is composed of atoms must come under this general law.[1] In his practical teaching, Democritus observes the distinction between the happiness which comes from within by the rational ordering of the soul, and that which comes from external causes, preferring the former to the latter.[2] A like disparagement of outward or sensible good is found in the doctrine of Anaxagoras, who is said to have attached value rather to the contemplation of the structure of the universe, than to the satisfaction of the appetites. Thus the Eleatic distinction between the world of sense and the world of reason has its ethical correlative in most of the Pre-Socratic philosophy, in the antithesis between the moral life of the reason and that of the appetites. Among the Sophists, the theory of Prodicus of Ceos alone has special reference to the will. He is the author of a fable on the choice of Hercules,[3] in which a distinction is implied between desire for pleasure on the one hand, and moral purpose on the other. It is plain from this famous story that where attractive objects lure the appetite, the moral agent has it in his power to resist and refuse them.

This antithesis between the rational principle on the one hand, and the sensual principle on the other,

---

[1] Lange, Geschichte des Materialismus, Art. Atom.
[2] Fragm. I. 2, 8. [3] Aristotle, Eth. Eud. I. 1215, b. 6.

which appears in the early philosophy, has never disappeared from moral science. It is recognized in modern language as well as in modern thought. We say that a man is overcome with grief, is overpowered by anger, or is under the dominion of appetite; we do not say that he is a victim to reason, or a slave to any cognitive process. And in the pathology of the mind we recognize emotional insanity, where the feelings are of such a kind or of such intensity as to set at naught the rational processes. The appetite belongs to its subject as really as the train of thought or reasoning, but it is recognized that self-control is the control of the passions by the reason. It may be added, however, that of late years psychologists have been made familiar with an obsession of the mind by suggestion,— some intellectual phenomenon, a fixed idea, which is sufficient to govern the normal passions and the normal process of knowledge. There is therefore justification in philosophy for Goethe's words : —

Zwei Seelen wohnen ach ! in meiner Brust.

CHAPTER FIRST

THEORIES OF THE WILL IN THE SOCRATIC PERIOD

In the accounts of the teaching of Socrates, we find that he dealt with the doctrine of the will upon its moral side. In some respects it is difficult to distinguish between his views upon this subject, and those which were held by Plato. While the interest in practical questions was not so pronounced as in the period after Aristotle, the leading philosophers of this era were deeply interested in questions of theoretical ethics. In treating of the theories of Socrates, Plato, and Aristotle under the general head of the Socratic period, I would not be understood as supposing that they held any particular theory of the will in common. While there is a general likeness between the doctrines of Socrates and Plato, the views of Aristotle on this subject are radically different. All three philosophers represent the highest development of Greek thought, and with them philosophy becomes a science.

The moral teaching of Socrates was generally influenced by the conditions surrounding him; the popular religion and the literature of mythology did not satisfy the minds of thoughtful men, nor sufficiently explain the universe. The demand for a more systematic treatment of such questions, especially questions of ethics, may be inferred from the inadequacy of the previous philosophy, and from the moral dilemmas of the Greek tragedies already noticed.

Just as Empedocles had found a correlation between will and pleasure, or rather between pleasure and the demands of the organism, so Socrates regarded the good as correlative to the will.[1] That which is willed is the good; the good is that which is willed. It appears from the account given by both Xenophon and Plato, that Socrates believed man would follow what he thought to be good. The aim of Socrates was not to correct the will, but to inform the understanding. Virtue is not acquired by voluntary practice. Virtue is knowledge.[2] It is therefore teachable. It is because virtue is knowledge that it is teachable.[3] It is not knowledge of particular good things, such as an individual pleasure or utility; it is knowledge of the universal good. This shows it to be in relation to the Socratic theory of conceptions.[4] Just as true science consists in such a knowledge as will make possible a definition of the thing known; so true ethical science consists in such a knowledge as will enable one to define the good sought. If the object sought is definable, it will be related to the genus good, and the knowledge of the genus is virtue.

---

[1] Xenophon, Mem. III. 9, 4; IV. 6, 6.
[2] Aristotle, Eth. Nic. VI. 1144, b. 17.   Plato, Laches, 194.
[3] Plato, Meno, 87, 89.   [4] Id., ib. 74.

When the man knows the good he will do it.
Pleasure is not the good, although the good is the
useful.[1] The virtuous principle is intellectual, not
emotional, or voluntary. If he who knows the good
will do it, and only the ignorant are vicious, then it
is knowledge which determines the will. This is
the conclusion which must be deduced from the
ethics of Socrates.

Of the Socratic schools, the Megarics alone made
the will an object of inquiry. But for certain reasons, the Megaric theory may be more conveniently
considered in connection with the teaching of the
Post-Aristotelian philosophers.

PLATO

Plato distinguishes between voluntary and involuntary actions. He discusses them in their
psychological and ethical relations. The theory
fundamental to his whole philosophy is the Dialectic, the theory of Ideas. The question may therefore be raised at the outset: what relation, if any,
have the Ideas to the voluntary actions of man.

The Ideas are universal essences, in this sense,
that they are the real being by virtue of which all
things are what they are. They are the forms or
archetypes of which all existing things bear the
image. The object of sense is what it is, not only
because it participates in the universal essences,
but also because it is a copy of a perfect pattern.[2]
The Ideas are, further, the noumena as distinguished

1 Plato, Protag. 358.
2 Id., Timæus, 28; Repub. VI. 501; IX. ad fin.

from the phenomena. The latter are unreal, and transitory; the former are real, and abide. The individual objects of the phenomenal world are known by the senses, and by opinion;[1] the eternal essences are known by the reason only. The Ideas are sometimes represented as dynamic essences, as forces, which produce effects in the phenomenal world;[2] and in the later philosophy of Plato, the Ideas are described as numbers, in conformity to the Pythagorean doctrine that the ἀρχή of the universe is number. All the Ideas have an essential connection with the Idea of the good; which is in accordance with the optimism and ethical character of the Platonic philosophy. This is the Platonic realism, which the schoolmen epitomized in the phrase *universalia ante rem.* It has been said that realism involves determinism, and that to hold the logical doctrine necessitates a denial of the freedom of the will. If this be admitted, Plato's doctrine of the will should be deterministic. If the Ideas be regarded in their dynamic aspect, it might be held that their relation to individual volitions excluded the idea of freedom. It is, however, impossible to rest satisfied with such inferences. For the chief obstacle to a clear understanding of Plato is the obscurity which surrounds his doctrine of the way in which the objects of sense and opinion are related to the Ideas. The former are said to share or participate in the latter; but the term used is not sufficiently explained for us to reach any par-

---

[1] Plato, Repub. V. 477, X. 596; Timæus, 51.
[2] Id., Phædo, 76.

ticular conclusion as to the relation between man's volition and the Ideas.[1] At times, however, the Dialectic is so closely related to the psychological and ethical theories, that complete separation of the two is impossible. In the *Phœdrus*, for example, – the soul is said to be immortal and self-moving, and immortal because self-moving.[2] While the context discusses the nature of indvidual souls, it is probable that the earlier part of the passage refers to the soul as Idea or universal. It is the divine as well as the mortal soul which is said to be the source and first principle of all motion; and it cannot be the individual human soul which is meant, where it is declared that if it did not exist, the whole heaven and all created things would stand still. In this universal soul the particular souls of gods and men participate. Particular souls are in a state of preëxistence in the realm of Ideas; and, guided by some god, each of them is led to the contemplation of eternal truth. They are compared to winged creatures which ascend to this ideal vision. But among those who are so guided, there are some which lose their feathers, and are unable to behold the truth. These fall, and in consequence of their fall are united to mortal bodies. In the *Timœus*,[3] the manner of the union of soul and body is thus described: The offspring of God received from him the immortal beginning or principle of the soul, to which they joined the body as its vehicle. In addition to the immortal principle, a mortal soul was

---

[1] Plato, Parmen. 130, 131. S. Thomas Aq. I. i. Q. V. 2.
[2] Plato, Phœdrus, 245.   [3] Id., Timæus, 44.

placed within the body. The latter was subject to passion, swayed by pleasure and pain, by rashness and cowardice. Each of these souls had its place in a certain part of the body. The immortal principle was put in the head; while the mortal soul was divided into two parts, the emotional soul, and the sensual or appetitive soul. The former was fixed in the region above, the latter in the region below the diaphragm. Both were subjected to the sway of the reason. The control of the appetites was effected by the immortal reason, which was reflected upon the shiny surface of the liver. The emotions were governed through the blood which passed from the head into the cavity of the thorax. This fanciful account is presented by Plato as a mere probability, and as founded on divine revelation. The threefold partition of the soul is further discussed in the *Phœdrus* and the *Republic*.

In the former of these dialogues the doctrine of Preëxistence is asserted, but there is no intimation that the emotional and appetitive principles are mortal. The elements or parts of the soul are compared to two winged steeds and a charioteer.[1] The latter is the reason, while the two former are the emotional and appetitive principles. The control of the horses by the driver is evidently only relative, for it is shown that the black horse which represents the appetites can bring the chariot to ruin by rebellious behavior. The souls of the gods are also compared to two-horse chariots, although neither horse is said to be unruly, and the

---

[1] Plato, Phœdrus, 245, 246 f.

charioteer meets with no mishap. If we unite the statements of the *Timæus* and of the *Phædrus*, we have the inconsistency of the emotional and appetitive souls in the gods, which souls are elsewhere declared to be mortal. But in the *Phædrus* it is expressly stated that the gods have these three souls, and that the two lower souls are parts of the mortal principle. One of these parts is the more noble, which is the emotional; the other is less noble, which is the sensual part. In agreement with the *Timæus* the *Phædrus* declares that the lower souls are swayed by the reason. The steed which represents appetite, upon seeing the object of pleasure, becomes excited, and unless steadily controlled, will bring the charioteer to grief. In the impulsive soul there is a rational element, and it is more obedient to the command of the charioteer. In each of the three souls there is an element of knowledge, for the appetitive soul has a knowledge of the pleasurable object, and the emotional soul has an apprehension of that which excites its anger or courage or ambition or fear. In each of the three souls there is also will, as well as knowledge. That which wills the satisfaction of appetite resides in the lowest soul; that which wills the facing of danger, the avoidance of cowardice and rashness, resides in the emotional soul. Will in a higher sense, as deliberate, conscious preference, is in the reason. This threefold division is explicitly recognized in the *Republic*.[2] The reason is the instrument of knowledge, or learn-

[1] Plato, Timæus, 69 f.   [2] Id., Repub. IV. 440 f.

ing; the emotional soul is subject to anger, fear,
courage, and the noble emotions; the lowest soul
desires the satisfaction of the appetites. The act
of volition is compared to answering a question by
assent; this assent, in the case of appetite, may be
forbidden by the reason.   There may be a collision
between the assent of the appetite and that of the
reason; or between the assent of the emotional
soul and the reason.   The emotional soul is likewise at times in conflict with the appetite, because
it is on the side of the rational principle. The
emotional soul is naturally good, but may be corrupted by education. The reason issues its commands to the θυμός,[1] dictating what it should follow
or fear; just as in the state, the philosophers control the lower classes of citizens. The reason rules
by virtue of its knowledge. And just as in the
state, the control of the laboring class is disas-
trous, so in the soul, disaster follows the dominion
of the appetitive part.

Plato rejects the Pythagorean doctrine that the
soul is the harmony of the body, on the ground
that it implies the control of the soul by the body.[2]
In the *Phœdo* however, the discourse of Socrates
includes a statement of the relation of soul and
body, which bears much likeness to the Pythagorean
teaching. So far is he from supposing that the
body is an advantage to the soul, in knowledge and
virtue, that he views the relation as a misfortune for
the soul, as a limitation and imprisonment of its
powers. And in the tenth book of the *Republic*,

[1] Plato, Timæus, 70.   [2] Id., Phædo, 86, 94.

the lower part is said to belong not to the essence of the soul, but to be incidental to its disfigured existence in the body.[1] We are not to conceive of Plato as teaching any doctrine of an Ego, or of one psychical principle acting by means of the three parts, as if these were faculties. The three parts are compared to the high, middle, and low musical notes of the scale. When the soul is harmonious, each of the three has its proper proportion in the acts of man. But the essence of the soul is rational; the conflict between reason and appetite is not a civil war in the soul, but rather a war of the higher soul with invaders. If we consider will in its aspect as an energy, power, or impulse, we may identify the emotional soul, θυμός, with that faculty; if, on the other hand, we consider will in its deliberative, decisive, aspect, as *arbitrium*, we may place the will in the rational principle of Plato's psychology.

But will in its more general sense cannot be attributed to one part to the exclusion of the others. In some passages Plato speaks as if the appetite swayed a man against his will. A man may be thirsty, and yet unwilling to satisfy his thirst.[2] There is something within him which invites him, but there is also something in him which prevents him. The different species of knowledge described by Plato all imply a certain activity of the soul. Opinion (δόξα) is the pursuit of knowledge by the soul.[3] Intelligence (νόησις [4]) is the longing of the

<hr>

[1] Plato, ib. Repub. X. 603, 610 et passim.

[2] Id., ib. IV. 439.   [3] Id., Cratyl. 420.   [4] Id., ib. 411.

soul after what is novel or unknown. To will
(βούλεσθαι) is said to involve the idea of taking aim,
and deliberating; the voluntary (ἑκούσιον) is con-
trasted with the resistance of necessity.[1] It is the
yielding of the soul to the movement of the will,
and not opposing it. Necessity is spoken of as
that which opposes our will, and things done from
necessity imply mistake and lack of knowledge.
The emotional soul (ὁ θυμός) is a rushing impulse;[2]
and thus the same term stands for the act as for
the faculty. The practical working of the triple
soul is further discussed in the *Republic*. Emotion,
which is a kind of desire, is also to be found
contending on the side of the reason. Both of
these principles may combine to keep in subjection
the appetites; the reason deliberates, and the emotional soul fights under the reason as its com-
mander. Where the lower parts of the soul are
deficient in knowledge, the deficiency is supplied
by the superior knowledge of the reason. The
latter is that which decides; and it is when reason
is asleep that the appetites are awake.[8] In this
account of the relation of νοῦς to ἐπιθυμία, we find
the germs of that theory of the will which views it
as executing the commands of the understanding;
as subject to the control of the reason, and carrying out its intentions. But it is only the germ,
and we are left in doubt as to whether acts in
obedience to appetite which imply the overpower-
ing of the reason are to be considered voluntary,
or whether only deliberate acts should be thought

[1] Id., ib. 420.   [2] Id., ib. 419.   [8] Id., Repub. IX. 571.

to deserve the name. Certainly the ethical teaching of Plato leads us to accept the latter alternative.

If we turn to the moral teaching of Plato, we find that his doctrine of virtue is essentially that of Socrates. It consists in knowledge.[1] Knowledge is its source, and it is manifested in the harmony of the soul. As has been shown, the pristine state of the soul was one in contemplation of the eternal Ideas, and the ethical end is to rise once more to a knowledge of these, particularly to a knowledge of the Idea of the good.[2] When the good is known, it will be realized in the individual life and in the community. The realization of the good in this sense is virtue. Virtue is not a habit of the will, nor does it depend upon conformity to a given moral standard. Its essence is knowledge. That which a man does is determined by that which a man knows. No one who does wrong does it voluntarily,[3] and so there are no voluntary actions which are bad. The threefold division of virtue corresponds to the threefold division of the soul. Each part of the soul has its own appropriate virtue.[4] But each of these virtues is due to knowledge. Temperance and courage, like wisdom, depend on proper knowledge.[5] It must then be inferred that the intemperate man and the cowardly man are involuntarily vicious, for they would be

---

[1] Plato, Meno, 87, 89 f., 97, 99; Repub. VII. 518.
[2] Id., Phædrus, 247; Repub. VI. 500, 505, 516, 517; Timæus, 37.
[3] Id., Protag. 356; Legg, IX. 860.
[4] Id., Repub. IV. 440 f.   [5] Id., Laches, 195.

D

temperate and brave if they had the proper knowledge. The knowledge of the particular good, the
good of mere opinion, which is derived from the
senses, is not sufficient. There must be knowledge
of what Socrates called the general good, that is,
of the Idea. If, then, knowledge of the good is
imparted to man, his will is determined by that
knowledge. It would follow that in such a case
he would practically have no choice; deliberation
would be superfluous. The will is determined by
knowledge, not as mere motive, but as necessary
cause.

It is significant of the equivocation which belongs
to discussions about the will, that philosophers
have differed with respect to the relation existing
between knowledge on the one hand and will on
the other. According to some, the more perfect
the knowledge, the greater the freedom; while,
according to others, it is only ignorant acts which
can be called free acts. Knowledge has a causal
relation to the will, they say, and it determines
the will. The conclusion to be accepted will depend very much on the meaning which is given
to the term freedom. If the Platonic doctrine
be true, it would seem that willing the good depends on knowing the good, and the will in well-
doing is absolutely determined by knowledge which
in so far as it is knowledge is involuntary. Plato
does not raise the question whether knowledge is
voluntary or not. Still, he does not define virtue
as a willingness to know, but as knowledge. It is
conceivable that a man should refuse to be taught,

and if the refusal is involuntary, the refusal is not vicious, but the ignorance which causes the refusal is vicious. If the refusal is voluntary, then it is virtuous; for no one voluntarily does what is wrong. Taking this doctrine in connection with that concerning the teachableness of virtue, it is difficult to see in what sense Plato can be said to have taught the freedom of the will.

In addition to the psychological and ethical view of the will, one may notice also the stress laid by Plato upon the relation of native character, and education to virtue. There is perhaps nothing more modern than the teaching regarding this which is to be found in the *Republic*. Just as it is maintained in other dialogues that virtue is teachable, so in the *Republic* it is said that education is necessary in order to morality. Rules are laid down for the proper training of those who are members of the community. Periodical siftings and promotions occur. The warriors of the state must be chosen and set apart from the laborers, and the rulers must be selected from the warriors. All men are not capable of being thus educated, and some remain in the lowest and least virtuous class through their defective apprehension. Still fewer are capable of becoming philosophers, and of rising to the highest kind of virtue.[1] The famous figure of the cave,[2] in which Plato represents men as bound, with their faces towards the shadows, and away from the light, illustrates the natural condition of a majority of men. To say that virtue is teachable does not

[1] Plato, Repub. II. 376 et seq.; X. 618.   [2] Ib. VII. 514.

mean that all men can be taught. It is in one respect the fault of native character and breeding. For this reason directions are given with respect to the procreation of offspring in the ideal state. It is taught that character is largely dependent on inherited characteristics.[1] But even in the pre-existent state of the soul the character is decided, and we are thus led to consider the Platonic view of the will in relation to the principle of necessity.

Necessity in the Platonic sense is only another name for fatal necessity, and is not to be understood in the more modern logical and metaphysical sense. In the tenth book of the *Republic*, a myth is narrated with some elaboration of detail.[2] The distaff of Necessity, or the distaff which re-volves on the lap of Necessity, is a centre about which are gathered the three Fates, Lachesis, Clotho, and Atropos. These are called the daughters of Necessity; and clothed in white robes, they sing in harmony with the warning sirens. Clotho sings of the present, Lachesis of the past, and Atropos of the future. A prophet approaches and takes from Lachesis the lots or apportionments of life. He then proclaims the decree of Lachesis. He ad-dresses the preëxistent souls of mortals. He sets before them a choice of virtue. Virtue does not take them, but they must take virtue. The choice of the life to be lived will determine the destiny of each soul. The choice is free. He who chooses is re-sponsible for his choice, and God is not responsible. The destiny taken, determines the future character

---

[1] Plato, Repub. V. 460.   [2] Id., ib. X. 616.

of each one. The preëxistent soul is thus free in its choice, and determines its own character. Upon making their choice, the souls go in order to Lachesis, who sends them to Clotho, who in turn conducts them to Atropos. The latter spins the threads of their destiny, and it is thenceforth irreversible. That the doctrine here presented is a doctrine of the freedom of choice in a preëxistent state, there can be no doubt. Plato teaches that the preëxistent soul is free, but has its character determined irreversibly before its union with the body. Just as Christian theology teaches that Man in a state of innocence was free, but lost his freedom by the fall of Adam, so Plato would affirm that the preëxistent soul is free, until it has chosen its lot in life. If it be asked, what makes one soul choose a bad, and another a good character, there is no answer in Plato. If it is the badness of the soul which makes the choice bad, then the character of the soul is determined antecedent to the choice of the character, and the latter becomes a useless formality. To explain why a soul with a character which is neither good nor bad, chooses one destiny rather than another is, however, impossible.

Plato ordinarily employs the myth to explain what is otherwise inexplicable. Whether this particular allegory is to be construed as containing his philosophical doctrine of character or not, the fact that it is introduced, shows the deterministic nature of his system. It is probable that he found it necessary to account in some way for the differences among men, in matters of morality.

For an inconsistency is manifested in the *Republic*, where the instability of the ideal state is referred to.[1] The decay of such a state is owing to the degeneracy of the citizens; but it is hard to understand why the virtuous should become vicious, if virtue depends on knowledge, or is one with knowledge. Upon such a principle a ruler becomes corrupt because he has forgotten the good, not because he wills the evil; for vice is involuntary. If the warrior becomes cowardly, it must be likewise due to forgetfulness; for cowardice is involuntary, and he who knows the good, will be courageous. A disordered people would thus be logically a forgetful people, if at any time they had been virtuous. It is not to be understood, however, that such conclusions were actually drawn by Plato or any of his school.

If the *Hippias Minor* be a genuine work of Plato, a view of the will is there presented which is inconsistent with the account which has just been given. There Socrates defends the opinion that voluntary wrong-doing is better than involuntary. But if the contention in the other dialogues is well founded, that no man does wrong voluntarily, it is idle to discuss the question whether voluntary or involuntary wrong-doing is worse. Aside from the doubtful authenticity of the *Hippias Minor*, the manner of Socrates at the close of the argument is so ironical, and his words so hesitating, that he may well be believed to reject the conclusion into which he seems to be forced.

[1] Plato, Repub. VIII.

But as I have said, I am always wandering up and down about these things, and never abide in the same opinion. Nor is it surprising that I, nor that common men, do this, if wise men like yourselves also wander about. But it is dangerous to us, if when we have come to you, we do not cease to wander.[1]

It seems to me, therefore, that if compelled to choose between the statement of the *Protagoras* and that of the *Hippias Minor*, it is more reasonable to consider the former the true Platonic doctrine.

ARISTOTLE

In the philosophy of Aristotle there is both a psychological and an ethical doctrine of the will. Will is considered as a faculty of the soul and as an element in all moral action. In the writings of Plato, opinion and knowledge are called faculties, but his conception, as we have seen, is that of parts or kinds of soul, and the word faculty is seldom employed. With Aristotle there is a connection between his theory of faculties and his definition of the soul itself.

Soul is defined as the first entelechy of a natural organized body.[2] By entelechy[3] is meant imperfect realization or actualization. Entelechy is midway between potentiality and completed actuality. Aristotle speaks both of faculties,[4] and of different species of souls; but he rejects the idea of parts. There is a nutritive soul, which is the entelechy of

<hr>

[1] Plato, Hipp. Min. 376.   [3] Id. 412, a. 22; 1050, a. 23.
[2] Aristotle, 412, a. 19 f.; 412, b. 5.   [4] Id. 414, a. 29 et al.

plant life; there is a sensitive soul, which is the entelechy of the sensitive animal; there is a desiring or motive soul, which is the entelechy of the emotional and moving animal body; and there is a rational soul, which is the entelechy of the intellectual and rational human being.[1] Some of the faculties are common to man and the lower animals, others are peculiar to man. Like Plato, Aristotle set forth no doctrine of personality. It is therefore not explained in what way the several faculties are related to the subject of thought, nor how they are related to one another. But with the operation of these faculties in conformity to the end ($\tau\epsilon\lambda$os) of each, entelechy becomes energy.

That which distinguishes man from the lower animals is the reason. The universal reason is God, but in man there is an individual reason. The relation of the particular to the universal reason in Aristotle's system has caused some dispute among commentators. Some prefer to regard his philosophy as pantheistic, but it seems more probable that Aristotle taught a theistic doctrine. While, according to his *Logic*, the universal is in each of the particulars, the substance of everything is individual. And it is not justifiable to interpret logical realism as pantheism, however close the connection between them may be thought to be. God is the first mover, but the soul is also said to move itself. As the soul is said to be moved by appetite, desire, and understanding, as well as by the image of external objects, the self-moving

---

[1] Aristotle, ib.

of the soul is to be construed as signifying spontaneity. For in the individual soul there is no absolute beginning of motion. God is not universal substance, for the only substances are singular substances. He is a substance along with other substances, and not the substance of substances. But in the first mover is the source of all other motion and the thought of thought.

There is a theoretical and a practical reason.[1] The former is always passive. It receives knowledge, but originates nothing. It is not a faculty of immediate knowledge, except in so far as the apprehension of first principles or axioms is concerned. The highest principles are not deductions; for all deductions rest ultimately upon certain evident truths ($\phi a\nu\epsilon\rho\acute{a}$), and these are known by the reason. The practical reason is not passive, but active and creative. Thus in Man the reason is both receptive and spontaneous. As theoretical it is *tabula rasa*, and receives the writing of experience.[2] When experience ceases, the writing must cease, and the passive reason is not immortal.[3] The theoretical reason knows what is true or false; the practical, what is good or bad. The practical reason may both deliberate and act. Its deliberation takes the form of the practical syllogism. The major of this is a universal in which the desirableness of some object or end is set forth. The minor is a particular in which some act is said to be sub-

---

[1] Aristotle, 430, a. 18; 432, b. 27.

[2] Id. 430, a. 1; ἐν γραμματείῳ ᾧ μεθὲν ὑπάρχει ἐντελεχείᾳ γεγραμμένον.   [3] Id. 430, a. 22.

sumed under the general conception. The conclusion which follows is a decision that the end is to be sought.[1] The intellect (Διάνοια), which is sometimes used to denote the opposite of body, is often synonymous with reason, for in the *De Anima*, practical intellect is used interchangeably with practical reason.[2]

In the soul there are two moving principles,—desire and reason.[3] Desire is caused by an object, and the object of desire is the occasion for the praxis of the reason. The praxis of the reason is its act when something is declared to be either pleasurable or painful. When the object is declared to be pleasurable, the reason pursues it; when painful, it avoids it. While desire and reason are the moving principles within the soul, Aristotle finds the remote cause of action in the object of desire. But desire is the immediate cause of motion. It may be either irrational, in which case it is called appetite (ἐπιθυμία),[4] or it may be of a certain end, in which case it is called will. There are, however, two kinds of will,—the will of an end and the will of means to an end. The lower desires, or appetites, are common to man and the lower animals. When there is a general will for an end, the means to the end are willed by a union of desire and reason, which may be translated deliberate choice (προαίρεσις). Desire may therefore be a will for an end, or a will for the means to an end. It is not necessary that there

---

¹ Aristotle, 434, a. 16.   ³ Id. 433, a. 9.
² Id. 433, a. 13.   ⁴ Id. 433, a. 21 ff.

should be deliberate choice in willing, but wherever there is deliberate choice, there must be a will of the end.[1]

Will in the general sense (Βούλησις) is said to be constituted or stationed in the reason.[2] The reason does not desire or will, but desire coöperates with reason; and the lower species of desire, the appetite, may contradict the reason. The means by which the object desired is effective on the desire may be either the practical syllogism already referred to, or may be a mental image or phantasm. In the former case, it is not necessary that the premises and conclusion should be fully and explicitly stated. The practical syllogism often has the form of an enthymeme. The highest form of knowledge possessed by the lower animals is the image-making faculty. Neither reason nor phantasy (φαντασία) are motive without desire.

The feelings are excited through the senses, and where there is sensation there may be either pleasure or pain. We feel the pleasure and pain as good and bad; so that the object of desire is the good, either real or imagined.[3]

These doctrines, which are to be found in the Aristotelian psychology, are further noticed in his *Ethics*. It has thus far been shown:—

1. That God is the first mover, but that the reason in man is spontaneous.

2. That the reason alone is not will, except so far as deliberation and judgment are will.

---

1 Aristotle, Eth. Nic. III. 4; 1111, b. 4 ff.
2 Id. 432, b. 5.　　　　　3 Id. 434, a. 5.

3. That it is desire which moves the soul, and that this is determined by the object desired.

It is impossible logically to conclude that Aristotle taught indeterminism in his psychology. The springs of action are proximately desire and reason; remotely, the spring of action is the object desired. The knowledge of the theoretical reason is not voluntary; the knowledge of the object which awakens the desire is not voluntary. The practical reason alone cannot move to action, and both practical reason and desire are moved by the object of desire.

The faculty of deliberate choice is spoken of as something lying between the reason and the desires, but partaking of the nature of each.[1] The dominant principle of action is either desire or deliberate preference, and there is no choice where there is no act of intellect. Things which happen through deliberate choice are likewise distinguished from those which happen according to fortune. But some light is thrown upon the psychological doctrine by a passage in which will and thought (ἡ νόησις) are represented as different aspects of the same conception.[2] Thought determines desire; and, on the other hand, desire is excited by the object which is presented to thought.[3]

This view of the will is still further developed in the *Ethics*. All practice and all deliberate choice are directed toward some good. There are

---

[1] Aristotle, 1065, a. 32; 700, b. 18, 23.
[2] Id. 406, b. 25.   [3] Id. 701, a. 36.

relative or intermediate ends to which man's action is directed, but these in turn are only means for the ultimate attainment of the good. The good does not seem the same to all men, for it may be either real or apparent. The chief good is happiness, and there will be as many kinds of goods as there are kinds of men, according to character and disposition. There is a good which is the end of appetite, but appetite is irrational. Yet, although it is irrational, it has a capacity to submit to the reason.[1] It is obedience to the reason which constitutes the virtue of appetite. The intellect also has its virtues. Corresponding to the distinction between the desires and the intellect is the distinction between ethical and dianoetic virtue. Wisdom and prudence are dianoetic, while liberality and temperance are ethical virtues.[2]

In relation to the will, the conditions of a virtuous act are as follows: —

1. It must be an intelligent act.

2. It must be a deliberate act, proceeding from προαίρεσις.[3]

3. It must be performed upon some fixed principle.

Thus the feelings are neither virtuous nor vicious. There must be deliberate choice of a course of action before there can be virtue or vice. Nor are the virtues faculties or powers. They are acts of de-

---

[1] Id. 1102, b. 13.
[2] Id. 1103, a. 4.
[3] Δι' αὐτα, for the sake of an end.

liberate choice, or at least they are not without
deliberate choice. Virtue is a habit. It is a habit,
not of knowing, but of willing; or, to speak more
precisely, it is a habit of deliberate choice beforehand. That which is to be willed or chosen beforehand is the mean between extremes. This mean
is determined, not by feeling, nor by passion, but
by the reason. Thus while virtue is essentially
dependent on the will, the object of virtuous action
is fixed by the reason. Ἔστιν ἄρα ἡ ἀρετὴ ἕξις
προαιρετική, ἐν μεσότητι οὖσα τῇ πρὸς ἡμᾶς, ὡρισμένη
λόγῳ καὶ ὡς ἂν ὁ φρόνιμος ὁρίσειεν.[1]

In this definition the rational element is twice
emphasized. The act is not only deliberate, which
implies a rational process, but it is defined by
reason (λόγος) and by prudence (φρόνιμος), which
refers to an intellectual virtue.

In the third book of the *Nicomachean Ethics*,
the nature of voluntary actions is more specifically
discussed. The distinction is here expressed by the
adjectives: ἑκούσιον and ἀκούσιον. Involuntary actions are those which are done either through compulsion, or through ignorance.[2] In the former case,
the coercion is from without, and in spite of man's
wish. But actions which are performed because of
threats (under duress) are mixed. They resemble
voluntary actions, however, for when they are performed there is an act of will, and the end of the
action is related to opportunity (κατὰ τὸν καιρόν).[3]
The will moves the body, and the beginning of the

---

[1] Aristotle, 1106, b. 36.
[2] Id. 1109, b. 35.   [3] Id. 1110, a. 14.

movement is from within the man himself.[1] In connection with this, Aristotle notices the question whether a man may be coerced by desirable objects, such as honor or pleasure. He decides that actions from such motives are not compulsory. They are performed because they are pleasurable; so that a man cannot complain that outward circumstances forced him to take a pleasurable course. Compulsion refers to the external force, and Aristotle's argument is that no act is virtuous which is forced upon a man from without.

Actions done through ignorance may be due to ignorance in general, or ignorance of what one should do under certain circumstances.[2] A drunken man, or an insane man, or a vicious man, acts through one kind of ignorance, in the sense that he does not know what he ought to do; but his acts are not involuntary. Yet a man may act under a misapprehension, by mistaking a friend for a foe, by doing something which is forbidden, in ignorance that it was forbidden, as in striking another accidentally when trying to assist him. These are involuntary actions. Thus the essence of the voluntary act lies in the person or doer himself. An act, however, does not have to be rational in order to be voluntary, for there are purely emotional or appetitive acts which are voluntary (from θυμός or ἐπιθυμία).[3]

As has already been said, deliberate choice is a species of will, and is essential to moral action.

---

[1] Aristotle, 1110, a. 11. ἡ ἀρχὴ ἐν τῷ πράττοντι. 1110, b. 4.
[2] Id. 1110, b. 18.   [3] Id. 1111, a. 25.

Children and the lower animals have will, but no deliberate choice.[1] The will in moral acts is therefore different from βούλησις or θυμός or ἐπιθυμία. The will or wish for the end may be directed to an object which it is impossible to attain, as well as to possible objects; deliberate choice is always of the possible, and of the possible only. Appetite is likewise opposed to deliberate choice; it is directed towards the pleasurable, but deliberate choice is not necessarily so directed. Will or wish in general is of the end, while deliberate choice is of the means to an end. The latter is not emotion, for it has a rational element; it is not mere opinion (δόξα), for opinion refers simply to what is true or false, not to the faculty of taking or choosing. As Aristotle says, deliberate choice partakes of reason and intellect, and a choice of some things rather than a choice of others.[2] The object of προαίρεσις is an object of both deliberation and desire. In relation to the practical reason, the decision reached by the deliberate act of the faculty of choice is the same with the conclusion of the practical syllogism.[3]

Aristotle does not agree with Plato that vice is involuntary. According to him the power to do involves also the power not to do. That virtues and vices are within the power of the moral agent is proved by the fact that men are held responsible

[1] Aristotle, 1111, b. 9.

[2] ἡ γὰρ προαίρεσις μετὰ λόγου καὶ διανοίας, ὑποσημαίνειν δ' ἔοικε καὶ τοὔνομα ὡς ὂν πρὸ ἑτέρων αἱρετόν. Aristotle, Eth. Nic. 1112, a. 15.

[3] ἐκ τοῦ βουλεύσασθαι γὰρ κρίναντες ὀρεγόμεθα κατὰ τὴν βούλευσιν. 1113, a. 11.

and punished for their misdeeds, unless these are done under external compulsion. Even faults committed through ignorance are punished, when the agent had it in his power to acquire the requisite knowledge. Plato was wrong in supposing that men were involuntarily depraved and vicious; for when a man becomes intemperate or indulges in other vices, he does so voluntarily. In ethical virtue the habit of willing may make the act involuntary, but volition was necessary to form the habit. But Aristotle does not meet the possible objection, that the morality of the virtuous act done on account of habit, is at variance with his definition of moral action, which involves deliberate preference. From his point of view it would seem that all acts proceeding from ethical virtue were moral only in the beginning, when the habit was voluntarily formed. That the term " *in our power* " does not necessarily refer to the so-called freedom of the will is evident from the identification of that which is voluntary with that which is in our power.[1] It may be said that all men strive after the apparent good, and are not masters of the imagination or phantasy which places before them the object desired. But Aristotle replies that a man is the author of his own habits, and is also the cause of his own imagination. Both of these are within him, and are not external to him. The phantasy is thus placed on the same footing as the will,— both are in our power; and a man is as responsible for his imagination as for his will. Aristotle re-

[1] Aristotle, 1111, b. 20 ff.

E

plies also to Plato, who taught that some men were virtuous and some vicious by nature. To this the answer is made that if a man be born with a knowledge of virtue, just as he is born with a power to see, so that he cannot be anything but virtuous, then virtue is as involuntary as vice.

Still, the *Ethics* of Aristotle do not seem to me to affect the conclusion which I have drawn with respect to his psychology, — that he held a doctrine of determinism. It must be remembered that in the defence of the voluntary character of virtue and of vice, he is not arguing in favor of any form of the doctrine of freedom. He had, rather, two definite objects in view. 1. He wished to refute the Platonic theory that vice is involuntary, and that no man would do wrong voluntarily. Virtue is to him a habit of willing; but the habit is determined by the intelligence (Διάνοια),[1] which is a faculty of knowledge, and by prudence, which is a dianoetic virtue. So, while virtue is theoretically a habit of the will, in order that the habit may be acquired, the intellect must know the mean between the extremes, as well as the fact that virtue consists in such action. The intellect so far determines the virtuous act. 2. He wished to establish his ethical theory for the sake of his *Politics.* The chief good is a political good, and the truly virtuous man is the truly virtuous citizen. The good to be aimed at is political, and all other goods are means to that end. At the very outset of his *Ethics* he declares that they are subordinated to

[1] **Aristotle, 1113, b. 3 ff.**

Politics. The acts of the citizen which are to be called moral are those which he does voluntarily, without external compulsion, and irrespective of legal penalties. Consequently, while there is no sign of the modern issue which is debated by determinists and their opponents, the declaration that only voluntary actions are virtuous or vicious does not imply indeterminism. It is not the action which is determined by motive, or effected by causes, or dependent on character, which he opposes to voluntary actions; but those which are done by compulsion or through ignorance. It may be added that the term *"in our power"* was in use among the Stoics,[1] who were certainly not indeterminists.

Aristotle does not, like the Atomists, attribute everything and every event to necessity. While he identifies God with fate and necessity, he recognizes an element of fortune or chance in the world. Although some uncertainty surrounds Plato's view, he had maintained that the development of the state seemed to be due to chance or fortune, but that a necessary principle had really brought it into being. Aristotle employs the term necessity as an equivalent of force, and from this point of view voluntary actions are of course not necessitated. The essence of the voluntary act is that it is in our power, and due to deliberate choice or to spontaneity. If we accept the doctrine that God is the first mover, that he is one with Necessity, and that he is the form-giving principle, the first efficient and final

---

[1] Epictetus, Enchir. I.

cause, it is difficult to exclude the will from his control. The action towards an end is determined. There is, however, a sphere in which the casual and fortuitous play a part. This may be shown most plainly by considering Aristotle's opinion concerning the principle of contradiction in relation to necessity. While the logical principle of contradiction is very conspicuous in his *Organon* and *Metaphysics*, he takes a peculiar view of the relation of this principle to future time. It applies absolutely to past and present events. It applies to the future only under certain limitations. The past is necessarily what it is. The present is what it is necessarily. But Aristotle denies that all things which are about to happen are about to happen necessarily, and he endeavors to demonstrate this by an examination of the disjunctive proposition. He holds that there is a beginning of future things, and a possibility of their being or not-being. Their being is not necessary, even as their not-being is not necessary. Things are not brought about necessarily, for that would leave no place for chance. All things, then, do not come into being of necessity; being must of necessity be when it is, and not-being when it is not; but it is not necessary that being should be, nor that not-being should not be. It is necessary that a naval battle shall happen or not happen tomorrow. It is not necessary that the battle shall occur, nor is it necessary that it shall not occur. It is only necessary that it either shall or shall not occur. It is, in other words, a contingent or fortuitous event. Chance is in antithesis to nature, which is something fixed and invariable. Chance is introduced to explain the variations due to deliberation and other contingencies. It is evident that Aristotle did not shrink from applying necessity to the will, except in so far as to maintain that if the future were necessarily determined, man would be unwilling to deliberate.[1] Nature is regular and may be predicted; but chance is irregular, and its events cannot be foreseen. Specifically, it is evident that Aristotle regards mere spontaneity as contingent, and actions directed towards an end as determined. As future events, the acts of the will are not necessary, but necessity, in a limited sense, applies to events which are past. Like many philosophers, Aristotle confounded the objective with the subjective in his treatment of modality, as may be seen still further in his opposing the necessary to the possible, so that some necessary events might seem to be impossible. He ascribes the contingent to fortune. It may intervene in voluntary as well as involuntary acts, in an external or in an internal manner. The problem left unsolved by Plato is not solved by Aristotle. Admitting that virtue is a habit, its beginning is not habitual, and the habit must have a beginning. Virtue is a habit of willing a mean between extremes, and so virtuous action must be determined by knowledge. If virtue is voluntary, the knowledge of the mean between extremes must be either voluntary or not.

[1] Aristotle, 18, 19.

If this knowledge is voluntary, it is not explained
by Aristotle why some men have διάνοια of the mean
and some have not.　If the knowledge is involuntary, there is a contradiction in Aristotle's theory
of virtue.

CHAPTER SECOND

In these two schools, theory is subordinate to practice, and the problem to be solved is the problem of life and of character. This may have caused that specialization of the conception of the will which we find in their writings. Voluntary acts were now discussed in relation to the principle of fatal necessity, moral responsibility, and certain logical categories. In this discussion Megaric and Academic philosophers also had a part; and their doctrines will be considered incidentally in this notice of the Stoic and Epicurean philosophy. Both Stoics and Epicureans recognize three parts of philosophy, which may be generally described as, 1. Physics, including Theology; 2. Logic; 3. Ethics. Their theories about the will are related to all of these parts. But I shall reserve for special treatment their discussion of voluntary actions in connection with logical principles, and shall first consider the physical and ethical principles of the two schools.

The Stoics were materialists; for they denied that anything exists except the corporeal. They were also pantheists, in that they identified the universe with God. Particularly among the later philosophers of the school, however, language was used which was quite consistent with belief in a personal God. They affirmed that even abstract notions were material. Some writers of the school identify God with a primitive material principle, but all recognize that there is a governor of the world: —

Κύδιστ' ἀθανάτων, πολυώνυμε, παγκρατὲς αἰεί, Ζεῦ, φύσεως ἀρχηγέ, νόμου μέτα πάντα κυβερνῶν.[1]

And Seneca says: —

sed eundem quem nos Jovem intelligunt, custodem rectoremque universi, animum ac spiritum, mundani hujus operis dominum et artificem, cui nomen omne convenit. Vis illum fatum vocare? Non errabis. Hic est ex quo suspensa sunt omnia, causa causarum. Vis illum providentiam dicere? recte dices. Est enim cujus consilio huic mundo providetur, ut inconfusus eat, et actus suos explicet. Vis illum naturam vocare? Non peccabis. Est enim ex quo nata sunt omnia, cujus spiritu vivimus. Vis illum vocare mundum? non falleris. Ipse enim est, totum quod vides, totus suis partibus inditus, et se sustinens visua.[2]

From this doctrine of God the Stoics drew the logical inference that all events were determined by him. As they found no difficulty in supposing the soul of man to be material, so they attribute to the material universe πρόνοια and *providentia*.[3] The old doctrine of Fate becomes the doctrine of fatal necessity to which all things are subject.

The soul is defined as πνεῦμα or breath, the Latin

---

[1] Cleanthes, in Stobæus, Ecl. I. 30.
[2] Seneca, Nat. Qu. II. xlv.
[3] Cicero, De Nat. Deor. II. 5, 22, 29; I. 8.

spiritus. It is corporeal, and embraces and pervades the entire body. It is one and not many; and the Stoics insisted on this unity more emphatically than did any of their predecessors. The soul has faculties. These are variously enumerated by different writers.[1] All knowledge originates with the senses, and there is nothing in the understanding which was not previously in the sense. It was not consistent with their view of the origin of knowledge that they should ascribe spontaneous activity to the soul in the act of knowledge.[2] Impressions are made upon the soul through the senses, and cause phantasms, which are apprehended; and the knowledge is preserved in the memory (μνήμη). From single perceptions are formed general ideas (κοιναὶ ἔννοιαι). The assent of the mind to knowledge thus received is voluntary. It may reject or accept that which is presented to it. Opinion of the truth or falsity of that which originates in the sense, is not compelled but is voluntary.[3] The ruling principle in Man which is sometimes identified with the soul itself is τὸ ἡγεμονικόν.[4]

Instead of separating the rational, sensual, and emotional principles and faculties in man, as Plato and Aristotle had done, the Stoics taught that the affections and appetites, as well as the reason and the will, reside in the ruling principle. But they distinguish various stages in volition, as follows: 1. Purpose; 2. Impulse; 3. Preparation; 4. Appre-

[1] Tertullian, De Anim. 14.
[2] Plutarch, Plac. IV. 11.
[3] Cicero, Acad. I. 14, 40.   [4] Cicero, Nat. Deor. II. 11.

hension ; 5. Choice; 6. Deliberate preference; 7. Will of the end ; 8. Decision (*arbitrium*).[1]

The soul comes open-handed into the world, and grasps first partially and then wholly the objects which are presented to it. The activity of the emotional states is attributed to the universal life of Nature, and yet these affections and impulses do not constitute virtue or happiness. To follow these is not the object of the virtuous man. Pleasure and pain are not the criteria of moral conduct. The virtuous life is not emotional, but rational; and the virtuous man must cultivate not the passions (πάθη), but apathy (ἀπάθεια), which is indifference to both pleasures and pains.[2] In the unvirtuous man, the ruling faculty or principle is the seat of the affections and impulses, which are opposed to virtue. In the virtuous man, it is the ruling principle, free from emotion and passion, which controls. While the ἡγεμονικόν is the seat of emotion and passion, it is both a rational and a voluntary power. So far it corresponds with the Νοῦς of Plato and Aristotle. The will is a principle not of emotion or passion. It is a principle of apathy. The voluntary element in both knowledge and action is natural to the soul. The Stoics held that virtue is voluntary, and also agreed with Socrates that virtue is teachable. The union of these two doctrines raises a difficulty which the school did not attempt to remove. If virtue is teachable, it is manifest that most men are unvirtuous from an incapacity to learn, rather than from an unwillingness to act. Yet the Stoics held

---

[1] Stobæus, Ecl. II. 162.   [2] Diogenes, VII. 117.

that knowledge, *i.e.*, assent, is voluntary. Chrysippus declared that man's nature predetermines the will to assent, and the will to act. The will is like a cylinder which is made so as to be capable of revolving, and has this capacity as part of its nature. It revolves when it is set in motion. It would not revolve from its shape alone, nor from its motion alone.

But the idea of a virtuous aristocracy which was characteristic of the systems of Plato and of Aristotle, is apparent in the teaching of the Stoics. They did not share the exclusive sentiment of the earlier philosophers, but sought to abolish the barrier which separated Greek and Roman from Barbarian. Yet the virtuous man is the exception, not the rule. In one sense virtue is voluntary, because the ruling faculty can control the affections and passions; yet, on the other hand, man's actions are determined, not only by overruling nature or fatal necessity, but by circumstances, by disposition and education. The individual volitions are determined, as well as the causes which lead to the willing of a particular end. Chrysippus maintained that law forbade the performance of bad actions to foolish men, but made to them no positive commands, because such persons were incapable of doing what is right.[1] The peculiarity of the Stoic determinism is its intellectual character. While the unvirtuous man has his will determined by his feelings and passions, the wise or virtuous man is theoretically he who resists his feelings, and rises

----

[1] Plutarch, Stoic. Repugn. 23, 24.

superior to pleasure and pain. Thus the will of
the wise man is determined, not by the desires or
affections, but by *ratio recta*.[1] The doctrine that
knowledge is voluntary, that the soul is one and
not many, and that both knowledge and will belong
to the ἡγεμονικόν, does not seem to have been thought
inconsistent with the denial of freedom.

The supremacy of the ruling faculty or principle
is well set forth by Cicero, who says : —

Natura est igitur, quae contineat mundum omnem, eum-
que tueatur, et ea quidem non sine sensu atque ratione. Omnem enim naturam necesse est, quae non solitaria sit, neque
simplex, sed cum alio juncta atque connexa, habere aliquem
in se principatum, ut in homine mentem, in bellua quiddam
simile mentis, unde oriantur rerum appetitus. In autem
arborum et earum rerum quae gignuntur e terra radicibus
inesse principatus putatur. Principatum autem id dico,
quod Graeci ἡγεμονικόν vocant: quo nihil in quoque genere
nec potest nec debet esse praestantius. Itaque necesse est,
illud etiam, in quo sit totius naturae principatus, esse omnium optimum, omniumque rerum potestate dominatuque
dignissimum.[2]

The opposition which was noticed in the philosophy of Plato and of Aristotle, between the
rational and emotional elements of the soul, is here
described as taking place within the ruling principle itself. In the vicious as well as in the virtuous man, it is the ἡγεμονικόν which controls. The
difference between the virtuous and the vicious is
that, with the former the rational principle or element is in the ascendant, while with the latter the

---

[1] Cicero, Tusc. IV. 15, 34.   [2] Id., Nat. Deor. II. 11.

emotional pr: ·nle or element controls. According to Plutarch, the Stoics taught that the rational control by the ἡγεμνοικόν effected virtue, and that this ruling principle was exposed to invasion by the sensual, bestial, and unreasonable passions. They become the masters of a man's actions. When the reason becomes corrupt, the judgments in moral matters become perverted. False opinion (δόξα) is at the root of all vice. The soul is moved in opposition to virtue, by what the Latins called *perturbationes*, and when such emotions control, false opinion arises. This explains why Epictetus and others declared that pain and pleasure depend, not on things themselves, but only on our opinions about them. The *perturbationes* and the false opinion are to be corrected by *recta ratio*. Chrysippus denied what was afterwards called the liberty of indifference, holding that it was repugnant to nature to suppose that there could be any effect without a cause. And in this statement we find, for the first time, this historic argument against indeterminism. He illustrated his meaning by the balance which is weighed down, now on one side, now on the other, but always in consequence of some active cause. There may be no manifest cause for a given volition, but there are always causes, which may be hidden, which secretly move and induce men, and so determine their volitions. In the face of this statement, he maintained, however, that certain volitions may be due to chance, that is, may be fortuitous.

That man should have natural emotions and pas-

sions at all is due to misapprehension; and so the
Stoics virtually accepted the Socratic doctrine that
no man errs voluntarily. They agree also with
Aristotle that emotions may be awakened by an
exciting phantasm, or image. The contradiction
in the Stoic ethics may be partially reconciled, if
we regard them as making virtue depend on both
knowledge and volition. Whichever element be
emphasized the result is the same. If strength of
will be required for self-restraint, the strength is
necessarily predetermined; and if knowledge be
required to prevent the control of passion, man errs
through ignorance, although the connection of assent with voluntary elements does not warrant one
in drawing the same conclusion as was reached
with respect to the determinism of Socrates. While
assent is voluntary, it does not follow that all
knowledge is voluntary, and that the virtue of
prudence which is.intellectual is controlled by the
will. Self-control and prudence were, according to
Stobæus, identified by the Stoics; and Seneca makes
virtue a habit of the will depending on *recta ratio*,
which is dependent on right knowledge. The
moral quality of conduct belongs not to the acts
of a man *per se*, nor is it conditioned by freedom
in willing. Acts are virtuous or not, according
to the intention of the agent. Whether the act
be performed or not, the intention to perform it is
sufficient to constitute a virtuous action.

In the Stoic philosophy, there is the same conception of man as being in slavery to passion which
was characteristic of the older ethics. When

Seneca arraigns the race for its wickedness, and enslaving passions, he is painting a picture of the age of Nero, and is expressing faithfully the general Stoic pessimism with respect to the rarity of virtue. The whole school was not successful in explaining how it was that a vicious man could ever become virtuous. By some of them it was described as a sudden change, like the "immediate conversion" of Christian theology. Yet it was not demonstrated that a man who was vicious could become virtuous. It was evident that a man could not always be taught to be virtuous, so that the will as well as the knowing faculties were involved; yet to suppose that the will was amenable to *recta ratio* was to suppose that the man was already virtuous, and was living in rational conformity to nature. The practical result of the Stoic discipline was to produce apathy amid the changes and fortunes of life. It would not be true to affirm that there is a necessary relation between such an attitude and a theory of predeterminism; yet it is interesting to notice that this apathy or ataraxia is characteristic of those oriental systems which combine pantheism with a doctrine of fatal necessity. The Christian doctrine of resignation to the will of God resembles the Stoic apathy, and yet very few of those who have been conspicuous examples of resignation have denied the freedom of the will. Self-abnegation has been thought rather to be an admirable illustration of free submission. The idea that a providence or fatal necessity has predetermined all that is to come agrees well with the practical submission to the course of nature, which can be neither averted, nor resisted.

Chrysippus endeavored to reconcile this determinism with man's moral accountability. He held that, while men do right or wrong because they are fated to do right or wrong, in either case they act according to their own character. While he defined Fate as "sempiterna quaedam et indeclinabilis series rerum et catena, volvens semetipsa sese et implicans per aeternos consequentiae ordines, ex quibus apta connexaque est,"[1] he illustrated the property of man in his own acts, by supposing a stone which is thrown from a height. It falls, not because of the impulse alone, but because of its property thus to fall. The man born with an evil character wills evil, in accordance with that character, just as the stone falls because it is heavy. As Cicero says: "Dum autem verbis utitur suis delabitur in eas difficultates, ut necessitatem fati confirmet invitus."[2]

The fact that the physics of the Epicureans are derived from the Atomists might lead one to expect that they would adopt also the Atomic doctrine of necessity. On the contrary, Epicurus avoided this by an ingenious device, and maintained that the will is free. He was without doubt led to this position by the subordination of theory to practice in his philosophy. The doctrine of indeterminism may have been accepted in order that moral quality might be attributed to the motion of the soul in

---

[1] A. Gellius, VI. 2.　　　　[2] Cicero, De Fato, 17.

the direction of pleasure. While accepting the Atomic materialism, that nothing exists except atoms and empty space, Epicurus attributes the world not to any necessity, but to a fortuitous *congressus* of atoms. The soul itself is composed of atoms, but the will is free. This is only one of a number of inconsistencies in the Epicurean philosopy. There are gods, but they are not related to the universe, and are indifferent as to its welfare; the pleasures of the mind are to be preferred to those of the body, and yet pleasure is the only good and pain the only evil. The test of truth is sensible perception, and yet it is true that there are invisible gods, and there are atoms which cannot be detected by any of the senses. If only atoms and the vacuum exist, the motion of the atoms in all its variety is hard to explain. While this is ascribed to chance, it would seem that chance was only a name for the mode in which the atoms affect one another, so that worlds rise and are dissolved.

In emancipating the universe from supernatural causation, Epicurus and his followers were not so successful in gettting rid of causality in the atoms themselves. Democritus had taught that the falling of the atoms through empty space, together with the whirlings and reboundings, produced the universe. But the Epicureans saw that it must be explained how, from this inevitable flux of things, free will could emerge. For here was a lifeless, uncaused universe, which was bound by no unchangeable principle, and yet was as likely as not to go on as it had begun. There was no reason why it should go on without deviation, and yet no reason why it should deviate. To introduce any outside cause to account for irregularities or peculiarities of volition would have been contrary to the principle of the school, *ex nihilo nihil fit.* The Epicureans attempted to meet this difficulty by, first, a modification of the old Atomic theory, and, second, a denial of the logical principle of contradiction.

They agree with Democritus that the soul is composed of atoms, and their further description of its structure need not here be repeated.[1] The soul is a principle of rest and of motion; and it is sometimes defined as $\pi\nu\epsilon\hat{\upsilon}\mu\alpha$. When the body is dissolved, the soul perishes. All knowledge is derived from the senses, and the test of truth is reality to the senses.[2] This was virtually the doctrine of Protagoras, and there is a sceptical element in the Epicurean logic.

The ethical end of conduct is pleasure, and prudence is needed in order that a man may employ the best means for attaining pleasure.[3] In the choice of such means, the will is free. The early Atomists had regarded the universe as under the control of necessity; but the Epicureans, in order to avoid the conclusion that necessity would upon this principle govern voluntary action, modified the Atomic philosophy. In the falling of the atoms, according to Epicurus, there is a deviation (*declinatio*) from their straight line of descent. And that

---

[1] Lucretius, De Rerum Natura, III. 216 f.
[2] Cicero, Acad. II. 32.   [3] Diogenes Laërtius, 128.

this deviation is possible is a ground for the doctrine that the will is free.

> Sed Epicurus declinatione atomi vitari fati necessitatem putat. Itaque tertius quidam motus oritur extra pondus et plagam, cum declinat atomus intervallo minimo. . . . Sequitur enim, ut si alia ab alia nunquam depellatur, ne contingat quidem alia aliam: ex quo efficitur, ut jam si sit atomus, eaque declinet, declinare sine causa. Hanc rationem Epicurus induxit ob eam rem, quod veritus est, ne, si semper atomus gravitate ferretur naturali ac necessaria, nihil liberum nobis esset, cum ita moveretur animus, ut atomorum accipere maluit, necessitate omnia fieri, quam a corporibus individuis naturales motus avellere.[1]

This accommodation of the original theory of the Atomists to his practical conclusions does not exhibit Epicurus as a consistent teacher. It is, in fact, a denial of some of the more important principles of Democritus, and sets aside the idea of a reign of law in nature. If there exists nothing except atoms and empty space, and if it is due to gravity that the motions of the universe occur, then it must be inferred that the *declinatio* is uncaused, or else the leading Atomic doctrine must be abandoned. The connection of the Epicurean physics with the doctrine of the will, and the Epicurean theory of indeterminism, is thus set forth by Lucretius:—

> Denique si semper motus connectitur omnis,
> Et vetere exoritur semper novus ordine certo,
> Nec declinando faciunt primordia motus
> Principium quoddam quod fati foedera rumpat,

[1] Cicero, De Fato, X.

> Ex infinito ne causam causa sequatur :
> Libera per terras unde haec animantibus extat,
> Unde est haec (inquam) fatis avolsa voluntas,
> Per quam progredimur, quo ducit quemque voluptas ?
> Declinamus item motus, nec tempore certo,
> Nec regione loci certa, sed ubi ipsa tulit mens.
> Nam dubio procul his rebus sua cuique voluntas
> Principium dat. [1]

The atoms of the soul, then, are excepted from the law of cause and effect, just as the physical atoms may decline or deviate in the universal descent, according to the law of gravity. This is the unexplained wandering of the atom. It is due to no principle of the soul apart from the atoms. And this is the Epicurean theory of freedom.

Reference has been already made to a discussion in the Post-Aristotelian period with respect to the relation of voluntary actions to certain logical principles. This discussion originated at an earlier day, and was at first a debate about the principle of contradiction, that a thing cannot both be and not be at the same time. Aristotle mentions the denial of this principle by certain philosophers, and the reference is supposed to be to Heraclitus. [2] By Euclid, the founder of the Megaric school, the possible and the actual were identified, for he maintained that whatever is possible is. Diodorus of the same school, and one of the most acute of the ancient dialecticians, taught more specifically

---

[1] Lucretius, De Rerum Natura, II. 251 et seq.
[2] Aristotle, Met. 1005, b. 25: τινὲς οἴονται λέγειν Ἡράκλειτον.

that the possible is not only that which is, but also
that which is about to be. And, he added, that
which is about to be is necessary. According to
Diodorus, nothing impossible can follow from the
possible.[1] It is impossible that any past event
should be other than it already is. If such a thing
had been possible at any earlier time, something
possible would have given rise to something impossible, which is absurd. For in this case the
event was never possible. Consequently it is impossible that anything should ever occur except the
actual. No act of man could have been differently
performed, and no act which has been performed
could have remained unperformed. All has been
determined in the past. The future is also predetermined, and all events that are about to happen
are about to happen necessarily. Aristotle had
denied the necessity and affirmed the contingency of
the future.[2] In this he was followed by Chrysippus,
who held that only events which had already oc-
curred were necessary.[3] They are necessary because
they are immutable, and whatever has been true in
the past cannot be changed from true to false. But
the future is contingent. Events are possible which
are never about to happen. The actuality of future
events is dependent upon certain contingencies; as,
for example, it is predetermined that a certain man
will be drowned if he goes to sea, but it is not predetermined whether he will go to sea or not. The

---

[1] See Zeller, Phil. d. Gr. II. 230.
[2] Aristotle, De Interp. 19, b. 5.
[3] See Cicero, De Fato, 6 et seq.

drowning being contingent upon his going to sea, and his going to sea being a contingent event, his drowning is also contingent. Chrysippus is of the opinion that even predictions of a divine oracle are not about to be fulfilled necessarily. The only predetermination, then, is contingent predetermination. The practical inference from this doctrine is that no man can say that because a certain end is predetermined, he need not employ means to further or defeat the end. Nor is the fact that one of two alternatives is predicated of the future a ground for affirming that one of the two will necessarily be true. One of the alternatives is true only under certain contingencies. If I say I shall either die or recover from this illness, I am not at liberty to conclude that action on my part is useless. Either alternative is predetermined only contingently; and the end is fixed only conditionally on the means to the end being realized. In opposition to both Diodorus and Chrysippus, the Epicureans denied the principle of contradiction. According to Cicero, Epicurus feared that if he should admit this principle, he must also admit that all things are determined by fatal necessity. Chrysippus had followed Aristotle in insisting upon the importance of this principle, and he speaks of it as an axiom. He feared that if he should deny it, his doctrine that all things are accomplished by fate would not be tenable. The supposition that there was a swerving aside (*declinatio*) of the atoms, was used by Epicurus in support of his denial of fatal necessity. In this way, he implied first of all that events can happen without a sufficient external cause; second, that fatal necessity does not control events; and, third, that the will of man is free. While Chrysippus made a distinction between antecedent and necessary causes, and held that only the former control the volitions, Epicurus seems to have excluded from his theory of volition whatever could be interpreted as moving cause.

Carneades [1] of the New Academy differs with both Stoic and Epicurean, yet is far removed from the position of Diodorus. While he agreed with the conclusion of Epicurus, he feared to adopt the theory of declination, lest he should seem to deny the principle of cause and effect. He preferred to appeal to the fact of free voluntary actions in order to disprove the doctrine of necessity. His argument against the Stoics is thus stated by Cicero: if all things are accomplished by antecedent causes, all things are bound together and are dependent on one another. If that be so, then necessity is the efficient cause of all things. And if that be true, nothing is in our power. Carneades therefore denies the consequent, and holds that inasmuch as there are certain things within our power, all things are not effected by fatal necessity. Carneades affirms that not even Apollo can predict the future. But he does not deny the principle of cause and effect. The cause of the volition is intrinsic not extrinsic; because it is in the nature of the will to be free from the law of external causation and external necessity.

[1] Cicero, De Fato, 11.

Whether voluntary actions are necessarily determined, and whether the principle of contradiction is applicable to future events, are two separate questions, and, as Bayle has shown, the connection of voluntary action with the disjunctive proposition was irrelevant.[1]

In general, it may be said that of course the past must remain as it is, and that there is no possibility of the present being other than it is. Whether the past might have been different under certain contingencies is another question which need not here be considered. Whether the principle of contradiction is applicable to the future may be easily seen in connection with any disjunctive proposition where the alternatives exclude one another. If I say: either James or John will die to-morrow, both of these alternatives may be true and both may be false, or either one may be true, while the other is false. By accepting one alternative I have not rejected all other possible cases. In logical language, the disjunction is not complete. But if I say: James will either die or not die to-morrow, the negative alternative embraces all other cases or conditions except the death of James. The proposition is equivalent to saying that if James does not die, he will live, that he cannot both live and not live, nor die and not die. It is not implied that he must die; it is not implied that he must live. It is not even implied that it is fixed whether he must live or must die. Nothing is said about either of the alternatives taken by itself. It

<hr>

[1] Bayle, Dict. Art. Epicure.

was therefore unnecessary for the Epicureans to dispute the validity of the principle of contradiction in order to establish their indeterministic doctrine. But if the Epicurean contention was unnecessary, the Stoic doctrine is inconsistent with itself. Let it be assumed that James will be drowned if he goes near the water, and that this has been predetermined by fate. If we understand by fate the operation of necessary causes, then I mean not that James will be drowned in spite of anything that he may do, but only that by a series of inevitable causes and effects the last effect will be the drowning of James. Either the end is predetermined or it is not predetermined; if it is, then the means to the end are predetermined, and contingency is excluded. To say that inaction on James's part is unnecessary because one of two alternatives must come to pass, is to assume that the true alternative is known. If it is not known, then by his inaction, if he escapes drowning, his escape will be effected; and by his action, if he is drowned, his death will be effected. To say that by venturing on the water he predetermines his death by drowning, is either to deny that his drowning is predetermined, or else to affirm that his venturing on the water is predetermined.[1] In addition to this, the whole argument between these various philosophers illustrates the effect of regarding

---

[1] Compare Lessing, *Der Freigeist*, I. 3. Dageht Er nun und spintisirt von dem was ist, . . . von der Nothwendigkeit, der halben und ganzen, der nothwendigen Nothwendigkeit und der nicht nothwendigen Nothwendigkeit.

necessity, possibility, and actuality as purely objective categories.

While the philosophy of Carneades is sceptical, other ancient sceptics carried their doubt to a greater extreme. The atheism and the denial of fate and necessity among philosophers of the later Greek schools were unfavorable to a belief in determinism. The sceptics did not hold that nature is *genetrix omnium*, but were disposed rather towards an individualism and subjectivism out of harmony with philosophical tradition and the popular religion. In particular, some of them denied the principle of cause and effect. They did not, as some modern philosophers have done, simply deny the connection between effect and cause, but they held it to be impossible that causes and effects should exist at all. Ænesidemus, of Cnossus, a contemporary of Cicero, was one of those who thus disputed the reality of causality.[1] It is probable that indeterminism was held by all the Greek sceptics. As an illustration of the connection between their theory of knowledge and their theory of volition may be mentioned their so-called suspension of judgment with respect to the events of life. Pyrrho had recommended apathy and indifference, because there is nothing certain. And if nothing is certain, nothing is either good or shameful. He was followed in this by Timon of Philus, his successor. Carneades, as we have seen, defended the

---

[1] Sextus Emp. Hypotyp. Pyrrh. I. 180. It may be added that Sextus himself denied the possibility of causes and effects. Adv. Math. 207 f.

freedom of the will, and the conclusion which he drew was that apathy (ἀπάθεια, ἀταραξία) was the proper attitude for the philosopher. Besides the suspending of judgment, the sceptics of the more extreme class also recommended the suspension of volition.[1] The combination of this conclusion with their denial of fatal necessity is worthy of consideration. The objection which had been brought to the determinism of Chrysippus was that human action is useless, if all is necessarily predetermined; and it has been seen how the objection was answered. The later sceptics maintained that human action is useless, because knowledge is uncertain, although the will is free. While one must accept with caution the extravagant stories which are told of the extremes to which the sceptics were led by their doubts, their philosophy was undoubtedly far more practical in its results than is the scepticism of more modern times.

[1] Ἀφασία and Ἀκαταληψία.

CHAPTER THIRD

THEORIES OF THE WILL IN CHRISTIAN THEOLOGY

In Christian theology, doctrines of the will have been complicated with doctrines relating to the prescience of God, the predestination of all events, original sin, and grace. Possibly, owing to these complications, the discussions concerning the nature and freedom of the will have been far more extensive and far more animated among theologians than among philosophers. Even if it be denied that these theological discussions have contributed much to our positive knowledge of the will, it must be admitted that they have often brought out very clearly, not only the different species of volition, but also the issues involved in the free-will debate.

The consideration of the will in Christian theology has prominence, because of the Christian conception of God as the personal and moral governor of the world, and because of the ethical character of Christianity as a system. The Christian conception of God is derived directly from the religion of Israel. Jehovah is rarely conceived of as a distant creator and first cause only. He is an active and intelligent power, who interferes repeatedly and directly in the events of nature and history. And he interferes in order to carry out to the end a preconceived and prearranged plan. In the execution of his designs, God is represented as acting either through human agency or without human agency. His purpose is accomplished, sometimes in conformity to natural laws, at other times by supernatural interposition or miracle. He is often represented as forming and executing his plans, contingently upon the acts of his creatures. But this anthromorphism is evidently not fundamental to the Hebrew idea of God. The prevailing conception in the old faith is of a God who governs all events, either by permissive decree or by positive agency. The call of Abraham, the choice of Isaac, the apostasy of Esau, the commitment of the divine revelation to the chosen people, the required ritual of tabernacle and temple, the rise and fall of kings, the fortunes of war,— all these are attributed to God's almighty power, and all are parts of the divine plan. This is also the conception of the New Testament writers; but in the Old Testament this theory of divine omnipotence and sovereignty is not brought into opposition with any scientific view of the will, and it remained for Christian writers first to notice this opposition. The germs of the great discussions of later theologians are contained only indirectly in the recorded sayings of Jesus Christ. It is in the Epistles of Paul that the first explicit suggestions of the great controversy are to be found. From his time down to a comparatively late date, theological interest has been attracted to questions which grow out of the old Hebrew conception of God's sovereignty, — the questions of predestination, of sin, and of grace.

St. Paul

If any excuse were needed for including a notice of the doctrines of Paul in explaining the development of philosophy, it might be found in the influence which his writings have had upon European thought. Like Plato and Aristotle, he has been cited as an authority in many differing schools. The Gnostics and the Manicheans appealed to his writings in support of their opinions; his views determined the course of Patristic and Scholastic thought; the sources of both Catholic and Protestant teaching are in his Epistles. While he taught no theory of systematic philosophy, there are implications of some modern philosophical doctrines in his teaching; and it is possible that his influence upon later philosophy has been too little considered.

Attempts have been made to trace a very close connection between the teaching of Paul and the Greek philosophy. In spite of the distinguished names connected with this attempt, I can find no proof of such a relation. The impression conveyed by the text of the Epistles is, that of a man who has a religious message to deliver, which he puts into words such as will be readily understood by those to whom they were first addressed. From a strictly philosophical point of view, Christianity is to be coördinated with those systems of practical philosophy which arose in the Post-Aristotelian period, which sought a standard of conduct, and practical rules of living. With these forms of philosophy, the teaching of Paul has some affinity, especially with the Stoic ethics; and there are also analogies between his thought and that of Plato. But the psychological terms used by Paul are mostly to be found in the LXX. translation of the Jewish Scriptures, and some are common to him and the Jewish philosophers of Alexandria. Beyond this, there is very little reason to believe that he was indebted for his ideas to any of the Greek philosophers. Where he uses terms of philosophy, he does it with a certain independence, and in a way peculiar to himself and other Christian writers. And yet no very definite psychology can be found in his writings. The most that one can hope to do, is to trace in his thought some elements which entered into the theories of fathers, and schoolmen, and reformers, and which indeed have not disappeared from scientific philosophy.

The object of Christianity as a practical system is, according to Paul, to make men righteous or holy.[1] The aim of his teaching is thus similar to that of the Greek ethical schools, which was to make men virtuous. The need of a solution of Paul's problem is evident from his own statement that the race of man is corrupt, and is dead in sin.[2] This theory, which is known as the doctrine of original sin and human depravity, underlies all Christian theories of the will down to the seventeenth cen-

---

[1] Titus, II. 11–14; Rom. XII. 1.
[2] Rom. I. 18 f.; III. 9–18; Eph. II. 1.

tury. What effects original sin has produced may
be best determined if we turn to the psychological
language of Paul's Epistles.

I. *The Psychological Terms of the Epistles.* The
most general of these is the heart (καρδία), which is
a Hebrew rather than a Greek form of expression.[1]
It has both an intellectual and a moral meaning.
It is a principle of thought, of intention, of desire,
and of faith, as well as of deliberate choice.[2] It
is emotional, for the love of God is shed abroad
in it;[3] it is a moral faculty, for the law is written
upon it.[4] It is the abode of Christ and the principle of inner character. It does not necessarily connote any moral quality, for there may be a bad
heart, as well as a good. The term soul (ψυχή) is
less often used than heart. It refers both to life,
and to that which in man is distinct from the body.[5]
The term reason occurs more frequently than soul.
It may denote a theoretical or a practical faculty.[6]
With (γνώμη) it is used to indicate a fixed way of
thinking or a conviction; it may mean the mind
or the moral faculty in man. It has both a good
and a bad connotation, according to the way in
which it is qualified. It is the "law of my members" which wars against the "law of my mind"
(νοῦς); but there are men with a "reprobate mind"
(νοῦς).[7]

The word body (σῶμα), so often used by Paul,

[1] LXX. Gen. VI. 5, VIII. 21; Eccl. VIII. 11.
[2] Rom. X. 1, 6, 8, 9, 10; 1 Cor. II. 11, IV. 5.
[3] Rom. V. 5.   [4] Rom. II. 15.   [5] Rom. II. 9, XI. 3.
[6] Rom. VII. 23, XII. 2; 1 Cor. I. 10, II. 16, XIV. 19.
[7] Rom. I. 28.

presents no difficulty of interpretation, in spite of
conclusions which have been drawn from his language. It is the ordinary mortal and natural body
of man, and it does not connote any bad moral
qualities.[1] Paul speaks of the mortal body, of the
appetites of the body, declares that it is subject to
redemption, and that it is to be changed so as to
become like the glorified body of Christ. Absence
from the body is presence with God.[2]

More difficult is the interpretation of the terms
flesh ($\sigma\acute{a}\rho\xi$) and spirit ($\pi\nu\epsilon\hat{\upsilon}\mu a$). The former is not
derived from Greek philosophy, but from the Hebrew
writers.[3] In the writings of Paul, it has the general
traditional meaning of human nature, or mankind.
But because human nature is corrupt, and is dead in
sin, to be in the flesh is *ipso facto* to be sinful and
morally dead. That it is not used in this unfavorable sense everywhere, is proved by the references
to Christ who was made of the seed of David according to the flesh;[4] there is the circumcision of the
flesh;[5] Christ came in the likeness of sinful flesh.[6]
In one instance it is used to denote not merely
human, but also animal nature of every kind.[7] But
theologically it has a bad meaning. It is the unregenerate principle in man. They that are in the
flesh cannot please God. To be carnally minded
is death. Flesh is the seat of the lower appetites

[1] Rom. I. 24, VI. 12, VII. 24, VIII. 23, XII. 1; 1. Cor. VI. 15,
XII. 12.

[2] Phil. III. 21; 2 Cor. V. 8.

[3] LXX. Gen. VI. 13, VII. 21; Is. XL. 5, 6.

[4] Rom. I. 3.   [5] Rom. II. 28.   [6] Rom. VIII. 3.

[7] 1 Cor. XV. passim.

(τὸ ἐπιθυμητικόν of Plato). In it dwells no good thing; it wars against man's higher nature; it cannot inherit the kingdom of God.[1] But ethically it is not to be identified with body; nor put in antithesis to soul.

Another more peculiar term is spirit (πνεῦμα). It may denote the Spirit of God or the soul of man. In the latter application, it is the regenerate part of man. It cannot be clearly distinguished from mind and heart. It is apparently the self-conscious spirit, the principle of real inner life. It is the true opposite of body (σῶμα), and is only once distinguished from the reason. Most commonly it is opposed to flesh, simply because the Spirit of God acts upon the soul, and not immediately upon the body. When the soul is regenerated, it is antithetical to the corrupt nature, whether the latter be corporeal or incorporeal.[2] Flesh does not apply to body alone as the Manicheans supposed; for to be carnally minded, not merely to be in the flesh, is moral death, and the carnal Ego is sold under sin.[3] The adjective spiritual (πνευματικός) refers to the regenerate soul and all its concerns.[4] The law of God is spiritual. There is the law of the spirit of life in Christ Jesus; Christians walk not after the flesh but after the Spirit. There are spiritual gifts, and those who have them are

---

[1] Rom. VIII. 3, 5, XIII. 14; 1 Cor. I. 26, XV. 50.

[2] Rom. I. 9, VII. 6, VIII. 10, 11; 1 Cor. II. 4, 11, V. 3, 5, XIV. 14, 15.   [3] Rom. VIII. 6, VII. 14.

[4] But compare πρὸς τὰ πνευματικὰ τῆς πονηρίας. Eph. VI. 12.

πνευματικοί, although this term is evidently not indicative of a caste or esoteric circle within the Church.[1]

II. *Sin and Grace.* From what has just been said, it will have been seen that all or nearly all the psychical principles in man are corrupted by sin. And Paul teaches that this condition is due to the fall of Adam. The death of man in sin brings upon him the curse of God, involving guilt and punishment; while subjectively man is unable to keep the moral law. The will is determined to evil by the birth of man in sin. This is of great importance in relation to later philosophy. For here is the origin of the doctrine taught for many centuries, that the human will is in slavery to sin, and that there is no free will in the sinner. Naturally the will is determined to sin because the character is sinful, and man cannot change his character. The change which enables man to escape the curse and to obey the law is effected by the grace of God. Grace produces faith, and Paul expressly says: (1) that man is justified by faith; (2) that man is saved by grace through faith.[2] Theologians are not at one as to what is meant by faith. It is not necessary that I should offer any particular interpretation either of the term justification or of the term faith, about which there has been so much dispute. But it is perfectly plain that Paul regards faith to be instrumentally the cause of justification, and grace to be efficiently the cause of faith. God is the author of faith,

[1] 1 Cor. XIV. 1, XII. 1.   [2] Rom. V. 1; Eph. II. 8.

and man is the recipient. Jesus Christ is the object of faith. ⌐ The breach between man and God is healed through faith, and the holy life begins with faith. Grace and original sin are antithetical. Just as birth into the human race carries with it the sin and corruption of the flesh, so the new birth by which faith is given to man enables him to live a holy life, and carries with it the beginnings of obedience to the moral law. The will which in the unregenerate is predetermined to sinful acts, in the regenerate is predetermined to a holy life.

III. *The Conflict of the Will.* For the first time in the history of thought, Paul presents from a subjective point of view the conflict of a man between two moral alternatives. While the aspects of this conflict are chiefly theological, it is evident, I think, that the subject involves principles of philosophy of no ordinary interest. Among interpreters, discussion has arisen as to the place which should be assigned to that part of Paul's writings in which this conflict is described.[1] Does it represent the man in a state of sin struggling to obtain grace and righteousness; or is the picture that of a man who has known the effects of grace, and who is seeking to attain to holiness, agonizing to overcome the corrupt principle which rebels against the changed character? It is perhaps needless to settle this question in interpreting Paul's conception of the will. If the chapter be taken in connection with the context, it would seem,

____
[1] Rom. VII. 14 ff.

however, that in the person of Paul is represented the man who has been already justified by faith, and who is at peace with God. In the sixth chapter of the Epistle to the Romans, the question discussed is whether such a man, who has escaped the unequal warfare with God, is obliged to keep the moral law. But in the seventh chapter, the question is not, must man keep the moral law, but why is he so incapable of keeping the moral law? The struggle is thus, apparently, not in the soul of the unregenerate man who is supposed to be dead in sin, but in the soul of the regenerate man who has been pardoned and is endeavoring to keep the law. In a state of sin, the will is determined towards the bad; in a state of grace, the will is determined towards righteousness; but not wholly so, for the flesh is not at once subdued, and there is a war between the good and the bad principles of action in the soul of him who has been pardoned. The conflict is described in a soliloquy, in which there is some confusion of psychological terms. · A series of good principles is enumerated in opposition to a series of bad principles. It is not the Ego warring with a principle of evil, nor is it the war of grace with the unregenerate Ego. It is the law which is spiritual (νόμος πνευματικός) in conflict with the carnal Ego ('Εγὼ σαρκικός); it is the Ego hating one course of action, and yet performing it; willing one course of action, and performing another. It is the Ego which serves the law of God, warring against the Ego which serves the law of sin, the Ego as rational (ἐν τῷ νοΐ) in conflict with an Ego which is carnal. It is opposition between the law of my mind or reason, and the law or principle of sin which is in my members ($\mu\epsilon\lambda\acute{\eta}$). The Ego is apparently the agent in either case, whether the spirit or the flesh conquers. There can be no doubt that Paul regards the attainment of holiness as progressive and not instantaneous, and so the conflict thus described is theologically free from difficulty. Philosophically, it is impossible that the Ego should be ranged on either side exclusively in this inner conflict. But it is ranged first on one side, and then on another; it is evident that there is something more than a mere impersonal conflict between two principles, good and bad. If we eliminate as impossible the idea that Paul was setting forth the modern psychological theory of a double personality, it is plain that he views the will as determined by one or the other of two conflicting motives, and acknowledges that without predetermining grace, it will be predetermined by sin which is resident in human nature even after grace has been imparted.

This interpretation of the seventh chapter of Romans is further justified by the continuation of the discussion in chapters eighth and ninth. The antithesis between the carnal and the spiritual is again emphasized. The carnal mind is enmity against God; it cannot obey the law of God. They that are in the flesh ($\grave{\epsilon}\nu\ \sigma\alpha\rho\kappa\acute{\iota}$) cannot please God.[1] The subjection of the creature to the vain principle

[1] Rom. VIII. 7, 8.

of the flesh is not voluntary, and the creature will be freed from the slavery of corruption. To those who are freed from the bondage of the flesh, a hope of glorification is offered.[1] If it be asked who are to be glorified, it is found that whom he did foreknow, he also did predestinate, and whom he predestinated, them he also called, and whom he called, them he also justified, and whom he justified, them he also glorified.[2] If this should be thought consistent with an indeterministic view of the human will, it is difficult to explain why in the ninth chapter Paul should be at pains to answer objections to determinism. It is quite irrational to defend indeterministic doctrine against objections which have force only against deterministic doctrine. It seems equally irrational to employ positive arguments which lead to determinism, if the proof of indeterminism be the end in view.

If those who are glorified are those who have been predestinated, then there has obviously been an election or choice of those who are predestinated, called, justified, and glorified. Not all the children of Abraham were elected, but only Isaac; not all the sons of Isaac, but Jacob only. The election was unconditional, for it was made before the birth of the children, and the election was not according to works, but according to the mind of God. This is not merely the choice of a nation, for not all are Israel which are of Israel; neither because they are Abraham's seed are they all children; but in Isaac shall thy seed be called. But

---

[1] Rom. VIII. 20.　　　[2] Rom. VIII. 29.

if God thus unconditionally decides who are to be elected, it is possible that a man may say that God is unrighteous. The Apostle's protest is not against the doctrine of unconditional predestination and determinism, but against the man who regards such a theory as impugning the righteousness of God. Moses received a manifestation of divine glory, not from anything which he had done to deserve it, but out of God's unconditioned determination. Pharaoh was not one of the chosen race, and God hardened his heart; the reprobation of Pharaoh as well as the election of Moses is expressly taught. Almost every objection which can be made to the doctrine here laid down is stated and answered; and the writer intimates that human criticism is out of place: who art thou, O man, that repliest against God? Why doth he yet find fault, for who hath resisted his will? The clay cannot find fault with the potter, unless it has authority to legislate for the potter. The vessel is not made dishonorable, but it is made a vessel unto dishonor. In the case of Pharaoh, which excited great attention in most of the later Christian theology, Paul seems to say: God is not the cause of evil in the mind of Pharaoh; but in any event God is the cause of Pharaoh's existence. And indeed it might be urged that if God foreknows the dishonor of Pharaoh, and yet brings Pharaoh into the world, the objection made to the doctrine of unconditional election applies also to that of conditional election.

It is possible that so strict an interpretation of a passage, which is in the main practical and hortatory, should not be offered; and it may be urged that Paul probably had no definite conception of the philosophical bearings of what he was affirming. Even admitting the force of this objection, the fact remains that in all theories of the will in the history of Christian theology the doctrines of Paul have been so extensively interpreted that I have been unable to give any account of the one, without a notice of the other.

The Greek Fathers

The earlier part of the Patristic age was a period in which Christian writers were chiefly engaged in defending the faith against Anti-Christian opponents, such as the Neo-Platonists and the Gnostics. Christianity was in conflict also with the old polytheism of the Greek and Roman religion. In this earlier period, emphasis was laid upon the unity of God, as opposed to the many deities of pagan religion and the Gnostic dualism. The government of the world was held to be in the hands of providence, and not under fatal necessity. To avoid the Gnostic conclusion that God is the cause of evil, the early Fathers contended that God had simply permitted evil, and that the free will of angels and of men was responsible for sin. This raised the question, first, as to the way in which man came to sin by his own free will; and, second, as to what effect the fall of man had upon the race. This became the subject of debate between Augustine and the Pelagians. Consequently the theories of the earlier Fathers were indeterministic, and the pronounced determinism of Augustine was a result of the rise into prominence of the doctrine of original sin.

The greater part of the later period of the Patristic age was occupied with purely theological disputes, first, as to the Holy Trinity, and then as to the person and nature of Jesus Christ. When such doctrines had been defined by general councils, the subject of man became a centre of interest. And this engaged the attention of the Latin Fathers in their opposition to the Pelagians.

The tendency of the Eastern Fathers to hold an indeterministic theory of the will arose from the fact that they were obliged to meet in controversy the pagans who believed in fatal necessity, and the Gnostics who made God the author of evil. While there were Gnostics who taught explicitly a doctrine of freedom, the views of the school regarding matter and the body were not favorable to a belief in indeterminism. The limitation of the soul by evil matter, which was a principle of both Gnostic and Manichean, would lead some to the logical conclusion that under such bondage the volitions of man must be determined by this corrupting influence. It was the Christian doctrine of original sin which was the chief cause for the appearance in theological discussion of the problem of the will. "This is that hereditary corruption which the Fathers called *original sin*, meaning by sin the depravation of a nature previously good and pure; on which subject they had much contention, nothing being more remote from natural reason than that all should be criminated on account of the guilt of one, and thus sin become common; which seems to have been the reason why most ancient doctors of the church did but obscurely glance at this point, or at least explained it with less perspicuity than it required. Yet this timidity could not prevent Pelagius from arising, etc."[1] Even Augustine was at first little disposed to develop a doctrine of the will in accordance with the theory of original sin. His earlier opponents were mostly Manicheans and pagan philosophers; and from a letter written by him shortly before the outbreak of the Pelagian controversy, it is plain that he had hitherto paid no particular attention to the questions which Pelagius had raised in Rome.

Justin Martyr, the earliest of the Patristic writers, teaches that God foreknows all that is about to come to pass, and that prophecy will most certainly be fulfilled. But he opposes the fatal necessity of the Stoics. While angels and men were created to obey the law of God, their punishment is foretold, because God foreknew that they would sin. For angels and men were created with free will, capable of virtue or vice, and therefore subject to reward or blame. It is not the fault of God that they have sinned.[2] Man was not made like the quadrupeds and other lower beings. He is endowed with freedom, without which he would have been undeserving of punishment and un-

---

[1] Calvin, Inst. II. 1, 5.
[2] Justin Martyr, In Apol. I. 28, 43.

worthy of reward. Justin, however, does not define will, nor give any psychological explanation of it.

Irenæus, who was one of the chief opponents of the Gnostics, teaches a doctrine of general predestination, and the unity of the divine plan, in distinction from dualism. He criticises those who attribute the creation of the world to angels, and declares that God alone is creator, who has predestinated all things according to his pleasure, by his word.[1] Man is endowed with reason, and in this respect is like God. He has free will, that is, he has power over his own actions. He is said to be a cause unto himself.[2] This expression which originated with Justin Martyr was afterwards adopted by Spinoza in his definition of God. If the theology of Irenæus be separated from his anthropology, his language when he refers to the sovereignty of God will be found to be as decided as that of Augustine. The Son of God is the revealer of the Father's will, and reveals the Father to whom he wills. Without the good will of the Father, and the agency of the Son, no man can know God.[3] One chapter of his work against heresies is devoted to a consideration of the freedom of the will. In this he presents a form of indeterminism. Man is called upon to obey freely, and not by any external or internal compulsion. God has commanded obedience, and the law has sanctions. Men are judged, not by their natures, but by their actions. They deserve no praise for having a good nature,

---

[1] Irenæus, Adv. Hœres, II. 2.

[2] Id., ib. IV. 4.   [3] Id., ib. IV. 6, 7.

nor blame for having a bad nature. Obedience is possible to the commands of God, whether the nature of man be bad or good. Irenæus defends the singular theory that if God had created devils and men who were predetermined to resist his will, it would argue impotence in God. The opposite of this has sometimes been held by advocates of predestination, that if a man has free will, the omnipotence of God is limited. It is interesting to find Irenæus taking a contradictory view. The man who does not obey the commands of God, is the cause of his own disobedience. Those who do not see the light are blind through their own fault, for the light is there. The fault is not God's but man's; he has been created a free agent with power over himself.[1]

Hippolytus, a disciple of Irenæus, and another opponent of the Gnostics, criticises Plato for his "fatalism," directing his attack against the Platonic statement that vice is involuntary. He criticises also the Stoics for their doctrine of fatal necessity, and the Epicureans for their belief in chance.[2] A treatise on the freedom of the will is attributed to Methodius, but is of doubtful authenticity, and of small importance. It teaches that man was created free, so that it might be possible for him to obey or to disobey the commands of God. Evil has come into the world as the effect of disobedience. Having originally had power, man has enslaved himself. While this exhibits

---

[1] Irenæus, Adv. Hæres, IV. 37.
[2] Hippolytus, Refut. I. 16-19.

some signs of the Pauline doctrine of inability, it is doubtful whether the writer of the treatise intended to speak except figuratively of the slavery of the will.

The ablest theologians among the Eastern Fathers, were Clement of Alexandria and Origen. Although they opposed the Gnostics, there are signs of Gnosticism in some of their own opinions. Clement attacked the theory that God is in any way the author of evil. He was the first to introduce a distinction which ever since his day has had a prominent place in theological literature. He affirms that God is not the cause of evil, but that God permits the existence of evil.[1] There was a purpose which God set before him, and which required for its accomplishment the creation of man.[2] When man sinned, God simply did not interfere to prevent the occurrence. Not to prevent an event, is different from causing an event. God is therefore not the cause of evil, except in so far as he did not interfere to prevent it. God foreknows all that is about to happen. The ground of predestination is this foreknowledge. Foreknowing, for example, that certain men will be righteous, God predestinates them unto eternal life. The devil had free will and was the cause of sin, and God is not responsible for the volitions of the devil.[3] Sin is the result of free inclination and choice. Yet while God permits evil, he overrules it for good. As God is not the cause of sin, so also

---

[1] Clement, Strom. I. 17.
[2] Id., ib. I. 3. [3] Id., ib. I. 17.

he is not the cause of the will to become righteous.
Christ saves men by drawing to himself those who
are willing to be drawn. Everything which did
not hinder man's free choice, God rendered auxili-
ary to well-doing, in order that the divine goodness
might be revealed.[1]

More specifically, Clement teaches that self-
determining choice has been imparted to the soul.[2]
Voluntary actions are of three kinds: (1) those
which are done according to desire; (2) those
which are done by choice; (3) those which are
done intentionally. There is a corresponding
threefold division of evils into (1) sins, (2) mistakes, (3) crimes. Both of these divisions are
obscurely drawn. Sins and mistakes are said to
be merely errors; voluntary sins are crimes.[3] To
commit sin lies within man's power, and depends
upon his volition. Will takes the precedence of
all other human powers, and the intellect is its
servant. In this Clement departs from the Platonic tradition, and defends the primacy of the
will.[4] God has set before men good and evil
objects of choice. Men are not made originally
virtuous or vicious. Sin is dependent on the will;
and faith as well as the intellectual powers is
subject to will.

Origen, like the other Greek Fathers, defends
indeterminism, although his doctrine of providence
is in accordance with belief in predestination. According to him none of the events which happen to

---

[1] Clement, Strom. VI. 6.
[2] Id., ib. II. 4.   [3] Id., ib. II. 15.   [4] Id., ib. II. 17.

man, happens by accident. All occurs in accordance with a plan so stupendous, and yet so carefully considered, that even the hairs of the head are numbered.[1] Nor does Origen shrink from admitting that some men perish in accordance with the will of God; as in the case of Pharaoh, whose heart God hardened. His less general treatment of the will forbids the supposition that he believed it to be determined. He makes a distinction between objects which have a cause of motion from without, and those which are moved from within. To the latter class belong animals, plants, possibly metals, fire, and fountains. Most animate things are moved by a phantasm springing up within them, which incites to effort. But the rational animal is incited to effort by something in addition to phantasm. There may be some external cause which incites the reason, but it is the latter which determines what the action shall be. It is not possible to distinguish the reason and the will completely in the writings of Origen. The incitement of the reason is not irresistible. In the presence of the same temptation one man will resist, another will yield. The action is not dependent solely on the external cause. Men are not dragged about as slaves; nor is the action of the will determined by the constitution of the body. In opposition to the Gnostics, Origen holds that the reason sits as a judge over all external incitements. It is probable that he means that choice is a function of the reason. In

1 Origen, De Princip. II. 11.

a fragment of Origen found in Jerome's epistle to Avitus, it is said that all men have free will, and that it lies with each one to improve or to degrade his life.[1]

The most striking aspect of Origen's psychology is his theory adopted from Plato, of the pre-existent soul. The conduct of man is determined not by the Creator, but by the will of man as a rational creature. When it is said that men are created to dishonor, it is meant that this is on account of their preëxistent characters and consequent free actions.[2] This suggests the theory of the Platonic myth, that it lies in the power of pre-existent souls to choose their own destiny. It may be noticed that this explanation is not sufficient to account for the preëxistent character of the soul, nor does it prove that acts of free will determine the character. This view of the will is to be found repeated throughout Origen's theology. He discusses the case of Pharaoh, and maintains that the statement of the Bible is quite in harmony with free will. It had been argued that if God hardened Pharaoh's heart, then Pharaoh's will was not free. In opposition to this Origen maintains that if Pharaoh had an earthy nature, so that he disobeyed God because of such a nature, there was no need that his heart should be hardened. If he had not an earthy nature, God would not have hardened his heart, because God would not cause a man to sin, unless the man's character was bad. Origen

---

[1] S. Hieron, Epist. ad Avit.
[2] Origen, De Princip. II. 10.

therefore does not hold the doctrines of original sin and depravity. The origin of repentance is in the heart of man. When men come of their own free will to God, he removes the stony heart. This view is enforced by the quotation of many practical exhortations from the Scriptures.[1]

The soul of man in its present state is one of three principles in man. Human nature is made up of spirit, soul, and body. Each part has its own will. It is difficult to determine in which of these three, the unity of the will is to be found. The psychical will is the most important morally. For the will of the soul is said to obey either spirit or body of its own free choice. It is better that the soul should follow altogether the will of the flesh, than that it should waver. For in such an extreme condition, there is a more favorable prospect of reformation. Men fail to come to God, not because of God's inability to draw them, but because of their wayward wills.[2]

The Latin Fathers

TERTULLIAN.

The thought of the Latin Fathers is so well represented in the writings of Augustine that it will not be necessary to consider their theories in great detail. Among them there is no more interesting writer than Tertullian. While in time, he

[1] Origen, De Princip. III. 1.
[2] See particularly Origen Περὶ τοῦ Αὐτεξουσίου, I. 1-7; De Princip. III. 4; Contra Cels. VI. 57.

belongs to the age of apologies, his doctrine has not been without positive influence on Christian theology. Yet his frequent inconsistencies, his declamatory manner, and his arbitrary distinction between matters of reason and matters of faith make it difficult to present a satisfactory account of his philosophical opinions.

His chief psychological treatise contains no systematic account of the soul. It is for the most part a fierce polemic against the theories of the Greek and Roman philosophers. His teaching has more affinity to the philosophy of the Stoics than to that of any of the Greek schools.

He rejects the Platonic theory of preëxistence, and holds that the soul is generated and propagated with the body. In conformity with this principle. he teaches that the soul is corporeal in its nature. He speaks even of God as corporeal.[1] While many have interpreted these expressions as evidence that Tertullian was a materialist, it seems more rational to regard them as manifestations of impetuous and inconsistent speculation. For he attacks the Gnostic doctrine that matter is coeternal with God.

The soul cannot be called an animal body (*corpus animale*) nor a non-animal body (*corpus inanimale*). For it is that which makes a body animal by its presence, and non-animal by its absence. In opposition to those who hold that the soul is incorporeal, from the fact that the soul can be moved from without by bodily objects, and can itself produce motion of bodies, it is proved that it is

[1] Tertullian, De Anim. XXI.

corporeal in its nature. *Conatus ejus extrinsecus foris parent.* Hands, feet, eyes, and tongue are moved by the soul.[1] Tertullian opposes also the Platonic threefold division of the soul, holding that there is reason in appetite and emotion, as well as in the thinking principle.[2]

The Traducian theory held by Tertullian does not, according to him, exclude the possibility of a subsequent change in the nature of the soul. A bad character will necessarily effect bad actions; yet, to use his language, divine grace can change stones into the children of Abraham, and a generation of vipers into the fruit of penitence: vis divinae gratiae potentior utique natura, habens in nobis sub jacentem sibi liberam arbitrii protestatem quod τὸ αὐτεξούσιον dicitur. This is the term used by the Greek Fathers to denote free will. It is a native power of the soul. Thus the nature of man is not fixed in evil, as some of the Gnostics taught, but can be changed by grace. Tertullian emphasized the efficiency of grace more than any of the Greek Fathers had done. Grace is more powerful than nature; and free will is drawn under the sway of supernatural power. Free will, however, is part of the essence of the soul. It belongs both to fallen and to unfallen man. God not only made man a free master of his actions, but also imposed laws upon him. This would not have been done, had not man had it in his power to disobey as well as to obey. The reason why exhortation and persuasion are effective is because of man's

---

[1] Tertullian, De Anim. I.–V.   [2] Id., ib. XVI.

free will. The original liberty of man was a manifestation of the goodness of God; for man was made in the image and likeness of God, a part of which is free choice. The sin of man is no reflection upon the goodness of the Creator.[1] In opposition to Marcion, Tertullian argues that if God had intervened to prevent the fall of man, and to keep the serpent away, Marcion might have said that it was a faithless Lord who abridged the liberty which he had first bestowed. The same free will which succumbed to the temptation becomes at length the conqueror of the devil, by obedience to the law of God. Man is responsible for his use and misuse of freedom. Yet the predetermination of events is stated very distinctly: nihil origine sua prius est in agnitione, quia nec in dispositione. Subito filius, et subito missus est, autem dispositum. . . . At quin nihil putem a Deo subitum, quia nihil a Deo non dispositum.

St. Jerome

The theory of Jerome deserves notice more on account of his prominent part in the Pelagian controversy than because his opinion has intrinsic importance. In his writings, there is a departure from the indeterminism of the earlier Fathers and an approach to the position afterwards occupied by Augustine. His psychological views are rare, and always unsystematically expressed. His references to the will are for the most part theological. These

---

[1] Tertullian, Anti Marc. II. 5, 6.

are scattered throughout his formal treatises and his letters. All the Patristic writers agree that Adam was originally endowed with free choice of good and evil. The only question is whether the will of fallen man is free, without freedom being given by the grace of God. This, as has been already said, unites the theological discussion of the will to the doctrine of grace. Jerome's theory is theologically defended by reference to the New Testament rather than to the reason.

1. He teaches a doctrine of providence in harmony with predestination. All things are controlled and directed by the providence of God. It was owing to the divine foreknowledge and predestination that the prophets were enabled to see the future, as if it were already past, and to make truthful predictions. *Predestinatio* is different from *propositum*. The former refers to the intention of God a long time prior to the event determined. The latter is applied to a plan in the immediate future :—

de quo . . . Paulus ait ; ut autem venit plentitudo temporis, misit Deus Filium suum ; qui ante venire non potuit nisi mysterium temporis impleretur.[1]

Jerome reproves those who seek to discover why God has willed as he has.[2] But he wavers between the theory of conditional and that of unconditional predestination. Among several strong passages in his commentaries is one in which he interprets the words *secundum propositum suae voluntatis*, in the

1 S. Hieron, Opera, IV. I. 330.   2 Id., ib. IV. II. 504.

Epistle to the Ephesians, as meaning, according to the purpose of God, independent of the will of man. And he explains the words in the Romans, *his qui secundum propositum vocati*, etc., by saying that men believe because they have been predestinated to eternal life. To the objection of the Pelagian that if God predestinates all human actions, he is commanding certain things which are impossible for man to perform, Jerome replies, that many things are ordained as lawful and proper, but that it is not the duty of every man to do them all.[1] Some commands do not apply to all men. Throughout his works, however, Jerome refers to the mystery which surrounds this subject: a me sententiae et dispositionis Dei causas requiris?

2. He teaches also a doctrine of indeterminism. While his defence of freedom is not in harmony with many of his statements concerning grace, he asserts very emphatically the doctrine of free will :—

sed liberum dedit arbitrium Deus, quod aliter liberum non erit, nisi fecero quod voluero.[2] Liberum arbitrium dat liberam voluntatem, et non statim ex libero arbitrio homo facit, sed Domini auxilio.[3]

While Jerome asserts that man has fallen, is in a state of sin, and cannot of himself do any good, the part that grace performs in man's obedience is not quite clear. Man is free, because he has grace. On the one hand it is said :—

---

[1] S. Hieron, Opera, IV. II. 497.

[2] Id., ib. IV. II. 478. [3] Id., ib. IV. II. 481.

sed si quid in me boni habeo, illo suggerente et adjuvante completur,[1]

which is in harmony with a moderate degree of freedom even in fallen man. On the other hand, the freedom of the will is ascribed wholly to grace:

ut enim liberum possideamus arbitrium, et vel ad bonam vel ad malam partem declinemus propria voluntate, ejus est gratiae, qui nos ad imaginem et simitudinem sui tales condidit.[2]

This difficulty arises in more than one of the Patristic theories. The will in fallen man seems to be determined to evil. It is freed by grace. If grace is given in consequence of man's will to have it, then freedom is not wholly lost in the fall; and if not, then the questions are raised,— first, is the sinner responsible for his sins, and, second, is the man in a state of grace responsible for his holy actions? These questions were discussed more fully by Augustine. The obscurity of Jerome's theory is further increased by his remarks on the hardening of Pharaoh's heart. Here he represents God as acting conditionally and not unconditionally. Pharaoh's heart was hardened not through the direct agency of God, but because of its native character, just as certain substances are not softened by the warmth of the sun: —

Alicquin unus est solis calor, et secundum essentius subjacentes, alia liquefacit, alia indurat, alia solvit, alia constringit. Liquatur enim cera, et induratur lutum : et tamen

<hr>

[1] S. Hieron, Opera, IV. II. 485.   [2] Id., IV. II. 486.

caloris non est diversa natura. Sic et bonitas et clementia Dei, vasa irae quae apta sunt in interitum, id est populum Israel, indurat.[1]

The same difficulties reappear from time to time in later theological discussions of the will. Some of the inconsistencies of the earlier Fathers are corrected in the philosophy of Augustine.

St. Augustine

Augustine's interest in the will is chiefly theological. He treats of predestination, sin, grace, and their effects, but contributes very little to the psychological doctrine of volition. In this respect, he falls behind some of his predecessors, notably Aristotle.

I. *The Nature of the Will.* Two terms are used by him to denote the faculty of will. The first of these is *voluntas;* the second, *arbitrium.* *Voluntas,* in addition to its executive signification, comprehends also the character, inclinations, and affections of man. In many cases it is synonymous with *arbitrium.* The latter denotes the will as a decision of the soul. Its primary meaning is presence — the presence of judges in a court. It was then applied to judicial decisions, and was adopted into philosophy to denote a decision of the soul or mind. Augustine sometimes speaks of *arbitrium voluntatis,* possibly to distinguish will from *arbitrium intellectus.* Yet Lucretius uses *arbitrium* to

---

[1] S. Hieron, Opera, IV. i. 182.

denote the act of the mind which executes the intentions.

According to Augustine, the creature is endowed with will by a creative act of the Trinity.[1] Whether he held that the individual soul was the result of a creative act, or was transmitted by the laws of ordinary generation, cannot be directly decided, nor is it of much importance to the present inquiry that it should be decided. Beings which have will, even if the will be evil, are to be ranked higher than those which have none. The will is defined as an act of the soul, either towards the not losing or towards the gaining of something without coercion,— *voluntas animi actus, cogente nullo, ad aliquid vel non amittendum vel adipiscendum.*[2] This act or motion is not physical. But it is felt far more intimately than any other fact. The will is almost the same with the person,— *voluntas est quippe in omnibus: immo omnes nihil aliud quam voluntates sunt.*[3] The soul is present in every part of the body, and is moved by the will spontaneously, and by nothing foreign to itself. Certain Manicheans had affirmed that the soul is moved *ab extra*, and had inferred that man is not responsible for his deeds. Augustine holds that every volition belongs to the man who wills, and that he is therefore responsible for his actions.[4]

It might be demonstrated that Augustine's doc-

---

[1] S. Augustin. Opera, III. Part I. 242. (The references are to the Benedictine edition of 1685.)

[2] I. 24; cf. VIII. 71, 85; X. 1261, 1263.

[3] VII. 354; X. 610.   [4] I. 13, 613; X. 717; II. 874.

trine of the will was modified at different parts of his career, according to the theological opposition by which he was confronted. He had been early trained in the philosophy of the Academy, and by education would be disposed to indeterminism. But he had afterwards become a Manichean, and his conversion from Manicheism to Catholic Christianity had produced in him a strong reaction against that heresy. With the Academic teachings he never altogether lost sympathy; but during his ecclesiastical life the Manicheans were among his most formidable antagonists. It is, however, interesting to remember that Augustine and his followers were accused of Manicheism by the Pelagians. During his earlier life as a Christian, he was also opposed to the doctrines of the Greek determinists and fatalists. There was nothing in the theories of these adversaries which made the defence of predestination and original sin essential to Augustine's apologetic. It was not until the Pelagian heresy arose, and agitated both East and West, that those principles which have since been called Augustinian were clearly formulated in Latin theology. And even after Pelagian doctrines had spread throughout the Church, we find Augustine expressing ignorance of the nature of the controversy.[1] In order to understand Augustine's theory of the will in relation to the doctrines of predestination and original sin, it is proper that some account should be given of the points in this dispute, which excited the whole Church to lively debate, and caused

[1] Vit. S. Augustini, ed. Bened. VII. c. viii.

the interference of the Holy See and of the Roman Emperor.

II. *The Pelagian Doctrines.* From the fact that Pelagius was a British monk, and had been at least familiar with the religion of the Druids, if not himself a Druid, it has been sometimes said that his doctrine of indeterminism was Druidic. There seems to be no necessity for such an inference, especially as there had been an indeterministic tendency among the Eastern Fathers prior to his own time. As he left no writings, it is difficult to say what he actually and uniformly taught. He made several recantations of his heresy, as did also his chief follower, Cœlestius, and it is not known to what form of doctrine they adhered. Pelagianism was without doubt primarily an ethical movement, which afterwards became a theological revolution. At Rome, at Carthage, and in the East the Pelagians contended that predestination led first to determinism and then to lawlessness. This opinion afterwards prevailed in the Semi-Pelagian monastery of Adrumentum. A powerful moral and theological impression was made upon the Christian Church, from Rome to Carthage, and from Carthage to Jerusalem.

In general, the Pelagians taught: that Adam's death was not a consequence of his sin; that the sin of Adam was not imputed to his descendants; that there is no original sin; that all sin is actual, and is the result of volition · that the will in each man is undetermined towards the bad or the good; and that even without the help of divine grace man can avoid sin. Men are thus the authors of their own salvation; the unaided will is sufficient for righteousness, and there is the liberty of indifference in every man. It follows, to cite the famous dilemma of Cœlestius: Si necessitatis est, peccatum non est; si voluntatis, vitari potest.[1] In the East the Pelagians encountered Jerome, and in the West they encountered Augustine.

III. *The Doctrine of Predestination.* This had already been taught by the Greek Fathers, but Augustine presented it in a much more decided form. According to him, all events are foreknown to God, because he has predetermined them.[2] The causes of predestination lie hidden from human sight, and man cannot discover them. In the same way, the righteousness of the divine plan is beyond the criticism of men. Reasoning from the omnipotence of God, it is shown that all events are either predestinated or permitted by him. Even the actions of the wicked are included in the divine plan, so that they may serve as lessons for the good. From the conception of God are deduced his immutability and the necessary counsel of his will.[3] So inclusive is the predestinating purpose of God, that in it are comprehended all inner and outer events, from the creation to the fall of man, and from the fall, to the beatification of the elect, and final punishment of the unjust. God's purpose is thus described in a classic passage from *De Civitate Dei:* —

[1] X. 168.   [2] IV. 1501; VII. 410; X. 17, 18.
[3] IV. 1479.

Verumtamen omnipotenti Deo, summo ac summe bono
creatori omnium naturarum, voluntatum autem bonarum
adjutori et remuneratori, malarum autem relictori et damna-
tori, utrarumque ordinatori, non defuit utique consilium,
quo certum numerum civium in sua sapientia predestina-
tum etiam ex damnato genere humano suae Civitatis im-
pleret : . . . Cur ergo non crearet Deus, quos peccaturos
esse praescivit; quando quidem in eis et ex eis, et quid eorum
culpa mereretur, et quid sua gratia donaretur, posset osten-
dere, nec sub illo creatore ac dispositore perversa inordinatio
deliquentium rectum perverteret ordinem rerum ? [1]

This leads to the consideration of Augustine's
doctrine of the will in relation to original sin and
grace.   It is virtually his answer to the Pelagians.

IV. *The Doctrine of the Will in Relation to Original Sin and Grace.* If God has predetermined
all events, this must be made to harmonize with the
doctrine of the origin of sin.   Augustine's method
of reconciliation is founded on two general principles.   The first is deduced from the character of
God.   Because God is good, he is not the author
of sin.[2]   Whatever idle speculations men may make
about God, and whatever inferences they may be
tempted to draw from the nature of sin, the fact
remains that God is good, and that evil cannot be
attributed to him.[3]   Sin is not the result of the
will (*voluntas*) of God.   It is the effect of God's per-
mission, and of a defect (*defectus*), that is, a failure
on the part of God to will certain positive results.
God is negatively, not positively, the cause of evil.
But evil wills are said to have no efficient cause.

[1] VII. 377.   [2] VI. 234.
[3] IV. 1244.   See De Libero Arbitrio, Liber II. ad init.

The second of these principles is that sin is originally due to the free will of man. This has some importance in the philosophical theory of Augustine. For in predestination he finds no contradiction of the freedom of unfallen man.

Animae rationali quae est in homine, dedit Deus liberum arbitrium. Sic enim posset habere meritum, si voluntate, non necessitate boni essemus. Cum ergo oporteat non necessitate sed voluntate bonum esse, oportebat ut Deus animae daret liberum arbitrium.[1]

Original freedom was lost at the fall of Adam. Since then, man has been the slave of sin; of himself he is unable to avoid sin and attain to holiness. No external obstacle hinders him. The cause lies within him; for his will is corrupt. Without the will, there is no sin.[2] Augustine speaks of a good will and a bad will, meaning in general the disposition and affections of a man. The natural will of man in this sense is predetermined to evil, because of original sin. Good and bad wills are compared to the roots of trees. The good will is the root of the good tree, and the bad will is the root of the bad tree. The fruits are good or bad according to the quality of their roots. The root although called *voluntas*, includes much more than the mere volition.

In permitting man to sin, God had an occasion for the exhibition of his glory in the work of redemption. This doctrine, which is one of the leading conceptions of Calvinism, has also been adopted in

[1] VIII. 98.   [2] VIII. 101.

effect by later optimists, who, instead of deducing
God's moral qualities from the phenomena of the
world, explain the existence of evil by causes lying
beyond the will of God and outside of his character.

The remedy for the evil of original sin is found
by Augustine, even as by Paul in divine grace.
When this is imparted to a sinful man, it may be as
the effect or consequent of an outward as well as of
an inward call (*vocatio*).[1] Grace is given to man,
and man responds freely. Man is separated from
God by sin, and cannot return of his own will.
He must seek a physician who can heal him, and
not try to heal himself.[2] This return to God lies
in his power, only by the help of God (*arbitrio ad-
jutorio Dei*). If men remain without *vocatio*, it is
the depravity of their own minds which makes them
sin. For that the grace of God enables a man to return to God, does not mean that man's will has no
part in the act. The return is voluntary. Free will
is not taken away by grace, but is established.[3] The
foreknowledge of God is held not to be inconsistent
with this view. Those who have been predestinated
to be delivered from sin have this grace.[4] They
are made free, because they have been chosen ; and
their own choice is the effect of God's choice. Sed
quia electi sunt elegerunt ; non quia elegerunt electi
sunt.[5] Inclinations and feelings are changed by
the grace of God, and so the volitions are changed.
Predestination is said to be the preparation for the
gift of grace ; and grace the gift itself. But the

---

[1] X. 717, 834.   [2] V. 352.   [3] X. 114.
[4] X. 839, 840 ; VII. 124 ; V. 762.   [5] X. 738, 812.

affirmation of efficacious grace does not involve the denial of second causes. The order of causes in the world has been fixed and foreseen by God. The will is a cause in the order of nature:—

et ipse quippe nostrae voluntates in causarum ordine sunt, qui cerus est Deo ejusque praescientia continetur; quoniam et humanae voluntates humanorum operum causae sunt. Atque ita qui omnes rerum causas praescivit, profecto in eis causis etiam nostras voluntates ignorare non potuit, quas nostrorum operum causas praescivit.[1]

The so-called fortuitous causes of the Greek and Roman philosophy are called by Augustine *latentes*; it is not denied that natural causes are efficient. They proceed ultimately from the will of God. They cannot be altogether separated from the will of him who is the author and founder of nature. Augustine explicitly rejects the conception of Fate, and that of fatal necessity. With respect to a decree of God, it may be said, however, *fatum est*. If it be held that our wills are controlled by necessity, so that we cannot will what we please, experience proves the contrary:—

necesse est ut ita sit aliquid, vel ita fiat, nescio cur eam timeamus, ne nobis libertatem auferat voluntatis.[2]

It is God's grace which operates (*operare*); it is man's will which coöperates (*co-operare*).[3] The change of will is experienced subjectively as a change of feeling or desire; so that even as man freely desires, so he chooses the good.

[1] VII. 123. [2] VII. 124.
[3] De Gratia et Libero Arbitrio, 33; cf. V. 832.

I

Is the will thus transformed, free or not? This is one of the obscure points in Augustine's doctrine. On the one hand grace restores the liberty which was lost at the fall of Adam; for Adam originally had free will.[1] On the other hand grace determines the will to what is good, just as before it had been determined by original sin. Augustine speaks of a freedom from righteousness, as well as a freedom from sin. The will to righteousness is effected by the grace of God. Whether Augustine's theory is compatible with freedom in the modern psychological sense, is doubtful. The perplexity and controversy which his doctrines have caused in the history of theology are a sufficient commentary on the difficulty of interpreting them consistently. There are parts of Augustine's writings in which he implies that the effect of grace is to restore the reason (*ratio*) to its lost supremacy in the soul. For he describes it as in the citadel of the soul,[2] swaying its movements, controlling its evil affections, and furthering righteousness of character and life.

As has been said above, men are held responsible for their actions. Those who deny that they are responsible, because their wills are determined by the grace of God, are accused of pride and irreverence. But those who have been predestinated and elected, and moved by grace, will persevere, and can never relapse into the state of depravity from which they have emerged.[3] Those who have simply the outward call, but are not predestinated, will not be saved.

[1] De Gratia et Libero Arbitrio, X. 765.   [2] VII. 370.   [3] X. 195.

St. Anselm

In general Anselm's theory of the will is the same with that of Augustine. Like the latter, he considers it principally in relation to original sin, grace, and righteousness. Like Augustine he lays emphasis upon the doctrine of predestination.

He does not define the term will as, according to him, it is equivocal. It may mean the instrument of willing (*instrumentum volendi*), or an affection of that instrument (*affectio ejusdem instrumenti*), or a use or practice (*usus*). It is placed on an equality with the reason, and priority is given to neither. There is something higher than both, which employs both as instruments. This higher something is the immaterial soul. As *affection*, the will is potential, and partly instinctive. The mother is said to will to love her child, not because she is always actually having the feeling of love, but because the feeling is not against her will, and will arise and become actual when an occasion is presented. The will belongs properly to man alone; the lower animals are subject to the appetites of the flesh (*appetitus carnis*). It may have either the just or the expedient as its object. But the will of what is just, is not innate, and is not always found in man. The unjust man does not will what is just; and the affection of willing what is just is not an inseparable property, for just men sometimes will what is unjust. But from the affections of willing justice and of willing injustice, man wills whatsoever he wills. The object

of volition may be either an end or a means to an
end; one may will righteousness in order to
be saved, or may will to be saved. The will
may be either positive or negative, that is, a man
may will to have or not to have. There is, furthermore, the efficient, the approving, and the permitting will. In relation to God, this distinction is
introduced to explain the existence of evil in the
world. In the philosophy of Anselm, the will
occupies a position midway between the two dispo-
sitions in man, the spirit and the flesh, the nature
which tends upward, and that which tends down-
ward. When the will joins itself with the carnal
nature, the soul is degraded; when it joins itself
with the spiritual nature, the soul is elevated.[1]

That which decides between two alternative
courses of action, is called by Anselm *liberum
arbitrium*. Following the doctrine of Augustine,
he holds free will to be a property of God and
of unfallen angels. The consideration of this
subject leads us from Anselm's general conception
of the will to his particular views respecting freedom and necessity.

I. *Freedom*. The conception of freedom may
be treated of in studying Anselm, either in relation
to the doctrine of sin, or in relation to the doctrine
of grace. By the freedom of the will he does not
mean the liberty of indifference, or the power of
contrary choice. He means: —

a. The liberation of the soul from sin, or the
preservation of righteousness in the unfallen.

<hr>

[1] Anselm, De Voluntate Libera.

b. The responsibility of the agent for his self-originated actions.

By freedom of the will is not meant the power of sinning or not sinning, inasmuch as God and the good angels have free will, and yet have no power of sinning. On the contrary, that will is said to be the most free, which has the least power of falling into sin.[1] Freedom is defined as power, and the greater the power, the greater the liberty.

Quoniam omnis libertas est potestas ; illa libertas arbitrii est potestas servandi rectitudinem voluntatis propter ipsam rectitudinem.[2]

The power to retain original righteousness shows a greater freedom than a power to either retain or desert it at pleasure. Sin was due, however, not to the curtailment of human freedom by any external coercion, but the willing to sin was within the souls of those who sinned, and thus the liberty of retaining original righteousness was lost. The act was spontaneous (*sponte*).[3] Losing the power to retain righteousness, man lost the power of willing what was right. The freedom which was lost was freely lost, and not forcibly taken away by temptation. It may be well to call attention at this point to the inconsistency of Anselm who finds liberty to consist in the power to retain righteousness, and who yet affirms that this righteousness was lost by an act of free will. In so far as the will sinned, according to his principles, it was not free, and freedom to sin is on these principles a contradiction of

---

[1] Anselm, De Libero Arbitrio, I.   [2] Id., ib. III.   [3] Id., ib. II.

terms. The will is so identified with a man that temptation is simply an occasion for the exercise of a will which in the fallen state has an intrinsic tendency to sin.[1]

There are two kinds of freedom, first, that which is neither caused by another, nor received from another, and which is possessed by God alone; secondly, that which is given by God and received from him. This belongs to angels and men. The unfallen angels had righteousness and freedom, and they preserved it; the others had it and lost it. Further, righteousness may be held separably or inseparably. It was held by all angels, separably, before the bad angels fell, and before the good were confirmed after the fall. It was held separably by man. It is held inseparably by God; and also by elect angels, and by men; by the former after the ruin of the fallen angels, by the latter after death.[2] From these principles we may conclude that free will consists in determination to righteousness, and the impossibility of doing anything but righteousness. Yet, Anselm does not adhere consistently to this view. The power to will anything but what is right is a weakness. It is only in a special and limited sense that we may affirm that Adam sinned of his own free will. If his will had been absolutely free, even as that of God is free, he would have had no power to sin. As in the doctrine of Augustine, it is grace which restores liberty to the fallen will. Without grace, the will is not free, and man is the slave of

[1] Anselm, De Libero Arbitrio, III.-V.   [2] Id., ib. XIV.

sin. In what way the slavery of sin limits the free will of man may be seen by the following passage from Anselm: —

Sine repugnantia et servus est, et liber. Nunquam enim est ejus potestatis, rectitudinem capere, cum non habet; sed semper est ejus potestatis, servare cum habet. Per hoc, quia redire non potest a peccato, servus est: et per hoc, quia abstrahi non potest a rectitudine, liber est. Sed a peccato et ejus servitute, non nisi per alium potest reverti: et rectitudine vero non nisi per se potest averti: et a libertate sua nec per se, nec per alium potest privari. Semper enim naturaliter liber est ad servandam rectitudinem, si eam habet: etiam quando, quam servet non habet.[1]

With Augustine, Anselm teaches also, that grace comes from God, and neither freedom nor righteousness has its source in man. A man may have it in his heart to hold the truth, because he knows it to be right to hold it. He has a right will (*rectam voluntatem*) and righteousness of will (*rectitudinem voluntatis*). If such a man be threatened with death, unless he consent to lie, he deliberates whether he shall sacrifice the right for the sake of his life or not, and makes a decision. The act of making the decision is *arbitrium*, and it is free. The man cannot have a right will, however, without the grace of God. That his will is right is due not to himself, but to God. If the will in the sense of *voluntas*, that is the disposition, be wrong, then the decision, or *arbitrium*, will be wrong. The wrongness of *arbitrium*, as of *voluntas*, is caused by the absence of grace. But a wrong decision is not

[1] Anselm, De Libero Arbitrio, XI.

given against the will: velle autem non potest invitus, quia velle non potest nolens velle; nam omnis volens ipsum suum velle vult.[1]

Actual sin is always a matter of the will. It is only potentially that sin is original. Original sin is manifest by its effects. Anselm defines it as follows:—

Originale igitur peccatum non aliud intelligo, quam quod est in infante, mox ut animam habet rationalem; quicquid prius in corpore nondum sic animato factum sit, vel post sive in anima, sive in corpore, futurum sit.[2]

Thus deprived of all righteousness (*justitia*) and consequently of all true happiness, men are, in the exile of this life, subject to sins which always confront them, unless the divine grace intervenes for their relief. Original sin has been transmitted from generation to generation, and the realism of Anselm implies the fall of the whole race really in the person of Adam. Episcopius seems to have been right when he associated realism with determinism to this extent, that whatever qualities as a sinner Adam once possessed, are really the qualities originally possessed by all sinners descended from him. If these qualities determine the will, the character is determined irrespective of the will, and the will is determined by the character. There is no sin actually in the person *per se;* but to sin one must will. The sinfulness of the will is due to the sinfulness of the character. In this sense the will

<hr>

[1] Anselm, De Libero Arbitrio,V.
[2] Id., De Concept. Virg. et Orig. Pecc. XXVII.

of fallen man is determined to evil. There is some difficulty in reaching a conclusion as to the extent to which the will is determined by the grace of God. If such power were at once given to the regenerate man that he could not fall again into sin, then it would be plain that freedom was completely restored by grace. To regain the power to do what is right, and to lose the power to do what is wrong are, according to Anselm's first principles, the highest kind of freedom. The grace of God does not make any one perfect in this life, and so the freedom of the will in this sense is not regained until after death. But a limited freedom is regained; for it becomes possible for a man to avoid sin, although actually he may not cease altogether from sinning. In so far as it is possible for him to sin, his sin must be determined by his sinful character, and in so far as he wills what is right, his right willing must be determined by the grace of God. What, then, is his responsibility for his evil deeds as a sinner, and what is his merit for his right deeds, done through the grace of God? It has been seen how this difficulty was met by Paul and by Augustine. Anselm's definition of liberty or freedom makes another kind of answer necessary.

The fact that original sin is inherited, and only actual sin is committed by the will, does not free the agent from responsibility. This is shown by the punishment of sin. All actual sins are sins of the will, and all punishments are punishments of the will.[1]

[1] Anselm, De Concept. Virg. et Orig. Pecc. IV.; cf. Proslogium, IX. X.

The realism of Anselm raises the question, why the other parts of man should be punished for that which is done by the will; and he replies, that the acts are punished not by the punishment of the person who commits them, but by the punishment of the will which has made the sins actual. All punishment is of the will, because all punishment is *contra voluntatem*. *Voluntas* is here used for the desires, and not merely for the deciding or executing power of the soul. Responsibility does not belong to infants who, although they have original sin, have no will; and only sins of the will are punished.[1] When men become intelligent, they become responsible. If it be asked why sin, even sin of the will is punishable, the answer is, because it is personal. That which makes righteousness righteous, and sin sinful, is that it belongs to a person who wills. Sin is a negation; it is really nothing. And if it be objected that it is unjust to punish nothing, the answer is that the punishment is not on account of the presence of nothing, but because of the absence of something, namely, righteousness. Nor is man excusable because he claims inability to do what he ought, just as a servant is not relieved of responsibility by his master for presenting such an excuse.

II. *Predestination and Necessity.* Prescience and predestination have no meaning in so far as they are related to God's view of the future; for to him all is present, and there is no past nor future. The knowledge of that which is about to be, the pre-

---

[1] Anselm, De Concept. Virg. et Orig. Pecc. I. II.

determination of all events, and the call of men, are all events in the present. But as God foreknows, he predestinates.[1] Anselm here differs from Augustine in holding that the prescience of God is the cause of predestination. And he quotes in proof of this the words of Paul: "whom he did foreknow, he also did predestinate." Two questions rose before the mind of Anselm, which were an inheritance from the ancient philosophy and from the earlier theology. The first was, what relation has predestination to necessity? and, second, what relation has predestination to free will?

Anselm says that the term necessary is often applied to that which is brought about by no force: saepe dicimus necesse esse quod nulla vi esse cogitur; et necesse non esse quod nulla prohibitione removetur. When it is said that God is necessarily immortal, or necessarily just, we mean that no force obliges him to be immortal or just; when it is said that a man will necessarily sin, it does not mean that he will be forced to sin. The chief peculiarity about Anselm's view of necessity is in the distinction which he makes between *necessitas praecedens*, and *necessitas sequens*. The distinction is derived from one already made by Aristotle, who held that necessity could not be predicated of future, but only of present and past, occurrences. The difference is that Anselm would regard any event which is about to happen, as about to happen necessarily, but would deny that any event could be said to be neces-

---

[1] Anselm, De Concord., etc., Q. I. 5.

sarily about to happen.[1] While the distinction is
not a valid one, and while it is apparently introduced
only to save from necessity the future free volitions
of men, it deserves notice as a significant part of
Anselm's theory. He sets out with the proposition
that God neither foreknows nor predestinates any
man to be just, *ex necessitate;* for without free will,
which is opposed to necessity, there is no justice or
righteousness. Still, it is admitted that all things
which are foreknown and predestinated happen
necessarily : necesse sit fieri quae praesciuntur, et
quae praedestinantur. Yet certain things which are
foreknown and predestinated do not happen with
that necessity which precedes and effects, but with
that necessity which follows the event: quaedam
tamen praescita et praedestinata non eveniunt ea
necessitate quae praecedit rem et facit, sed ea quae
rem sequitur.[2] As predestination does not precede
but follows foreknowledge, God who foreknows all
contingent events does not predestinate them before
they are foreknown. He is thus put, according to
Anselm's theory, in the position of one who consents
to events, not after they have happened, but after he
has known that they are about to happen. Nothing
is predestinated, therefore, which is not foreknown.
The free or spontaneous acts of men are foreseen
to be about to happen; the foreknowledge does not
make them necessary, for they are foreseen as

---

[1] Anselm, Cur Deus Homo, I. xvii. Est namque necessitas
praecedens, quae causa est ut sit res; et est necessitas sequens,
quam res facit.

[2] Id., De Concord. etc. Q. II. 3; cf. De Voluntate Dei, V.

about to happen according to freedom. It is likewise seen that a necessity will follow them, even if there is no antecedent necessity. For the conception of antecedent necessity is inconsistent with free will, inasmuch as all necessity is either *coactio* or *prohibitio*. Necessity can be predicated of future events only hypothetically, and not absolutely. Of any future event, it is not said that it will occur necessarily, but only that if it occur it will occur necessarily. This, according to Anselm, is only a conclusion from the principle of contradiction, that a thing cannot be and not be at the same time; if, therefore, the event will occur, it is inconceivable that it should not occur at the same time, and this constitutes the necessity of the future. The fact that it is foreseen, or predestinated, does not affect it either in the way of coaction or prohibition. Without discussing the logical validity of such a position, about which there is grave doubt, it may be said that Anselm's treatise *De Concordia*, etc., fails to give a consistent account of the determination of the bad will in original sin, and of the foreknowledge and predestination which are so explicitly divorced from necessity.

Necessitas sequens has no particular meaning in relation to future events. To know that an event which is about to occur will occur necessarily, is an affirmation either that the event is foreknown as about to occur, in which case it is impossible that it should not occur; or else it is foreknown that it is about not to occur, in which case there is no *necessitas sequens*. But it is difficult to see that Anselm has proved that *necessitas sequens* is distinguishable from *necessitas praecedens*, if it be held that God foreknows and predetermines the future. Psychologically, the man not knowing whether the event is predetermined or not, may regard it as not yet necessary, and consequently the supposed necessity of the future will not affect his action. That on which Anselm rests necessity is not so much the principle of contradiction as that of identity, as appears from his conclusion:—

Necessitate ergo omne futurum, futurum est; et si est futurum, futurum est, cum futurum dicitur de futuro; sed necessitate sequente, quae nihil esse cogit.[1]

St. Thomas Aquinas

The philosophy of Thomas Aquinas is the most perfect result of mediæval scholasticism. While his theory of the will in some respects resembles that of Augustine and Anselm, he surpasses both in the scientific treatment of the subject. His system is characterized by uniformity of method, coherence of parts, variety and precision of distinctions, and extraordinary logical consistency. His theory of the will, like that of Spinoza and that of Hegel, can hardly be stated, except in relation to the other parts of his philosophy. The terms of his psychology are equivalents, for the most part, of terms used by Aristotle. His definition of the soul as the *actus* or actuality of an organic body is

[1] Anselm, De Concord.. etc., II.

Aristotelian, and so also is his conception of the faculties and their relation to the essence of the soul. But his doctrine of the will is far more complete than that of Aristotle, and has had a very remarkable influence, not in the Catholic Church alone, but also in the theology of the Reformers.

I. *The Soul and its Faculties.* He rejects the theory of preëxistence, and affirms that the soul first has its *esse* in the body. Traducianism he regards as heresy.[1] The soul is not situated in any particular part of the body, but is the life and energy of the whole body,—est tota in qualibet parte corporis sui.[2] The body is both its object and instrument. It is united to the body as form and mover,—forma et motor.[3] Instead of making the vegetative, sensitive, and other principles, different souls, as was done by Aristotle, he regards these several principles as genera of mental powers; and of these there are five,—the same with those mentioned by Aristotle, and in certain places called by the latter Δύναμις. The soul is that which makes the body real, and it is also the *esse animatum.*[4] Where there is soul, there is life. In its lower genera it is to be found in the lower animals; but not the rational soul. The Gnostics and Manicheans had claimed a knowledge for the lower animals, so that they had attributed to these rational faculty, and had even maintained that beasts might pray. Thomas Aquinas teaches that the soul of man alone is rational among corporeal

---

[1] Summa Theol. I. Q. XC. 2, 4. [2] Id. I. Q. VIII. 2.
[3] Id. I. Q. LXXV. 3; Q. LXXVI. 1. [4] Id. I. Q. LXXVI. 3.

beings. And reason and intellect differ only *secundum perfectum et imperfectum*. As individual substances, souls are persons. And by substances is here meant, not the Greek Οὐσία, but the Latin *subjectum, quod substitit in genere substantiæ*. The soul as *subjectum* is one person. There is, however, a plurality of faculties, and the soul differs from its own faculties or powers, so that the latter have a real existence, though not as substances. All the powers of the soul have their roots in its essence; and when the attention is attracted to the operation of one power, it is withdrawn from the operation of another, because the soul can have but one intention.[1]

Of the five genera of powers enumerated by Thomas Aquinas, those which are chiefly related to his doctrine of the will are the appetitive and the intellective.[2]

Intellect is active and not passive.[3] It moves itself; but it may be either speculative or practical. These are not two faculties, but one.[4] The first is contemplative, and the second is externally operative. The speculative intellect *per extensionem* is the practical. Appetite is a faculty or power of the soul. It seeks that which the soul does not yet possess, and delights in this. Its movement is either towards or away from some object. There are three kinds of appetite: the natural, the sensitive, and the intellective or rational. The first of these is a more general name for the property of all

---

[1] Summa Theol. I. ii. Q. XXXVII. [3] Id. I. Q. LIV. 4.
[2] Id. I. Q. LXXVIII. 1. [4] Id. I. Q. XIV.

the faculties in so far as they pursue any object: *appetitus naturalis est inclinatio cujuslibet rei in aliquid ex natura sua.*[1] It may be said to accompany every operation of the soul. But appetite has not necessarily a bad meaning, for *appetitur summum bonum, id est Deus.* There are two kinds of motive power in the soul: one of these commands, and the other executes motion; one is *vis appetitiva*, the other is *vis motiva*. One of these moves the body, and the other is that whose act is not to move, but to be moved (*cujus actus non est movere, sed moveri*).[2] The sensitive appetite is moved by thought and also by imagination. But appetite alone is directly motive. Cognition cannot effect motion except through appetite. The sensitive appetite pursues all objects which appear good to the senses. Its acts are called passions. It may be either *concupiscibilis* or *irascibilis*, but in either case is subject to the control of the reason.[3] The rational appetite is the will,[4] and its acts are called volitions. The object of the rational appetite is the good *simpliciter*. Distinguished from the will (*voluntas*) is the intellect or understanding (*intellectus*). There is no will without reason or intellect; those things which are without reason tend towards an end, on account of natural inclination. Both intellect and will are natural properties of the soul, and the soul cannot be without them. The intellect tends towards things as they are in it,

---

[1] Summa Theol. I. Q. LXXVIII. 1.

[2] Id. I. Q. LXXV. 3.   [3] Id. I. Q. LXXXI. 1, 3.

[4] Id. II. I. Q. I. 2; II. I. Q. VIII. 1.

K

but the will as they are in themselves,—*intellectus* is also necessary to *voluntas*.

II. *The Distinction between Voluntary and Involuntary*. As has just been said, will is a rational appetite. Following John of Damascus, Thomas Aquinas defines voluntary action as motion and action from one's own inclination, that is, action from an internal principle: *motus et actus a propria inclinatione, id est quod agere sit a principio intrinseco*.[1] It does not involve any external result, and may be wholly within the soul. In order that action should be voluntary, there must be action with reference to some end. The action must be intrinsic, and not effected from without. The beginning of volition lies within the soul, and in this consists the spontaneity of man: *et ideo cum utrumque sit ab intrinseco principio, scilicet quod agunt, et quod propter finem agunt, horum motus, et actus dicuntur voluntarii*.[2] But in order that there should be intrinsic action *ad finem*, there must be knowledge. The greater the knowledge of the end which is sought, the more voluntary will be the action. In saying that the principle of voluntary action is intrinsic, Thomas Aquinas does not mean that it is the first principle, so that it is not moved from without or caused. It is a first principle *in genere appetitivi motus*. There is action towards an end even in the lower animals, who act according to intrinsic causes; but voluntary actions belong, properly speaking, to rational beings.

The act of will is either mediate or immediate.

---

[1] Summa Theol. I. II. Q. VI. 1.   [2] Id., Ib.

Immediate volition is the act itself of willing; mediate is effective only through some medium, as in willing to walk, in which the body is the medium. In the first case it is simply a certain inclination proceeding consciously from some intrinsic principle, while natural appetite is unconscious. Violence and coaction cannot be applied to the will, since the very nature of the latter is that it is not coerced from without. It acts from inclination, not from force. When it is moved by some appetite according to its own inclination, the movement is voluntary and not violent. The two terms are antithetical.[1] Actions done through fear are midway between voluntary and involuntary. *Per se* the act performed through fear is not voluntary, but it becomes voluntary in the avoiding act to escape the evil which is feared. Acts done through fear are therefore not necessarily compulsory.[2] Acts done through concupiscence, however, are voluntary. The object of such desire is a supposed good; and will is an appetite which seeks the good, either real or imagined. More important is the doctrine of actions done through ignorance. Aristotle had said that actions done through ignorance are involuntary, and with this Thomas Aquinas agrees.[3] That cannot be willed *in actu* which is not known. And this doctrine is complementary to one already stated, that intellect is essential to will.

III. *The Will and the Motive.* I use motive here in a very general sense, as meaning that which

---

[1] Summa Theol. I. ii. Q. VI. 4.   [2] Id. I. ii. Q. VI. 7.
[3] Id. I. ii. Q. VI. 8; cf. Aristotle, Eth. 1110, b. 18.

moves the will, because a large part of the theory of Thomas Aquinas is devoted to explaining the relation, in this respect, of the various powers of the soul to volition.[1]

1. *The Intellect as Motive.* As has been said above, there is no actual will without intellect, and there must be an end in view as object of the will.[2] The object to which the will tends is presented not by the will itself, but by the intellect. The volition is compared in this to the art which must be known in order to be practised. The helmsman must know how to steer in order to guide the ship.[3] It rules the will not by inclining it; for the will is itself an inclination towards the real or apparent good. It rules the will by demonstrating to it the object which is good, and by ordering or governing it; but there is no will in the intellect, although the latter is active. Nor is the intellect subject to the will, except that the former may be directed by the latter. In order to will there must be intellect, and the latter is superior to the former. The will is, however, mistress of her own actions, and comprehends both *velle* and *non velle*.[4] It therefore has power to move itself. Just as the intellect moves from premises to conclusions, so the will, in that it desires the end, moves itself towards willing the means to secure the end: —

Manifestum est autem quod intellectus per hoc quod cognoscit principium, reducit seipsum de potentia in actum,

---

[1] Summa Theol. II. Q. IX. 1.   [3] Id. II. I. Q. VIII.
[2] Id. II. I. Q. IX. 1.   [4] Id., Ib.

quantum ad cognitionem conclusionum ; et hoc modo movet seipsamet similiter voluntas per hoc quod vult finem, movet seipsam ad volendum ea qua quae sunt ad finem.[1]

The moving of the will by the intellect, and the moving of the will by itself, are different; by the intellect the will is moved according to the nature of the object; by itself, according to the reason of the end. In this respect there is an analogy between the *intellectus* of Thomas Aquinas and the practical reason of Aristotle.

2. *The Sensitive Appetite as Motive.* The object of the will is the good, either real or apparent. The sensitive appetite is an inclination towards the good, and so is capable of moving the will *per modum objecti.* It sets a good end in view, towards which the will may be directed. To say that the sensitive appetite may move the will is equivalent to saying that the will may be moved by the passions. But this is not to be understood as meaning that the sensitive appetite can dictate to the will: —

Voluntas igitur simpliciter praestantior est quam sensitivus appetitus ; sed quoad illum in quo passio dominatur, inquantum subjacet passioni praeeminet appetitus sensitivus.[2]

3. *An External Principle as Motive.* In one sense external principles may move the will, but only indirectly. Between the object which moves the will and the act of the will itself deliberation must intervene: hoc autem non potest facere nisi consilio mediante.[3] For example, when one wishes

<hr>

[1] Summa Theol. I. ii. Q. IX. 3. [2] Id. I. ii. Q. IX. 2.
[3] Id. I. ii. Q. IX. 4.

to be cured of a disease, he deliberates as to how this may be accomplished, and concludes that he has need of a physician. He wills according to this conclusion. It cannot be said that he has willed to have the volition to have the physician or to be cured, for this would proceed *ad infinitum*. The motive in the first instance is the external object, but the will is not compelled by the external object, because there has been intermediate deliberation. For it is the will itself which wills, although it may be moved to will by something beyond it. The motion would be violent (*violentus*), if it were contrary to the will; but in that case the action would be not voluntary but involuntary.

4. *God as Motive.* By the doctrine that God is motive, I mean the answer of Thomas Aquinas to the question whether God moves the will. God is both cause of the will and cause of the movement of the will. The existence of will as a power of the rational soul is owing to God, and each will is ordained to the willing of the good in general. God may move the will, not only towards the good in general, but also towards a particular good. To will anything by nature, is to will according to the tendency of the inclination in the direction of the good. As a natural motion, the motion of the will is intrinsic, that is, it is according to its own nature. Even in moving a stone the motion is intrinsic, that is, it is according to the nature of the stone; it is not natural to the stone to move, but, being moved, it is moved in accordance with its own nature.[1]

[1] Summa Theol. I. II. Q. IX. 6.

Predestination is a certain foreordination by God from all eternity of those things which, by the grace of God, are to be accomplished in time.[1] The term grace is in the definition, not because it is of the essence of the act, but because of its intimate relation to the result.[2] Predestination is a part of the providential government of God. Strictly speaking, it is applied only to the foreordination of the good; and the contrary term, reprobation, is applied to the predetermination of the bad. Predestination cannot be originated by man nor obstructed by man. It may be furthered and assisted by human instrumentality, by second causes, such as good works and the prayers of the saints. The cause of predestination is found not in man but in God. It is not because their merits are foreseen that men are predestinated.[3] The will of God is the efficient cause of predestination. It is eternal. It does not impose necessity on events nor remove contingency. Reprobation is a permissive act of God by which some men are permitted to fail of salvation. In the mind of God, predestination is active; but the mind of the predestinated is passive to the act of God. The free will of man is responsible for acts done when the man has been reprobated and deserted by grace.[4] He who is thus reprobated cannot obtain grace.

It pertains to providence to order things to an end. Necessary causes are prepared for necessary events, and contingent causes for contingent events;

[1] Summa Theol. III. Q. XXIV. 1. [3] Id. I. Q. XXIII. 5.
[2] Id. I. Q. XXIII. 2. [4] Id. I. Q. XXIII. 3.

but the providence of God is eternal. He sees all things as present. The future is therefore as certainly fixed as the past; but the voluntary actions of men are contingent.[1]

Grace may be either operative or coöperative, prevenient or subsequent. These distinctions are Augustinian. God is the cause of *operare*, and moves the soul; but the soul moves and is moved by coöperating grace. There is also a prevenient grace which is antecedent to man's voluntary act, and subsequent grace which comes as the result of man's coöperation with prevenient grace. The doctrine of Thomas Aquinas cannot therefore be reconciled with the Jansenist interpretation of Augustine. If the soul be prepared for the reception of grace, this preparation is the effect of grace.[2]

IV. *Voluntas and Liberum Arbitrium.* There is a general analogy between *intellectus* and *ratio* on the one hand, and *voluntas* and *liberum arbitrium* on the other. To know (*intelligere*) means the simple acceptance (*acceptionem*) of anything. Hence principles especially are said to be known. And this knowledge is direct, *sine collatione*. The knowledge of reason (*ratiocinari*) is the passing from one principle to something else, that is, to the knowledge of something else.[3] Analogically, there is the will of an end, which seeks something on its own account; and there is choice, which seeks the means to an end (*voluntas de fine qui propter se appetitur,*

---

[1] Summa Theol. I. Q. XXII. 4.   [2] Id. II. i. Q. CXI. 2, 3.
[3] Id. I. Q. LXXIX. 8.

and *eligere est appetere aliquid propter alterum consequendum*). The choice is an act of *liberum arbitrium*. But just as intellect and reason are not two faculties, but one, so *voluntas* and *liberum arbitrium* are the same faculty in different acts.[1] Free will (*liberum arbitrium*) is a faculty (*facultas*), for it has potestatem expeditam ad operandum; et sic facultas ponitur in definitione liberi arbitrii. It is a power (*potentia*) in so far as it can operate (*ut potens operari*), and it is also a habit (*habitus*) in so far as it is fitted or adapted to operate (*ut aptus ad operandum bene vel male*).[2]

It is an appetitive not a cognitive power, although it is said that the free judgment is an act of the free will. Any design is determined first by the opinion of the reason (*per sententiam rationis*), and, second, by the acceptance of the appetite (*per acceptionem appetitus*).[3] In so far as we apprehend, the faculties are intellect and reason; in so far as we are appetitive, the faculties are will and *liberum arbitrium*. The essence of free will is its power of choice.[4] If man did not have this, advice, precept, prohibition, would be in vain. The lower animals have an action *naturali judicio*, which takes place without any deliberation about alternative courses. Man acts, however, by free decision (*libero judicio*), and chooses between alternate volitions: quia per vim cognoscitivam judicat aliquod esse fugiendum vel prosequendum. The free will is not subject to the control of the passions or to the sensitive appe-

---

[1] Summa. Theol. I. Q. LXXXIII. 4. [3] Id. I. Q. LXXXIII. 3.
[2] Id. I. Q. LXXXIII. 2. [4] Id. I. Q. LXXXIV. 3.

tite in general. Such inclinations are under the sway of the reason, and are obedient to the reason. But free will holds itself in a state of indifference with respect to choosing well or ill: liberum arbitrium indifferenter se habet ad bene eligendum vel male. There seems to be a circle in the reasoning of Aquinas with respect to free will in relation to intellect. As has been shown, intellect moves the will, and without intellect there is no will. It has also been shown that will moves the intellect, while intellect is implied in every act of will. The motion of the will *ab intrinseco* is not inconsistent with either of these statements; but where the will is not moved *ab intrinseco*, it is moved either by an object or by the representation of an object. The sensitive appetite may rebel against the reason, but the will as an appetite is always rational.[1]

What is called choice (*electio*) consists in a certain motion of the soul towards the good, as its object. It is not a deliberative syllogism concerning the good which is to be willed; it involves comparison, but the comparison is made by the intellect, and choice is the result of the comparison. Ignorant choice is made, when there is no knowledge of that which is to be chosen.[2] Choice is not subject to necessity. A man is able to will or not to will, to act or not to act. The conclusion which moves the will is not a necessary conclusion, because the premises are not necessary; it is only under certain conditions that choice is necessary; and the fact that choice is necessary only under certain

---

[1] Summa Theol. I. Q. LXXXIII. 1.   [2] Id. I. II. Q. XII. 1.

conditions is the ground for affirming that it is contingent. Where the conditions attending either alternative to be chosen seem equal, there is nothing to prevent the intrusion of some condition which will overbalance choice of one alternative and effect choice of the other.[1]

It seems hardly necessary, after the full statement of the doctrine of sin in the theories of Augustine and of Anselm, that much should be said of this aspect of the theology of Thomas Aquinas. Like other Catholic theologians, he maintained that sin may be original as well as actual. It affects not the faculties or powers of the soul, but the essence of the soul itself. By sin man lost free will (*liberum arbitrium*). This was the loss not of natural liberty, which is the effect of coaction, but of liberty from fault and from misery. The result is that free will is not sufficient for righteousness unless it is moved and assisted by God. The choice of the good is determined by ourselves : supposito tamen divino auxilio.

V. *Necessity in Relation to the Will.* Necessity is either material or formal. According to another division, it is necessity either of coaction or of the end. In general, that is said to be necessary which is not able not to be (*quod non potest non esse*). Material necessity is from some intrinsic principle, as when it is said that a compound of contraries is corruptible; formal necessity is of another kind, as when it is said that the angles of a triangle are

[1] Summa Theol. I. II. Q. XIII. 6.

equal to two right angles. Necessity of the end is another name for utility, as when without a certain thing a certain course cannot be taken, on account of some extrinsic cause. Necessity of the end is implied, when it is said that food is necessary to life, or a horse for a journey; but the extrinsic cause may be some agent; the will may be forced by this extrinsic influence; and this is the necessity of coaction. This last form of necessity is altogether opposed to voluntary action. The essence of will is that it should be an inclination, and inclination cannot be coerced. Necessity of coaction removes all merit from an action. But the necessity of obedience to a precept is not a removal of obligation or merit.[1]

The contingent is the opposite of the necessary, for it is that which can either be or not be: quod potest esse et non esse. There is an element of necessity in every contingent event. When, for example, Socrates is said to run, his running is contingent, but it is necessary that Socrates should be moved if he runs. Actions of the will are included in the predetermining purpose of God, but are not absolutely determined, for choice is contingent. And because choice is not necessarily determined, but is contingent, the will is free, although the future is certain.

While Thomas Aquinas has expressed himself with regard to the will in a manner which it is difficult to misunderstand, he has been variously interpreted. There is certainly no Pelagian nor Semi-

[1] Summa Theol. I. Q. LXXXII. 1.

Pelagian doctrine in his theology; nor, on the other hand, is there any justification for the statement of a modern critic, that he makes God a relative being, discourages the individual, and reduces him to despair or to moral indifference.[1]

The doctrine of Thomas Aquinas was opposed by the leading philosopher of the Franciscan order, Duns Scotus. He denied the primacy of the intellect, and affirmed the primacy of the will. In his theology there is a tendency towards a Pelagian view of the human will in its relation to God and to original sin. This opposition did not cease with the death of the two leaders of the conflicting schools, and the debate was continued by a succession of Dominican and Franciscan doctors, who were called respectively Thomists and Scotists. According to Duns Scotus, the will determines itself, and is not determined by the intellect. Acts of the will are contingent, and there is the power of contrary choice; the intellect, however, is necessarily determined. The will has, indeed, an office in knowledge, coöperating with man's receptive capacity. In this doctrine Duns Scotus seems to have anticipated what Kant afterwards explicitly taught, that in the act of knowledge the spontaneous activity of the understanding must supplement the mere receptivity of the sensibility. In his practical philosophy, Duns Scotus is far from hold-

[1] D'une part, en effet, il fait de Dieu lui-même un être relatif, dont la volonté est l'esclave de l'intelligence. D'autre part, il fait plus que d'humilier l'individu : il décourage et le réduit au désespoir ou à l'indifférence morale.—A. Weber, *Hist. de la Philosophie Europ.* 241.

ing the doctrines of predestination and determinism, even in the moderate form in which they were presented by Thomas Aquinas, and yet the former, by insisting on the primacy of the will in God, goes so far as to maintain that everything which exists outside of God has its origin in the will of God. God wills necessarily only his own essence; all else is *secundario volitum*.[1]

CALVIN

Questions concerning the will, which among the later Schoolmen had chiefly a theoretical interest, became of vital importance among the Protestant Reformers and their opponents. Scarcely had the disputes between the Thomists and the Scotists begun to die out, when a controversy arose between the leader of the Reformers and the most eminent scholar of the revival of letters. Luther's work, *De Servo Arbitrio*, was followed by the *Tractatus De Libero Arbitrio*, of Erasmus. The doctrine of Justification taught by the Reformers explains in some degree their theories of the will. In the Reformed theology, justification is not a process which goes on within the soul of man, but is an act of God; it does not imply that man is made just or righteous, but only that he is putatively righteous, owing to the grace of God. It is God who justifies by imputing righteousness to the believer, and the condition or instrumental cause of justification is faith. Instead of winning par-

---

[1] Compare Erdmann, Grundr. der Gesch. der Phil. I. 417–419.

don by means of the sacraments and good works, the soul acquires pardon by an act of faith. And faith, the Reformers taught, is imparted by the free grace of God. Inasmuch as they supposed this grace to be bestowed antecedent to any act on the part of the individual soul, it was necessary that they should explain why some men are justified and led into holiness, while others are left in sin and misery. Logically they were obliged to maintain that the justification, sanctification, and perseverance of man must be attributed to the sovereign will of God. Any more ultimate explanation than this, they did not seek to give. The choice of some to the exclusion of others, to be the recipients of this saving grace, was thought to be a secret of the divine plan. This choice was called by the theologians *election*, and the doctrine of election in the early Reformation as well as in later times has sometimes been made a shibboleth of party. Rightly or wrongly the Reformers believed that they were logically obliged to lay great emphasis on this doctrine. Universal predestination involves a predestination of means as well as of ends. And among certain of the Reformers the importance of the human will was minimized, while great emphasis was laid upon the grace of God. There were some advocates of the doctrine of election who were reluctant to attribute the reprobation of the non-elect to the will of God, either as permissive or efficient cause. But the more logical writers in taking the first position were compelled to take the second. To say that man could will to be saved only by the grace of God, and without the grace of God would be lost, was to establish a certain causal relation between the favor of God, and the will to be saved. And the violent and exaggerated expressions of Martin Luther, his scornful allusions to human righteousness, and his bold statements concerning the efficacy of grace doubtless encouraged Antinomianism, and libertinism, and made many rest with fatalistic complacency upon the divine purpose, and look upon their own conduct as non-essential.

Erasmus, in the treatise just referred to, opposed the extreme doctrine which had been expounded by Luther, and taught a moderate theory of predestination, which was not greatly at variance with that of many Catholic theologians. For other reasons, his teaching was held to be repugnant to the Catholic faith, and his work was condemned by the Council of Trent. There is, however, no necessary opposition between an extreme doctrine of predestination and the leading dogmas of the Catholic Church. At first sight it would appear that a departure from the Augustinian position with respect to predestination and grace harmonized better with the Latin view of justification. If a man believes that he is freely justified without any sacramental means, and without good works,— in short, simply through faith, and that saving grace has been bestowed anterior to any good work of his own, he will have no difficulty in harmonizing that view with extreme predestination. If on the other hand a man believes that he is justified by works, he will be less inclined *practically* to the view that his justification and perseverance have been predetermined before the foundation of the world. Yet there is really no logical difference between the two men in their relation to predestination. If the first man has been predestinated to have faith, he will have faith, and will persevere; and if the second man has been predestinated to be baptized and to do good works, he will be baptized and will do good works. There is no more difficulty in supposing the predestination of a sacramental act, and of a good work, than there is in supposing the predestination of faith and perseverance. If a failure to lead a holy life in one case imperils the soul, or loses the soul, it is a sign that the man was not predestinated to eternal life. If a man who has professed faith, does not show signs of sanctification, it may be inferred that he has not been elected. But in both theories, whether election be conditional or unconditional, the elect are held to be known only to God. Upon this last point all schools of theology which teach election are at one. The Catholic Church has indeed always been very circumspect in its teaching concerning predestination. If, on the one hand, Augustine and Thomas Aquinas are decided in their doctrine, Jansenism was condemned by the same high authority which silenced Pelagius. It is in a certain school of Protestant theology that the most extreme form of predestination has been taught. Into the refinements of this discussion during the sixteenth and seventeenth centuries, it is not

L

necessary for me to enter. Nor is it of especial importance that any further notice should be taken of the issue between Luther and Erasmus. The dispute between Calvin and the Arminians, however, has an important bearing on the theory of the will. This brings us to the opening of the period of modern philosophy; but the discussion is as old as the Apostolic age. It has made an immense literature, which is less read than formerly. The different shades of opinion involved, and the wide geographical extent 'of the dispute, make it impossible, even if it were advisable here, to do more than trace in outline the doctrine of the will in the works of John Calvin, and in those of Episcopius perhaps the ablest Arminian theologian.

The psychology and ontology of Calvin, in spite of his rejection of a great deal of Catholic dogma, are not radically different from those held by some of the Fathers and Schoolmen. He distinguishes the essence of the soul from the essence of the body, and gives a classification of mental faculties. Although man was made in the image of God, his soul is distinct from the essence of God. In general the soul has two faculties: intellect or understanding, and will.[1]

Sic ergo habeamus, subesse duas humanae animae partes, quae quidem praesenti instituto conveniant, intellectum et voluntatem. Sit autem officium intellectus, inter objecta discernere, prout unumquodque probandum aut improban-

---

[1] Calvin uses *appetitus* as a synonym of *voluntas* (*appetitus seu voluntas*), Inst. II. ii. 2.

dum visum fuerit: voluntatis autem, eligere et sequi quod bonum intellectus dictaverit, aspernari ac fugere quod ille improbaverit.[1]

Thus it is the office of the intellect or understanding to discriminate between objects, and to decide whether they are to be approved or disapproved; it is the office of the will to follow and to choose what the understanding declares to be good. It is the intellect which governs the soul, and the will is subject to knowledge. Avoidance and pursuit in the appetite resemble affirmation and negation in the intellect.

Ergo animan hominis Deus mente instruxit, qua bonum a malo, justum ab injusto discerneret: ac quid sequendum vel fugiendum sit, praeeunte rationis luce videret, unde partem hanc directricem ἡγεμονικόν dixerunt philosophi. Huic adjunxit penes quam est electio.[2]

Will is therefore used by Calvin, not only as a synonym for the act of volition, but for the appetite, whether sensitive or intellective. The first man had these two faculties, intellect and will in perfection; and his will was free. Had he so chosen he might have had eternal life. Adam fell because his will was capable of being inclined in either of two ways. His choice of good and evil was free. Calvin disposes summarily of the objection that God might have made man incapable of falling into sin. He replies that God was under no necessity to give man any other kind of will. Adam had the power to remain righteous had he chosen to exer-

---

[1] Calvin, Inst. I. xv. 7.   [2] Id., ib. I. xv. 8.

cise it. But he freely fell. The sin of Adam has polluted the nature of his posterity and all the powers of men are depraved. In this way all the volitions have become corrupt. Defending this extreme doctrine, Calvin opposes those who regard the free will as arbiter between the dictates of the reason and the appetite, as if man were capable of choosing the good and avoiding the bad; and he denies that virtue and vice are in our own power, inasmuch as original sin has taken away our power, and has even corrupted the faculty by which good and evil are recognized. This view of free will which he opposes, he attributes to all philosophers (*haec ergo philosophorum omnium sententiae summa est*) and he blames theologians who have adopted the same opinion. The Patristic teaching generally meets with his disapproval. He criticises Chrysostom for his defence of free will; and even the Anti-Pelagian arguments of Jerome fail to satisfy him, for the latter taught that man begins and God completes: liberum arbitrium quid esset, quum in omniun scriptis identidem occurrat, pauci definierunt.[1]

According to Peter Lombard, there are three kinds of Freedom: 1. Freedom from necessity, 2. Freedom from sin, 3. Freedom from misery. Calvin criticises this arrangement on the ground that no distinction is made between necessity and coaction. According to him original sin necessarily determines the will to evil, but this necessity acts upon the will, not against the will. Grace deter-

---

[1] Calvin, Inst. II. ii. 4.

mines the will to good, but this again is necessary determination, and not involuntary nor coercive.

Calvin opposes another distinction which was adopted by the Schoolmen,—that between operative and coöperative grace. He regards this distinction as obscuring the fact that a good will comes altogether from the grace of God, for the term coöperate implies a good will, and this again implies that the grace of God is not essential to such a will. Calvin would therefore deny absolutely the ability of the will to will what is good, unless determined necessarily thereto by the grace of God. And to speak of the will coöperating with grace, according to him, implies that the will may resist the grace of God. He admits that when men sin they sin voluntarily; but to call this free will is to say that man has control over his whole heart and mind, so that he is able to incline to whatsoever he please. On the contrary, Calvin, in insisting that man is depraved, holds that this depravity makes man unable to will what is good; for it has affected the faculties of knowing as well as those of acting. The emotions are depraved as well as the deliberations : —

Quum ergo ratio, qua discernit homo inter bonum et malum, qua intelligit et judicat, naturale donum sit, non potuit in totum deleri : sed partim debilitata, partim vitiata fuit, ut deformes ruinae appareant.[1]

Sic voluntas quia inseparabilis est ab hominis natura, non periit : sed pravis cupiditatibus devincta fuit, ut nihil rectum appetere queat.[2]

[1] Calvin, Inst. II. ii. 4.
[2] Id., ib. II. ii. 12.

Calvin places choice in the will, however, and not in the understanding. Choice depends on right reason, that is, on right deliberation. Man naturally desires what is good, according to his natural inclination, which does not involve deliberation. It is therefore no argument in favor of freedom that man naturally desires what is good. He must know what is good according to the right reason, and when he knows it, he must choose it, and when he has chosen it, he must pursue it : —

Nihil ergo hoc ad arbitrii libertatem, an homo sensu naturae ad bonum appetendum feratur: sed hoc requiritur, ut bonum recta ratione dijudicet, cognitum eligat, electum persequatur.[1]

The inability of the natural will towards the good is removed by grace. This grace is not prevenient merely, but irresistible. There is no power in man to resist or oppose efficacious grace; although, as has been said, it does not force man against his will. The sacred Scriptures are appealed to by Calvin to support this position.

The most ingenious and original part of Calvin's theory is that in which he opposes those who present objections to this deterministic doctrine. To the Pelagian objection that unless sin is of the will there is no sin, and if sin is avoidable it is voluntary, Calvin replies that the essence of sin is not in its being freely committed, but in its being voluntary, and that determinism does not deny the fact but only the freedom of will. Another Pelagian

---

[1] Calvin, Inst. II. ii. 26.

objection was that unless virtues and vices are voluntary, there is no ground for rewards or punishments, because there is no merit nor demerit. Calvin replies that punishments are justly inflicted because those who sin are guilty of evil actions by their own will. Rewards, on the contrary, do not depend upon our own merit, but on the divine benignity. This is closely related to that other affirmation of Calvin, that men are good because they are elect, and their election is due, not to their own efforts, but to the mercy of God. Another objection raised, is that all exhortations and warnings are in vain unless man has free will. The burden of Calvin's answer to this is taken from Scripture and from the writings of Augustine; but the rational argument is that exhortations and warnings are secondary causes which determine the will. Calvin's attempt to strengthen his case by an appeal to the writings of Augustine is only partially successful, even if we accept the authority of the latter as decisive, for, as has already been shown, the teaching of Augustine concerning the will is by no means free from ambiguity.[1]

Although there is no direct evidence that such was the case, I believe that the theory of the will afterwards defended by Hobbes was in great part derived from the works of Calvin. The similarity of language, as well as the similarity of doctrine, points to this, especially in those passages in which determinism is defended against the objections of opponents. In the case of Hobbes the subject is

[1] Calvin, Inst. II. iii.

discussed with greater regard to psychological principles, and more weight is assigned to the emotional elements in man. While Hobbes had no theological purpose to serve, there is a striking parallel between his scriptural citations and those of Calvin.

With respect to Calvin's doctrine of Predestination, very little need be said. In most points it covers the same ground which has been already traversed in connection with the theories of Paul and Augustine. According to Calvin, however, the prescience and predestination of God should be sharply distinguished. To God, the past, the present, and the future are as one; all is present. Predestination is *decretum Dei*. By this decree is determined what shall happen to every man. Some are predetermined to salvation; some are predetermined to damnation. Each man being created for salvation or for damnation is predestinated to either life or death. By an immutable and eternal decree, God has fixed the salvation or the perdition of every man once for all. Calvin admits that this view is unpopular; but God, he maintains, is a law unto himself, and cannot be held accountable to any other law, much less to human law. God owes nothing to any man. The most striking part of this discussion is that in which Calvin rejects the traditional dogma of the " permissive decree," which affirms that God did not predetermine, but only permitted the fall of man, and the perdition of the non-elect. It is absurd, he maintains, to say that God did not determine positively the destiny of his principal creation. And in reply to those who contend that such a doctrine makes men indifferent about their moral conduct, he shows the actual results produced by such teaching.[1]

Such ambiguities as were to be found in this extreme theology of Calvin were effectually removed by some of his most acute disciples, and while some interpreters are disposed to find the theory of Calvin himself less uncompromising than I have shown it to be, there is no ambiguity whatever in the writings of such men as Beza, Twiss, Edwards, and others of the supralapsarian school.

EPISCOPIUS

Opposition to the doctrines of the school of Calvin arose among the Reformers of Holland. The leader of these was Arminius, and their views are best represented in the writings of Episcopius. According to these early Arminians, the distinctive doctrines of Calvin and of Beza are nothing less than an affirmation of fatal necessity.

According to Episcopius, the term will is used in three ways: (1) as a faculty, *facultas volendi* ; (2) as the act of willing, *actus volendi;* (3) as the thing willed, *res volita.*[2] The mistake of the determinists has been that they have distinguished faculties which should not be separated. These faculties are judgment and will, or, to speak more precisely, intellect and will. These are not two faculties, but one. Will without intellect is brute will (*brutam voluntatem*). Will is not merely active,

---

[1] Calvin, Inst. III. xxi.   [2] Episcopius, Disput. I. VI.

it is also intellectual. Voluntatem et intellectum non esse duas animae potentias realiter ab ea et a se distinctas; ex hac distinctione orta esse omnes circa doctrinam de libero arbitrio difficultates.[1]

Voluntas enim non est facultas quaedam distincta necdum diversa ab intellectu, uti neque intellectus facultas aut potentia quaedam est diversa a vita divina . . . vita enim divina, et anima humana immediatum sint tum intellectionis tum volitionis principium . . . quia si voluntatis est potentia distincta aut diversa ab intellectu tum necessè est ut voluntas et volitio omnis caeca sit, et stulta sive irrationalis, prout suo tempore demonstrabimus fusius.[2]

Episcopius was led to insist upon this identification of the will with the intellect, in order to oppose a prevalent doctrine that the will was determined by the intellect. He wished to restore the primacy of the will, not by raising it altogether above the intellect, but by recognizing it as intellect. In so doing, he brought back the will to a closer relationship with the moral agent. He would make the will not the slave of the intellect, which waits until another faculty has determined whether or how it shall act. Will is a self-determining principle, just as the intellect is a self-determining principle. If this doctrine can be established, then there is of course no servitude of the will to the intellect, and so far the freedom of the will is defended. But the defence of indeterminism is simply removed to another arena. It must be shown that the acts of the intellect are voluntary. The only other alterna-

[1] Episcopius, Tract. de Lib. Arbit. II.
[2] Id., Inst. Theol. IV. ii. 20.

tive is, that the dictates of the intellect are offered to the will, which has power to decide freely and intelligently, prior to action. This would involve the contradiction of two principles of intellect in the soul, one voluntary, and the other involuntary. It is probable that Episcopius wished to avoid such a contradiction. He would identify intellect and will, not in order to show that intellect is voluntary, but that volition is intelligent. Hence the statement that will without intellect is *brutam voluntatem.* It is worthy of notice that his countryman, Spinoza, not long afterwards, followed the example of Episcopius, in affirming the unity of intellect and will. But Spinoza drew another conclusion, holding that the identification of the two faculties was a reason for denying the freedom of the will.

Will, according to Episcopius, is free or has liberty. And by liberty is meant the dominion of man over the acts of intellect and will: per hominis libertatem intelligi dominium ejus in actiones voluntatis et intellectus quarum aliae sunt familatrices et imperatrices.[1] Free will is that which is able to act or not to act, or to do this or that, when all things requisite for action are present: liberum arbitrium, quod positis omnibus ad agendum requisitis, agere potest aut non agere, vel hoc vel illud agere.[2] It will have been seen that Episcopius does not adhere to the principle that the will and the intellect are one; for he distinguishes in the former of these two passages the act of one from that of the other. The contradictory of freedom is necessity. It is

---

[1] Episcopius, Tract. de Lib. Arbit. I.   [2] Id., ib.

therefore not sufficient to define liberty as freedom
from external coercion.   The objects of free choice
are goods (*bona*) either real or apparent.[1]

In connection with this theory of Freedom, Episcopius denies the doctrine of Original Sin: corrup-
tionis istius universalis nulla sunt indicia nec signa;
imo non pauca sunt signa ex quibus colligitur naturam totam humanam sic corruptam non esse.
The cause of sin was the free will of man: fuit
ipsa hominis libera voluntas spontaneo et libero
motu sese determinans, et convertens ad objectum
a mente seducta propositum et affectui desidera-
tum.[2]   And as the free will of man is the cause
of sin, so it is this free will which makes him responsible.   Into many of the theological implications of this teaching, it is not necessary to enter.
But Episcopius argues especially against the opinion
that future events are necessary because they are
certain, and so are known to God.   He admits that
there is foreknowledge and prediction of future
events; but this does not determine them necessarily.   They are foreknown as contingent.[3]   Of
two alternatives, one is certain;   but because the
end is certain, it does not follow that the means
are determined necessarily.   Thus the foreknowledge of our actions on the part of God does not
determine them.   God is not the cause of sin, but
simply permits it.   On this point Episcopius opposed Socinius.[4]   The latter denied the prescience
of God, on the ground that this would exclude con-

<hr>

[1] Episcopius, Tract. de Lib. Arbit. VI.   [3] Id., ib. IV. ii. 17.
[2] Id., Inst. Theol. IV. v. 2.   [4] Id., Bod. Inept. VIII.

tingent events. In like manner Calvin insisted that the future was necessary because it was foreknown by God. While there is less uniformity among the Arminians than among the Calvinists in the matter of doctrine, the opinions of Episcopius were adopted and taught by many noted divines upon the Continent, among whom the most important were Courcelles, of Amsterdam, Limborch, a relative of Episcopius, and Le Clerc. The Arminians might claim in their favor the traditions of the early Patristic age; while the principles of Calvin with respect to original sin, and the determination of the will, are more closely related to the views of Augustine and Anselm.

CHAPTER FOURTH

THEORIES OF THE WILL IN BRITISH PHILOSOPHY FROM BACON TO REID

AT the beginning of the modern period, the gradual emancipation of philosophy from scholasticism, and the change of method are not very evident in the treatment of the will. Writers on psychology and ethics were still inclined to confine their attention to the theological aspects of the subject. They continued to discuss it in connection with the doctrine of predestination. The revolution in metaphysics and psychology was not immediately apparent in the philosophical consideration of human agency. That which had been disputed with so much energy among the Reformers, at length became an object of purely philosophical interest. Whether we look at the thought of the Continent or at that of Great Britain, we find everywhere the conception of will governed by theological opinion. It was not until the publication of Locke's *Essay* and Spinoza's *Ethics* that the subject of voluntary action became actually independent of theology.

The methods of English philosophy, derived directly or indirectly from Bacon, did not effect uniform results. The period after Locke, which includes the English writers of the eighteenth century, in which the prevailing method was empirical, was noisy with the disputes of those who affirmed and those who denied the freedom of the will. Until the time of Hume, there was no radical departure from the earlier views of the nature of the will; and the discussion of freedom was for the most part theological. From what has been said of the rise of Calvinism and Arminianism, it may be inferred that the issue between the two was likely to appear in philosophy itself. In England during the sixteenth and seventeenth centuries, when the public policy was largely affected by theological interests, it is not surprising that matters of theology should intrude upon scientific discussions. Thus we find Hobbes justifying his doctrines by appealing to Scripture as well as to reason. The final cause of Berkeley's metaphysical theory was the refutation of atheism and materialism. Even Hume is associated in the popular mind with attacks on religion, more than with his valuable services to the advance of philosophy.

In the period from Bacon to Hume, there is a development from empiricism to scepticism. Bacon defined the method; Hume showed its logical results. All subsequent philosophy is related affirmatively or negatively to the principles of Hume. Affirmatively he is the father of later English associationalism and agnosticism, and of French positivism. Negatively, his works form the starting-point of the later German philosophy, and of Scottish thought from Reid to Hamilton.

FRANCIS BACON

Bacon is the apostle of a method, rather than the founder of a school. He applies this method to the realm of nature, and pays less attention to that of mind. His psychology is fragmentary, his ethics are unsystematic, and in metaphysics he shows a dislike for the subtleties of the mediæval Schoolmen. He lays emphasis, however, upon the regularity and universality of causation. He criticises those who speak of fortune rather than of Fate. He finds fault with Epicurus for preferring the idea of chance to that of a single principle under which all phenomena may be united.[1] There is a Providence or divine purpose concerned with the most minute events.

In classifying *facultates animae*, he distinguishes will from intellect, reason, phantasy, memory, and appetite.[2] The science of the will is a part of ethics. Intellect and will are twins. Both fell in the fall of man. Intellect lost its original illumination, and will lost its freedom. The action of the will is determined by the understanding. It is the function of the latter to determine, of the former to act. Voluntary motion may be incited by imagination, and the latter faculty may control the reason. The freedom lost by man, according to Bacon, is the moral not the natural freedom of the will,—as was taught by the theologians. Through divine grace, the will becomes an instrument in the attainment of virtue.[3]

[1] Bacon, De Augmentis, II. XIII.

[2] Id., ib. IV. III.   [3] Id., ib. VII. I.

While these statements might have been made by a philosopher of almost any school, they have a certain interest as the opinions of one whose influence was felt in all subsequent English philosophy.

Thomas Hobbes

It has often been denied that Hobbes was a follower of Bacon in anything except in time. There is, it is true, hardly any mention of Bacon in his works; his method is not Baconian, but analytic and deductive; he attaches very little value to experiments in natural science; and his respect for older systems is quite different from the hostility of the author of the *Novum Organum*. It is, moreover, difficult to show that any actual influence was exercised by Bacon on the mind or on the philosophy of Hobbes. It is known, however, that the two philosophers were friends; that both of them were profoundly affected by the revival of interest in natural science during the sixteenth century; and that the problem before each of them was the interpretation of nature. Bacon's view of nature was general, and his attention was not confined to any particular department of knowledge. Hobbes would interpret human nature, and his philosophy is concerned chiefly with the interpretation of man as an individual, and of men collectively in civil society. In order to ask and answer the political question, he first asks and answers the anthropological question. He will first examine the body natural, and then proceed to examine the body politic. Like Bacon, he disregards authority as a test of truth, although the political and religious character of his age made it important that he should show the accordance of his doctrines with the Scriptures. But this is different from saying that his doctrines are derived from a religious source. Unlike Bacon he employs the syllogism in his philosophical discussions, but he insists that the premises shall be well established in order that the conclusions may be valid. But just as Locke from the psychological point of view sought to reconstruct human knowledge on a natural basis, so Hobbes from a political point of view seeks to explain the foundation of civil society. While he does not recognize his own method as empirical, it is evident that his appeal is mainly to experience. Next to his political theory, his teaching concerning the will is the most important part of his philosophy.

Like Bacon, Hobbes emphasizes the principle of causation. Every effect has a necessary cause, and the cause is always sufficient to produce the effect.[1] The object of the philosopher is to seek the causes of given effects, and the effects of given causes.

The passions of the mind are of two kinds: (1) appetites, (2) aversions. The "small beginnings of motion within the body of a man, before they appear in walking, speaking, striking, and other visible actions, are commonly called endeavor."[2] When the endeavor proceeds towards a definite object by

<hr>

[1] Hobbes, I. 108.   [2] Id. III. 39.

which it has been excited, it is called appetite or desire. Appetite is the approach of the soul to a desired object; while aversion is the retiring from that which is not desired.[1] He criticises the Schoolmen for supposing that there could be mere appetite without actual motion. Some appetites are innate, others are acquired. Living creatures have sometimes appetite and sometimes aversion to the same thing, as they think it will be for either their good or their hurt. Prior to the actual satisfaction of the appetite there may be a "vicissitude" of appetites and aversions, — a hesitation between two courses of action. This vicissitude Hobbes calls deliberation.[2] This lasts as long as the agent has it in his power to obtain what is desired, or to avoid what is not desired. In order to action there must be one last appetite which is satisfied, or in accordance with which the action is performed. This last appetite is will.[3] Accordingly, the will is defined as "the last appetite in deliberating." Two conditions of an action about which there is deliberation are laid down: (1) it must be future, and, (2) there must be some possibility of the action being done. Hobbes expresses his meaning clearly when he says: "It is all one, therefore, to say *will* and *last will*; for though a man express his present inclination and appetite concerning the disposing of his goods, by words or writings, yet shall it not be counted his will, because he hath still liberty to dispose of them other ways; but

---

[1] Hobbes, I. 407 f.   [2] Id. 408.
[3] Id. 409.

when death taketh away that liberty, then it is his will."

Actions are voluntary, or involuntary, or mixed. A voluntary action is that which has its beginning in will. All others are involuntary or mixed. An involuntary action is one which is done " by necessity of nature," as when a man falls or is pushed. A mixed action is partly voluntary, partly involuntary; as when a man goes to prison. He may walk voluntarily, but he walks to prison involuntarily.[1]

Hobbes is the first philosopher to investigate the train of thought in relation to the will. Our thoughts proceed in two ways: either without design, and under no control of will, or else regulated by some desire or design.[2] In the former case the links are bound together by the principle of association; in the latter case, the course is directed to a certain end. There is also a distinction made between spontaneous and voluntary actions. All voluntary actions that are not done through fear are spontaneous,[3] and are said to be done of a man's own accord. In such actions there is no necessity for deliberation. It may be added that Hobbes would call voluntary, even the automatic movements of the body as in walking.

The will is not the effect of any other faculty, that is *volitio* is not the effect of *voluntas*. Neither is will the cause nor the effect of appetite : voluntas non est appetitus causa, sed ipse appetitus.[4] The

---

[1] Hobbes, III. 48, 120, 138, 197.
[2] Id. III. 13, 50, 61.
[3] Id. IV. 243.
[4] Id. II. 95 (Latin).

Schoolmen were mistaken who defined the will as a rational appetite. For, according to this definition, there could be no voluntary act against reason. The will is an appetite "resulting from a precedent deliberation."[1]

The power of an agent and efficient cause are the same. Power and act thus correspond to cause and effect.[2] Cause refers to that which has already produced a result. Power refers to the future. There is also passive power which is to be identified with material cause. Active and passive power together constitute the entire cause. The effect follows just so soon as the cause is entire. The action in like manner follows just so soon as the "power is plenary." Where the power is not plenary, the act is impossible.

Setting out from these metaphysical and psychological statements, Hobbes treats of the will in relation to the ideas of necessity and freedom. He sets forth the doctrine that the will is necessarily determined. Like Calvin and others, he seeks to establish this by an appeal to the Scriptures. But his argument is principally philosophical. And his writings upon this subject are probably the most important that have appeared in defence of determinism.

Hobbes deals with a question which vexed the later Greek philosophers. With respect to disjunctive judgments concerning the future, one of the alternatives *must* be true. If it shall either rain or not rain to-morrow, one of the alternative events

[1] Hobbes, I. 409.　　　　[2] Id. I. 127.

will happen necessarily. That the alternative is indeterminate and contingent, means only that we do not know which of the two alternative events will come to pass. To say that a thing is, and to say that it is contingent is one and the same. But Hobbes maintains that contingent causes are, properly speaking, no causes at all. They can effect nothing without concurrent causes. There is nothing casual; for even events like the fall of dice are to be attributed to necessary causes. A contingent event is only one for which we do not perceive the cause. These principles are applied to voluntary actions. The will is an effect among other effects. It is determined by necessary causes. There are no contingent acts of will. If it be asked whether will may not be excepted from this law, an answer may be found in the psychological part of Hobbes's theory.

The importance which Hobbes gives to the principle of causation underlies his whole view of voluntary action. His determinism rests not on the rather vague relation of the will to the predetermination of God, but to the union of all events by virtue of this general law. In this respect he effected a radical change in philosophy, and since his day a principal point of controversy has been whether the will is an effect among other effects, governed by necessary causes, or whether its action is an exception to the law. But Hobbes is not content to defend his determinism upon metaphysical grounds alone; he founds a great part of his argument upon principles of psychology, and recognizes the questions of responsibility involved by his denial of freedom. These various aspects of his theory may be given in order.

1. All causes are effects of a first cause, and all effects so proceeding from this first cause are necessary.[1] That is said to be necessary "which is impossible to be otherwise, or that which cannot possibly otherwise come to pass. Therefore necessary, possible, and impossible have no significance in reference to time past or time present, but only time to come."[2] A sufficient cause is one in which nothing is wanting to produce the effect. The same is a necessary cause. If an act of the will has "a sufficient cause, it is necessarily produced."[3] From this point of view, all events are necessary, and no events are contingent. Even chance events are caused necessarily.[4]

2. Hobbes is not satisfied with a mere dialectical defence of his theory of determinism. In a truly Baconian passage he appeals to experience. In the last analysis determinism must be proved empirically. Having already shown that the will is the last appetite after deliberation, and that volitions proceed from the will and from nothing else, he seeks to demonstrate psychologically that the will is determined. By liberty or freedom is meant that which is unhindered, as water which is free to flow so long as it is not prevented from flowing, and as will which is free, except in so far as it is forcibly restrained. "Liberty is the absence of all im-

---

[1] Hobbes, IV. 261.   [3] Id. IV. 274.

[2] Id. V. 105.   [4] Id. IV. 276.

pediments to action that are not contained in the nature and intrinsical quality of the agent."[1] A spontaneous action is one which is not preceded by deliberation. A free agent is one who can either act or refrain from acting;[2] and his freedom consists in the absence of external impediments to action. Voluntary actions can be called free only in the sense that they are not prevented. The deliberation which precedes the action is not will, for will is the last appetite after deliberation. The contention of Hobbes that will is an appetite, and that the appetite is necessarily determined, shows him to have been far from holding a theory of "self-determination." To resolve to do a thing, is to will to do it after deliberation.[3] But no man can determine his own will; for the will is an appetite. In this respect it is like hunger. No man can determine whether he shall be hungry or not. There is some confusion in Hobbes's doctrine at this point. He affirms that it is within man's choice whether he shall eat or not eat; but that he has no liberty whether he shall be hungry or not. He holds that the appetite of hunger is caused necessarily; it is therefore not apparent why he considers the appetite of the will, which effects eating or not eating, to be less determined than the appetite of hunger. From his arguments elsewhere, it is plain that he regards all choice as determined; and in close connection with the doctrine just stated he affirms that "if a man determine himself, the question will still remain, what determined him to determine himself

<hr>

[1] Hobbes, III. 196; IV. 273. [2] Id. IV. 240, 275. [3] Id. V. 34

in that manner."[1] This contradiction is not explained.

While there is no question of the freedom of the
will to act, there is no freedom to act in a particular way. The will cannot suspend itself, that is, it
is impossible to will not to will. Furthermore, the
will is always related to the present. Future purpose is not will.

Except in his statement that some appetites are
native to the soul, Hobbes does not explain why it is
that extrinsic motives produce different effects in
different men. For the theory which attributes
acts of the will to necessary causes should especially seek to explain why in any particular case certain causes effect certain volitions. Hobbes does
not dwell upon intrinsic causes of volitions. It is the
natural efficiency or effaciousness of external objects
which affect the appetite, and determine the acts of
voluntary agents. The last dictate of the understanding is something which, as it were, tips the
scale, and effects the particular action. " *The last
dictate of the judgment,* concerning the good or bad,
that may follow on any action, is not properly the
whole cause, but the last part of it, and yet may be
said to produce the effect *necessarily,* in such a manner as the last feather may be said to break a
horse's back, when there were so many laid on before as there wanted but one to do it."[2]

3. The moral consequences of this theory are
also discussed by Hobbes. In fact, the particular
attention which he gave to voluntary action arose

<hr>

[1] Hobbes, V. 34.   [2] Id. IV. 268.

from a dispute with Bishop Bramhall concerning the relation of the will to the will of God and to certain moral principles. Bramhall, as is well known, was an Arminian bishop of the English Church. In the presence of the Marquis of Newcastle, he disputed with Hobbes, and the dispute was continued in writing. In the long and able defence of his opinions, Bramhall thus enumerates the consequences which he supposes follow logically from the doctrine taught by Hobbes. His objections are not all of equal force; but they summarize quite fully the main arguments which were once employed in opposition to determinism.[1]

a. That the laws which prohibit any action will be unjust. Hobbes replies that it is the will to break the law which makes the act unjust, and not the necessity of the act. If any one justifies his failure to keep the law, on the ground that he was necessitated to break it, his punishment will act as a cause that others are deterred from crime.

b. That all consultations are vain. It is replied that deliberation or consultation is a necessitated means to a necessitated end, and is therefore not superfluous.

c. That admonitions to men of understanding, are of no more use than to children, fools, and madmen. The same answer is here given as was given *t- b.*

d. That praise, dispraise, reward, and punishment are in vain. Praise and blame, reward and punishment, are not in vain, says Hobbes; for they are all causes which determine the volitions.

<hr>

[1] Hobbes, IV. 252.

e, f. That councils, acts, arms, books, instruments, study, tutors, medicines, are in vain. As in his reply to *b*, Hobbes here holds that because an effect shall necessarily come to pass, it does not follow that it shall come to pass without any cause. Nor will there be neglect of religious duties, and of prayer, in case determinism be accepted. These depend for their efficacy upon the power of God, because all things proceed from his eternal will. That which gives moral quality to acts is not the freedom of the agent in willing. Sinful acts are sinful not because they are free, but because they are voluntary.[1] Hobbes departed from the ancient theological opinion that freedom of the will consists in freedom to do right, or follow the good. According to him, there is no freedom to do right or to do wrong. Right and wrong actions are necessarily determined, and are right and wrong because they are voluntary.

4. His theological doctrine requires some consideration, in so far as it is related to philosophy. All causes are the effects of prior causes, until the first cause is reached, which is God: Deus ergo, qui videt et disponit omnia necessitatem videt omnium actionum a sua ipsius voluntate proficis centium. . . . Nisi enim voluntas Dei necessitatem voluntati humanae imponeret, et per consequens actionibus omnibus ab ea dependentibus; libertas voluntatis humanae omnipotentiam et omniscientiam et libertatem Dei tolleret.[2] The acts of God are said to proceed from his power rather than from

---

[1] Hobbes, IV. 259.   [2] Id. III. 160 (Latin).

his will.   Like the ancient Fatum, the divine decree is described as *verbum Dei.*   While Hobbes was an opponent of political liberty, and while his theories of the state were opposed by the Puritans, we find him in theology taking up a position like that of the Calvinistic Reformers.   He regards the doctrine of free will and the denial of predestination to be modern inventions of the Catholic theologians, particularly of the Jesuits.   He holds that the foreknowledge of God is not the cause of anything, but that God simply foreknows that which has been already determined.   He faces without flinching the problem as to the origin of evil. God is the author of all causes and effects, but is not the author of sin.   God cannot commit sin, for the reason that it ceases to be sin if it is the will of God that it should happen.   But lest it should appear that he is denying the reality of sin, Hobbes makes a distinction between the author and the cause of sin.   The author of a thing is one who orders it to be done; and in this sense God is not the author of sin.   But God is the cause of sin. If it be objected that men are unjustly condemned, Hobbes would reply that this objection still leaves the difficulty, why God elected some, and did not elect others; and yet punished them in advance of their doing good or ill.[1]

He does not think that his theory is inconsistent with the idea that God is moved by the prayers of pious men.[2]   Such prayers do not alter the eternal decrees of God; but just as the gift bestowed has

---

[1] Hobbes, III. 501 (Latin).   [2] Id., II. 124.

been predetermined, so it has been predetermined
that it should be bestowed in answer to prayer.   It
is like the slave of Zeno who pleaded that he was
predetermined to commit theft, but who had also
been predetermined to be beaten for it.   The means
are predetermined as well as the ends.[1]   It may be
added that Hobbes's doctrines commended themselves as little to the Calvinists as to the Arminians,
and to this day it is often ignorantly said that he
was both a materialist and an atheist.

LOCKE

The inconsistencies and ambiguities of Locke's
philosophy cause some difficulties of interpretation.
Theoretically, his method is empirical; but the
results reached cannot be derived from experience
alone.   A more rigorous application of his method
gave rise to the philosophy which began with Voltaire and Condillac, and ended in the French materialism of the eighteenth century.   A more liberal
interpretation of Locke's theory of ideas found
expression in the philosophy of Berkeley, and indirectly in the scepticism of Hume.   The first
principles of Locke are that experience is the
source of all ideas; that ideas are the objects of
the understanding when a man thinks; that the
channels of experience are two in number, sensation and reflection; one is outward, the other inward.   The mind is *tabula rasa*, and there is
nothing in the understanding but what was previ-

1 Hobbes, IV. 551.

ously in the outer and inner sense. Setting out from such principles, it was inevitable that Locke should encounter difficulties in explaining the activity of the soul. In spite of his avowed method, he is far from teaching consistently that the mind is a mere passive surface, upon which experience writes its records. Experience gives, it is true, simple ideas of sensation, such as color and sound, but there is also the experience of reflection. Among the ideas of the inner sense are certain faculties or powers. These faculties exhibit the soul as spontaneous and active. Locke holds, indeed, that the faculties are simply the powers of the one mind, which is working in different ways. The power is receptive as well as productive. There is spontaneous activity [1] in the formation of complex ideas, such as space, time, cause and effect, and substance. The faculties of the mind may be referred to two *genera:* perception or thinking, and volition or willing.[2] The latter is enumerated among the simple ideas of reflection.

Locke's theory of the will comprehends a consideration of power and of freedom.

I. *Power.* This is a simple idea derived from sensation and reflection.[3] We obtain it from our observation that we can, at will, move the several parts of our bodies, and that other bodies produce changes upon each other. In general, the idea of power is caused by our experience of change. The possibility of anything having any of its simple

[1] Locke, Essay on the Human Understanding, Bk. II. xii.
[2] Id., ib. Bk. II. vi.   [3] Id., ib. Bk. II. vii.

ideas changed is power. By *simple ideas* in this sense are meant the qualities of that which is changed. Power is thus passive as well as active. It is, moreover, "a principal ingredient" in our idea of substances.[1] It involves the complex idea of relation, although it has been defined as a simple idea. But in this doctrine Locke shows a disposition to associate power with the conception of cause. He holds, also, that the mind receives a better idea of power from reflection on its own operations than from external sensations. All actions of which we have any idea reduce themselves to two, thinking and motion, which are apparently correlative to the faculties already mentioned, — perception and volition.

It having been affirmed that the mind has the idea of power, it is next shown that we find within ourselves a power to begin or forbear, continue or end, several actions of our minds, and motions of our bodies, barely by a thought or preference of the mind ordering, or, as it were, commanding, the doing or not doing such or such a particular action. This power is the will. Its particular exercise in any direction is volition or willing.[2] The forbearance of that action consequent to such order or command of the mind is called voluntary. And whatsoever action is performed without such a thought of the mind is called involuntary. Elsewhere he adds that volition is an act of the mind knowingly exerting that dominion it takes itself to

[1] Locke, Essay on the Human Understanding, Bk. II. xxi.
[2] Id., ib. Bk. II. xxi. 4, 5.

have over any part of the man, by employing it in, or withholding it from, any particular action. It is the power of the mind to determine its thought. Stripped of all disguises, will is nothing but the power or ability to prefer or choose.[1]

In these statements there is some confusion of definition. Locke seems to hesitate whether to define as volition the executive act of the mind, or the acts of decision and choice. But he holds that one faculty does not determine the action of another.[2] For example, the understanding does not determine the will, nor the will, the understanding. It is the mind which determines the will.

In order that there may be volition, the object of the will must be in our power. Deliberation precedes the will, but does not determine the will, unless a feeling of uneasiness be excited: "We are seldom at ease, and free enough from the solicitation of our natural or adopted desires; but a constant succession of uneasinesses out of that stock, which natural wants or acquired habits have heaped up, take the will in their turns; and no sooner is one action despatched, which by such a determination of the will we are set upon, but another uneasiness is ready to set us on to work."[3] There will be a constant rise of alternative desires, some of which will claim immediate satisfaction, and the main uneasiness which would otherwise determine the will may be kept waiting; but this at last "stands upon fair terms with the rest, to be satis-

---

[1] Locke, Essay on the Human Understanding, Bk. II. xxi. 14.
[2] Id., ib. xxi. 19.   [3] Id., ib. xxi. 45.

fied; and so, according to its greatness and pressure, comes in its turn to determine the will." Locke maintains, rather inconsistently, that the mind may suspend volition, and decline to prosecute a desire, until it has further deliberated.[1] According to his own principles, such a suspension of the will would be an act of will, and this would imply that some particular uneasiness had prevailed.

II. *Freedom.* From the account just given, Locke's determinism is manifest. He draws a strange distinction between will, and liberty or freedom. Liberty, according to him, does not belong to the will. For liberty is itself a power, and belongs to agents, not to the powers of agents. It is not the will but the agent which may be properly called free. The question is, therefore, not whether the will, but whether the man, is free. To ask whether the will is free would be like asking whether one power had another power. According to Locke, man is free, in so far as he can choose the existence or non-existence of an action by the direction or choice of his mind. Wherever there is preference or choice of what lies within the power of a man to perform or not to perform, the man is free. If it be asked whether man, then, wills what he pleases, the answer must be affirmative.[2] For freedom consists in being able to act or not to act, according to choice.[3] The action must be externally possible, however, and the contrary action must also be possible. The power of

---

[1] Locke, Essay on the Human Understanding, Bk. II. xxi. 47.
[2] Id., ib. xxi. 14-21.   [3] Id., ib. xxii. 27.

N

contrary willing cannot belong to a man, if its contemplated object be impossible. Locke overthrows all this doctrine, however, when he offers a definition of liberty "to the learned world." "Liberty," he says, "is a power to act or not to act, as the mind directs."[1] This definition, although it is supposed to refer to liberty in willing, shows the inconsistency and confusion of Locke's thought. Liberty in acting is confounded with liberty in willing.

That which causes the mind to determine the will, however, is some "uneasiness."[2] The term is rather indefinite. Hobbes had made no generic distinction between will on the one hand, and desire or preference on the other. With this Locke does not agree. He appeals directly to self-consciousness to establish his view of volition. And although he holds that the will and desire may be opposed to one another, yet he defines the uneasiness which moves the will as desire; and, conversely, calls desire the uneasiness of the mind on account of some absent good. That which immediately determines the will, from time to time, to every voluntary action is the uneasiness of desire, fixed on some absent good — either negative, as indolence to one in pain, or positive, as enjoyment of pleasure. The greater good does not determine the will, for man may will the lesser good. According to Locke life would be unbearable were it not that uneasiness carries with it its own remedy

---

[1] Locke, Essay on the Human Understanding, Bk. II. xxii. 71.
[2] Id., ib. Bk. II. xxi. 29. 31 f.

by moving the will to act in avoiding it, and taking the first step in the way of happiness. The
desires are "springs of action" which have been
put in man as an endowment of the All-wise Maker, –
"suitably to our constitution and frame, and knowing what it is that determines the will." It is,
however, the present desire rather than the contemplation of the prospective good which most
easily determines the will.   "A little burning felt,
pushes us more powerfully than greater pleasures
in prospect draw or allure."[1] In defending this
view, Locke criticises effectively the intellectual theory of human action, according to which
the mere knowledge of an absent or prospective
good is sufficient to determine the will. The spring
of action is within us, not beyond us. It is not
the natural object which determines the will, but
the desire or uneasiness of the soul. When some
one spring of action is in control to the exclusion
of any other, the will is supreme.

Thus any vehement pain of the body, the ungovernable
passion of a man violently in love, or the impatient desire
of revenge keeps the will steady and intent; and the will,
thus determined, never lets the understanding lay by the
object, but all the thoughts of the mind and powers of the
body are uninterruptedly employed that way by the determination of the will, influenced by that topping uneasiness
as long as it lasts; whereby it seems to me evident that the
will or power of setting us upon one action in preference to
all other is determined in us by uneasiness.[2]

[1] Locke, Essay on the Human Understanding, Bk. II. xxi. 34.
[2] Id., ib. Bk. II. xxi. 38.

Although Locke has previously said that one faculty does not determine another, the above passage implies that the will may determine the understanding, and be in turn determined by the feelings. For it is not the natural object which moves the will or effects the uneasiness. Yet Locke says, also, that it is happiness which produces or determines the uneasiness. Where there are conflicting desires and incompatible feelings, the most pressing desire determines the. will. In the expression "most pressing desire" may be seen an equivalent for what some later writers have called "the strongest motive."

But if it is the mind which determines the will, what is meant by mind? According to Locke, substance is a mere collection of qualities united by the imagination. Power is one of these, "a principal ingredient of substance,"[1] volition is another. The sum of these qualities is substance. If, therefore, the mind determines the will, it must be the other qualities of various kinds which determine the will. In any event the spring of action lies beyond the will, and itself determines the mind to will. Unless the mind were uneasy, it would not will in one way rather than another. All that can be concluded as to the determination of the will by the spring of action, is that Locke finds the latter to lie within not without the mind. Judgment, it is true, may correct the desires; there is no compulsion of the mind in willing. But the conclusion is clearly deterministic. This appears further from

1 Locke, Essay on the Human Understanding, Bk. II. XXIII. 7.

Locke's statement, that liberty may be hindered by external obstacles, but that a man who ceases to be a free agent by outward restraint recovers his liberty when he recovers his understanding, and his power to act or to forbear.[1] Necessity in relation to the will is found in cases where there is no power to act or to forbear in accordance with the direction of thought. Where there is no thought, there is no freedom. But both thought and motion may be present and liberty be absent.

If one were disposed to insist upon a strict interpretation of Locke, it might be urged that the mind should have no freedom, because it has no spontaneity. According to the principles of his method, it would be difficult to prove the spontaneity of the mind, which is *tabula rasa*. If we overlook this inconsistency, it appears that while the mind may arbitrarily move the will at discretion, it is itself moved and determined to will by the uneasiness which is the spring of action; and the uneasiness is produced by an external object. In the Patristic and Scholastic philosophy, the will was so identified with a man's character and inclination that the depravity of the man involved the depravity of the acts of will. Voluntary acts were determined by original sin. The moment the will is separated from the character as Locke separates it, and has a place given to it of independence in the hierarchy of mental faculties, it loses its identification with the self, the true nature of the man, and becomes

---

[1] Locke, Essay on the Human Understanding, Bk. II. xxi. 9, 10, 11.

subject to judgments and desires, which in their nature are involuntary rather than voluntary. Belief in freedom may be impossible, if it be supposed that the character is enslaved by evil; but such a view is more easily harmonized with the idea of freedom than with the doctrine that the faculties of the mind are so many separate powers. This is especially true, if these faculties collectively constitute the substance of the soul. Cousin saw this, and in his mistaken criticism of Locke appealed to the self-consciousness of the reason to refute the theory.[1] There is no more vital doctrine in the *Essay on the Human Understanding* than the doctrine of Substance. It is possible that Locke himself felt the difficulties attending his metaphysical theory when he suggested that God might have endowed matter with a power of thinking. And while this admission was vigorously attacked by Stillingfleet, it was taken up by the French school and taught as a dogma by the materialists. In Great Britain, it was Locke's doctrine of substance which prepared the way for Hume. According to the French writers, the several faculties were functions of a material unity in the brain; according to Hume, the unity was an illusion, for he failed to "catch" self in the act of perception.

From Locke's meagre statements it is hard to determine the relation of his theory of volition to morality. Moral good consists in the conformity of voluntary actions to some standard, with sanc-

---

[1] V. Cousin, La Phil. de Locke, 155.

tions.   The good or evil which attends upon such actions constitutes reward or punishment respectively.   Such sanctions must be known, otherwise the wills of men will not be determined to virtue. He fails also to consider voluntary action in the light of cause and effect.   In the *Essay* his discussion of the causal relation is limited to the consideration of the physical world.   It need not be said, therefore, that he does not follow Hobbes in regarding will as a necessary effect.

The tendency to deny the primacy of will, as well as sharply to distinguish the faculties from one another, is henceforth apparent in British philosophy.   One faculty of the mind is set over against another.   The judgment is independent of the will. The bond of union between them is not clearly explained.   They are "united by the imagination." Such a view shows a reaction against the scholastic view.   But the intellectualism which prevailed in European philosophy through the powerful influence of Thomas Aquinas harmonizes at some points with the conclusions of Locke.   To say that the intellect determines the will is to say virtually that the idea of reflection, which is called judgment, controls the idea of reflection, which is called volition. In the former case the faculties are supposed to have a real union in the spiritual substance of the soul.   In the latter case, the substance of the soul is a congeries of qualities which are called either ideas of reflection, or powers, or faculties.   That mere ontological principles do not lead to any particular doctrine of freedom is demonstrated by the

fact that Spinoza, with his monistic theory of substance, reached deterministic conclusions not far
removed from those of the English psychological
school. It was upon the general psychological
foundation of Locke that Collins and Priestley
built their extreme theories of necessity, to which,
however, I can only refer, without giving them
more extended consideration.

Before considering the theory of Locke's immediate successor in British philosophy, I may call
attention for a moment to an interpretation of his
philosophy in France, which may be more appro-
priately mentioned here than in connection with
the development of the continental philosophy in
general. Voltaire and Condillac are philosophically
responsible for the French misunderstanding of
Locke, and so indirectly responsible for the dogmatic materialism of the philosophers just before
the Revolution. Voltaire was an admirer of both
Newton and Locke. He brought their writings to
the notice of the French public. In his *Traité de
Métaphysique*, Voltaire readily expresses his indebtedness to Locke; but he does not recognize
reflection as one of the sources of ideas, and maintains that all our knowledge is derived from the
senses.[1] In another treatise, he teaches that the
present is born of the past, that the Great Being
who holds the chain of events cannot permit it
ever to be broken, and that inevitable destiny is
the law of all nature. He denies that man is free
to will, although he is free to do as he will. There

---

[1] Voltaire, Tr. de Met. Chap. III.

must be a cause for every volition; otherwise man, and not God, would be master of the world:—

Il est impossible qu'il veuille sans cause. Si cette cause n'a son effet infaillible, elle n'est plus cause. . . . Il faudra toujours reprimer les méchants ; car s'ils sont déterminés au mal, on leur repondra qu'ils sont prédestinés au châtiment. [1]

Condillac, while agreeing with Voltaire that all knowledge is derived from the senses, affirms that the will is free. In his *Traité des Sensations*, he compares man to a living statue, which comes into being without any previous experience, and receives knowledge wholly from without. Condillac's dissertation on liberty is supplementary to his *Traité des Sensations*. He supposes that the statue which has received the ideas of sensation finds itself at length affected by desires which are of equal force, so that no one of them can prevail over the others:—

Elle flotte entre plusieurs objets, et elle se porte pas plus à l'un qu'à l'autre. [2]

Through experience, the statue finds that unless it resists certain desires, it will suffer pain, and in consequence of pain will feel remorse. It is therefore led to deliberate as to the preferable course of action, when several alternatives are presented to it. It resists some desires and follows others. It may even choose that which it least desires; [3] and when the feelings are violent, there will be no de-

---

[1] Voltaire, Il Faut Prendre un Parti, XIII.
[2] Condillac, Diss. sur la Liberté, 2.
[3] Id., ib. 8.

liberation. In case the desires are moderate, there will be deliberation:—

Or quelles que soient ses connaissances, nous avons vu qu'elle en sait assez pour être sujette au repentir: elle en sait donc assez pour avoir occasion de déliberer.[1]

The consequence of this deliberation will be that in some cases the desire which most tempts the statue will be that which is conquered or controlled. Such an act is called choice; and when choice has once been made, the statue knows by experience that it had the power to choose the opposite. Liberty is the power of doing or not doing in order to action. It is through liberty that choice is possible:—

Car la liberté n'est que le pouvoir de faire ce qu'on ne fait pas, ou ne pas faire ce qu'on fait.[2]

It is not a question whether one has the power in general to will or not to will; but whether when one wills there is also power not to will, and when one does not will there is also power to will.[3] But without the act of deliberation there is no liberty and no choice. Liberty, however, does not consist in independent determinations, without reference to the action of objects on the subject of the volition. Following the terminology of Locke, Condillac holds that an uneasiness (*inquiétude*) is caused by the absence of desirable objects, and that through experience choice is regulated so that the most use-

---

[1] Condillac, Diss. sur la Liberté, 10.
[2] Id., ib. 12.   [3] Id., ib. 14.

ful and desirable ends may be attained. Knowledge of the means is requisite to secure the end sought. It is this which constitutes freedom, and not the ignorant will of the end. Liberty is thus the effect in determination of deliberation:—

Confiez la conduite d'un vaisseau à un homme qui n'a aucune connaissance de la navigation, le vaisseau sera le jouet des vagues. Mais un pilote habile en saura suspendre, arrêter la course ; avec un même vent il en saura varier la direction ; et ce n'est que dans la tempête que le gouvernail cessera d'obéir à sa main. Voilà l'image de l'homme.[1]

The writers who afterwards drew materialistic conclusions from Condillac's theory of knowledge rejected the doctrine of Indeterminism which has just been presented. They followed Voltaire in his determinism, but their defence of the latter doctrine is not deserving of special mention.

BERKELEY

As Locke's theory of ideas was ambiguous, it is not surprising that Berkeley should have found in it a justification for denying the existence of matter. It is not possible, however, to trace any connection between Berkeley's theory of knowledge and his doctrine of the will. He is an opponent of determinism, and regards it as a consequence of a false theory of the concept. So far there may be some ground for considering his nominalism as the cause of his indeterminism. Yet Hume, who held

---

[1] Condillac, Diss. sur la Liberté, 18.

substantially the same logical doctrine, was a determinist.

The nature of the will is discussed incidentally in the *Principles of Human Knowledge*, and the problem of freedom in *The Minute Philosopher*. According to Berkeley, the only existences are God and created spirits. A spirit is one undivided active being. In so far as it perceives ideas, it is called *understanding*, and in so far as it produces or otherwise operates about them, it is called *will*. Berkeley will not recognize these as distinct from each other nor from substance in general. Spirit is known, not *per se*, but only by its effects; but will, soul, and spirit "do not stand for different ideas, or in truth for any idea at all."[1]

He says:—

I find I can excite ideas in my mind at pleasure, and vary and shift the scene as oft as I think fit. It is no more than willing, and straightway this or that idea arises in my fancy: and by the same power it is obliterated, and makes way for another. This making and unmaking of ideas doth very properly denominate the mind active. Thus much is certain, and grounded on experience, but when we talk of unthinking agents, or of exciting ideas exclusive of volition, we only amuse ourselves with words.[2]

Thus the activity of the soul is identified with will, and the ideas themselves are attributed to the voluntary agency of God.

In the seventh dialogue of *The Minute Philosopher*, determinism is opposed by Euphranor, who

[1] Berkeley, Principles of Human Knowledge, XXVII.
[2] Id., ib. XXVIII.

represents the opinions of the author. The discussion grows out of a theological consideration of the will in relation to divine grace. It is said that there has been no more fruitful topic for controversy than the doctrine of grace, which has engaged the attention of Jansenist and Molinist, of Calvinist and Arminian. The .question is raised as to whether grace is a real influence, provided nominalism be true. The reply to this is *ad hominem;* if grace cannot be real because it is an abstract, then there is no real color, nor man, nor animal. But all such general names stand as representative of classes of ideas. Berkeley's indeterminism may be best presented by arranging the arguments of his opponents in a series, and then showing how these are answered.

I

1. Corporeal objects strike on the organs of sense, and the impression is conveyed to the brain by the nerves. In consequence of this, there is an outflow of motion, which is called volition. Therefore so-called voluntary human actions are simply mechanical. They are falsely attributed to a free principle. There is then no foundation for praise or blame, for reward or punishment.

2. Man is like a puppet; the threads or wires are invisible, but he is not independent of them.

3. Subjectively the process of volition is as follows: (*a*) The understanding considers; (*b*) the judgment decrees; (*c*) this determines the will to action; (*d*) the will executes. There is therefore

no freedom. In freedom there must be indifference, a power to act or not to act, without pre-
scription or control. But no matter what moves
the judgment, the will is controlled by it and cannot
be free. Neither knowledge nor appetite is voluntary. And in addition to these reasons, the future
must be fixed, because God foreknows it.[1]

II

The reply made by Berkeley to these assertions
and arguments is as follows: —

1. It is confounding two distinct ideas to affirm
that motion and will are the same. And if this
identity be denied, the first argument of the determinist fails.

2. Certainty and necessity are not the same; in
the former notion there is nothing that implies
constraint; it may be foreseen that an event is
about to happen, and yet be foreseen that it
is about to happen through human choice and
liberty.

3. The abstractions of the determinist pervert
the truth. In ancient times, when philosophers
denied the possibility of motion, they were met by
those who walked before them. In the same way,
man is a free agent, because he freely wills. This
argument resembles that of Dr. Johnson in opposition to Berkeley's idealism.

4. It is not judgment that determines the will,

---

[1] Berkeley, The Minute Philosopher, VII. xix. 20.

but I, being active, determine my own will. Thus,
although one may not be able to defend the abstract
idea of freedom, there is no doubt that the individual act is free.

5. A man is free in so far as he can do what he
will. To act according to will is to be free. To
pursue the matter any farther is to assert that man
can will as he wills. Such subtleties are absurd,
for the notions of guilt and merit, justice and rewards, in the mind of man are antecedent to all
metaphysical disquisitions; and according to those
received natural notions it is not doubted that
man is accountable, that he acts, and is self-determined.[1]

6. The whole argument of the determinist, in
short, is an excellent illustration of the sophistry
of abstract ideas. One of the disputants remarks,
that all arguments which can be urged against liberty are referable either to realism or materialism.
Yet human minds are far from being mere machines
or footballs, acted upon and bandied about by corporeal objects, without any inward principle of
freedom or action. The only true notions of liberty that we have, come from reflecting upon ourselves and the constitution of our minds.

That Berkeley's attitude against determinism
was so decided may be partly ascribed to his em-
phatic opposition to materialism. The two doctrines were naturally associated in his mind, so
that in refuting the latter he was led to oppose the
former.

[1] Berkeley, The Minute Philosopher, VII. xxii.

HUME

The radical effects of Hume's scepticism are well known. The originality of his views with respect to the nature of the will is often overlooked. It is interesting to find in his theory of the nature of volition an anticipation of conclusions which have been presented in our own time as the result of psychological inquiry.

According to Hume, all the perceptions of the mind may be divided into impressions and ideas. The former are those which enter the mind "with most force and violence." They include all our sensations, passions, and emotions, as they make their first appearance in the soul. The ideas are "the faint images of these in thinking and reasoning."[1] Impressions are of two kinds, original and secondary, or those of sensation and of reflection. The first include all the impressions of the senses and all bodily pains and pleasures; the second are the passions and other emotions resembling them.[2] The passions are either direct or indirect. Direct passions are those which arise immediately from good or evil, from pain or pleasure.[3] "Of all these direct passions, there is none more remarkable than the will."[4] Properly speaking, it is not to be included among the passions; but they cannot be understood without a knowledge of it. In his treatise on the passions, he thus defines the will;

[1] Hume, Treatise of Human Nature, Bk. I. Part I. 1.
[2] Id., ib. Bk. II. Part I. 1.   [3] Id., ib. Bk. II. Part I. 1.
[4] Id., ib. Bk. II. Part III. 1.

it is "the internal impression we feel, and are conscious of, when we knowingly give rise to any new motion of our body, or new perception of our mind." This is incapable of closer definition, and any further description would be likely to cause confusion. In order that Hume's theory of voluntary action may be fully explained, it is expedient that his doctrine of cause and effect should be recalled.

I. *Cause and Effect.* There is a natural principle of union in our ideas, which may be described as the principle of association. An example of such union is presented in the ideas of cause and effect. From the empirical doctrine of knowledge already laid down, Hume was unable to arrive at any justification for the idea of power or of necessary connection. A cause has no power to produce an effect, and the effect is not necessarily connected with its cause. "We have no other notion of cause and effect but that of certain objects, which have been always conjoined together, and which in all past instances have been found inseparable."[1] Why they should be thus inseparable is something which we cannot explain. We know only that such is the case, and can give no reason for it. The invariable succession of phenomena in the past is the only warrant that we have for the same sequence in the future. The invariable antecedent is cause; the invariable consequent is effect. Any different conclusion from this is excluded by Hume's doctrine that we know only impressions and ideas. It

[1] Hume, Treatise of Human Nature, Bk. I. Part III. 6.

o

is because we have no impression of any connection between cause and effect, that we have no idea of such a connection. The relation is one of antecedent to consequent and no more.[1]

II. *Power.* All ideas are derived from impressions or some preceding perceptions. If we have any idea of power, therefore, there must be some instances in which power is perceived to exert itself. According to Hume, such instances can never be discovered in body. It has been held by some, he says, that there is an innate idea of God, and that God is the cause of every change in the material world. But having rejected the theory of innate ideas, Hume concludes that there is no reason to suppose that there is any principle of activity in the Deity. It is equally impossible to derive any idea of power from matter. It is found in none of the qualities of matter. We deceive ourselves when we suppose that we have any idea of efficacy or power. "All ideas are derived from and represent impressions. We never have any impression that contains any power or efficacy. We never, therefore, have any idea of power."[2] One other alternative, however, remains to be considered, and that is whether we derive the idea of power from the action of our wills.

III. *Voluntary Action.* Hume proceeds to examine the opinion that we feel an energy or power in our own mind; and that, having in this man-

---

[1] Hume, Treatise of Human Nature, Bk. I. Part III. 2. Inquiry concerning the Human Understanding, I.

[2] Id., Treatise of Human Nature, Bk. I. Part. III. 14.

ner acquired the idea of power, we transfer that quality to matter, where we are not immediately able to discover it. In accordance with the doctrine of cause and effect already explained, the will is said by Hume to have "no more a discoverable connection with its effects, than any material cause has with its proper effect. So far from perceiving the connection betwixt an act of volition and a motion of the body, 'tis allowed that no effect is more inexplicable from the powers and essence of thought and matter."[1] Nor does the will seem to have any greater power over our mind than over the material object. The control which we have over our thoughts is limited. We perceive a constant conjunction of ideas in the mind, but no connection between them which involves power or efficacy. "No internal impression has an apparent energy, more than external objects have." It follows from this that there is no faculty of will; and that what we suppose to be a feeling of power over our bodies or minds is a mere impression, which has no apparent energy. This might be translated into the language of modern psychology to mean that we have no knowledge of any control of the body by the will except in the feeling which arises when the body is voluntarily moved.

IV. *The Necessary Determination of the Will.* The greater part of Hume's discussion of the will is concerned with this particular aspect of the subject. In spite of his empirical principles, he asserts that necessity governs all material phe-

---

[1] Hume, Treatise of Human Nature, Bk. I. Part. III. 14.

nomena. "Every object is determined by an absolute fate to a certain degree and direction of its motion, and can no more depart from that precise line in which it moves, than it can convert itself into an angel or spirit, or any superior substance."[1] Necessity governs also all mental phenomena. It has been shown already that Hume denied the necessary connection of cause and effect. It is further evident that constant union of ideas, together with the mind's inference, constitute necessity. Wherever we discover these, there is necessity. And such a necessity he observes in the mind. His proof of this shows some advance in the inductive method as employed in psychology. Like causes he finds produce like effects in the history of mankind.

a. There is a difference in the physical qualities of men; yet all are subject to substantially the same physical causes. In like. manner there is a difference in the mental qualities, and again all are subject to the same principle of union or causation. The only way of avoiding this conclusion is to deny this general uniformity in human conduct. "As long as actions have a constant union and connection with the situation and temper of the agent, however we may in words refuse to acknowledge the necessity, we really allow the thing."[2] It may be answered that necessity is regular and certain, while human conduct is irregular and uncertain. Yet when we observe apparent irregularities in the

[1] Hume, Treatise of Human Nature, Bk. II. Part III. 1.
[2] Id., ib.

material world, we do not deny the uniformity of causes, but try to explain the irregularities by referring to other causes which may have been overlooked. We do not deny the principle of cause and effect in the external world because of these exceptions; and we have no more reason to deny them in the case of the will. Madmen, it is admitted by all, have no liberty of will, and yet their actions are far more irregular than those of men who are supposed to be both sane and free.

b. The similarity in the characters of men gives an assurance that their wills will be determined by like causes. Just as a prince who makes laws expects the obedience of his subjects, or a general who issues orders anticipates that they will be carried out, so it is to be concluded that the actions of the will are determined by causes; for the latter doctrine is established by the same kind of moral evidence. In judging of the actions of men, we rely upon causation as much as we do in judging of the phenomena of nature. Necessity is of the essence of causation, consequently the belief in freedom, by removing necessity, removes also causation, and leads directly to belief in chance. "As chance is commonly thought to imply a contradiction, and is at least directly contrary to experience, there are always the same arguments against liberty or free will."[1]

If such inductive considerations lead to a belief in the determination of the will, it is fair to inquire why men so commonly affirm that voluntary actions

[1] Hume, Treatise of Human Nature, Bk. II. Part. III. 1.

are freely performed. To this Hume replies that, in the first place, it is difficult for men who have acted to persuade themselves that they might not have acted differently. They are conscious that their action has been spontaneous, that they have not willed on account of any external compulsion, and so they confound that which is opposed to violence with that which is opposed to causation and necessity. "Few are capable of distinguishing betwixt the liberty of spontaneity, as it is called in the schools, and the liberty of indifference; betwixt that which is opposed to violence and that which means a negation of necessity and causes." In the second place, men are deceived by the apparent mobility of the will into supposing that what seems so easy to think of, viz. an alternate course of action, might have been easily carried out, and so they imagine that this is the liberty of indifference. There is "a false sensation or experience even of the liberty of indifference, which is regarded as an argument for its real existence."[1] Hume considers this idea to be an illusion. No matter how capricious and irregular the actions may seem to have been, and no matter how we may act so as to attempt to prove that we are free, we are always bound by necessity. While we imagine that we are acting quite freely, the spectator can commonly infer what the motives of our actions are, and what our character is, from the actions themselves. And if he were acquainted with all the elements of our situation and temper,

---

[1] Hume, Treatise of Human Nature, Bk. II. Part III. 2.

and our secret springs of action, he would be assured that our wills were determined necessarily.

Hume notices the prevailing tendency in philosophy before him to place the reason in opposition to the passions; to make rational motives superior to emotional motives. This doctrine he opposes. Reason alone can never move the will. There are two general processes of what he calls the understanding: one of these is demonstration, the other reasoning on probability. The former, which is called abstract or demonstrative reasoning, does not influence our actions directly, but only guides our judgments with respect to causes and effects. Nor does probable reasoning affect the will; it shows only the causes and effects of emotions. Reasoning alone cannot dispute with passion and emotion or prevent the will. There is no conflict between reason and passion; for the former is really subject to the feelings. It is a part of Hume's doctrine that passion is a more real element in the nature of man than is any thought of the understanding. "When I am angry I am actually possessed with the passion, and in that emotion have no more reference to any other object than when I am thin or sick, or more than five feet high."[1] The passion is always an original, while a rational process is a copy or representation. Furthermore, the passions are unreasonable only on rare occasions. Such occasions are, first, when it happens that the facts about which the passion arises are unreal; and, second, when wrong means are chosen

[1] Hume, Treatise of Human Nature, Bk. II. Part III. 3.

to secure certain ends.   In all other respects reason and passion are in harmony.   What is thought by many to be the determination of the will by the reason in opposition to passion, is in reality the determination of the will by certain more tranquil feelings, which from their tranquillity assume the appearance of rational processes.   Strength of mind and self-control are thus only the predominance of the calmer feelings in controlling the will.

It has sometimes been said that the denial of free will is disadvantageous to religion.   Hume holds, on the contrary, that a belief in necessary determination is indispensable to good morals and religion.[1]   The doctrine of necessary determinism teaches that there is a necessary relation between a man's disposition and his actions.   If the wills of men were free, it would be absurd to punish evil-doers.   For it would be the infliction of punishment on a man who was not responsible.   "According to the hypothesis of liberty, therefore, a man is as pure and untainted after having committed the most horrid crimes as at the first moment of his birth, nor is his character any way concerned in his actions, since they are not derived from it, and the wickedness of the one can never be used as a proof of the depravity of the other."[2]   Hume would, therefore, turn the tables on his adversaries by showing the injustice of gauging moral actions by the liberty with which they are performed.

Such are the main arguments by which he en-

---

[1] Hume, Treatise of Human Nature, Bk. II. Part III. 2.
[2] Id., ib. Bk. II. Part. III. 2.

deavors to prove the determination of the will. I
do not think it worth while to point out the manifest inconsistency of his theory with the principles
which he affirms in the beginning of his *Treatise
of Human Nature*. Those who recall his conception of the origin of knowledge, and his doctrine
of cause and effect, will be disposed to dispute
the cogency of his arguments. Upon Hume's own
principles, there is no good reason why the will
should be thought to be necessarily determined,
unless it is because such determination has always
been observed. For the denial of any necessary
connection between cause and effect leaves it possible that there should be volition unconnected
with motives and entirely disconnected with character. John Stuart Mill, who afterwards held with
few modifications Hume's theory of causation, defended a like theory of determinism.

Reid

The philosophy of Reid may be considered both
as a dogmatic reply to Hume, and as the beginning
of the later development of Scottish thought. It
has especial importance because of the influence
which it has exerted not only in Great Britain but
also in America. In relation to the philosophy of
the Continent, Reid may be placed at the head of
those who appealed to what the Germans called *der
gesunde Menschenverstand;* he is a "common-sense"
philosopher.

He adopts the old division of the faculties of the

soul into understanding and will.[1] The first of these is a faculty of knowledge and speculation; the second is a faculty of action. Consequently, he speaks of intellectual and active powers. By the latter, as well as by the former, man is distinguished from the brutes. The brutes follow the strongest impulse, and seem to have no capacity for self-government. They deserve, therefore, neither praise nor blame for what they do or fail to do. They may be governed by discipline, but not by law. Man, on the contrary, acts from motives of a higher nature. He has a conception of duty, and feels that when he does his duty, the action is meritorious, and when it is left undone, the action is worthy of blame.[2]

I. *The Conception of Active Power.* Reid criticises Hume's definition of active power: it is not as Hume said, "A lively idea related to or associated with a present impression." While declining to define the conception, Reid explains it as follows:—

1. It is not derived from any of the external senses, nor from self-consciousness. So far Hume was right in opposing Locke.

2. Power is one of those things of which we have only a relative and indirect impression; that is, power is known not *per se* but only by means of its effects.

3. Power is a mere quality, and has no existence independent of the subject to which it belongs.

[1] Reid, Active Powers, Introduction.
[2] Id., ib.

4. But the degree of power belonging to anything cannot be inferred from the effects produced, for a given thing may not manifest the amount of power which it possesses.

5. There are some powers which have a contrary, and some which do not. Vice is the contrary of virtue; but there is no contrary of power. There are only conceptions of privations of power, such as weakness or impotence.[1]

The exercise of active power is called action. While all power is to be traced ultimately to God, there is a relative power which the mind has over its own operations.

II. *Active Power and the Will.* The only conception which we get of active power in relation to its cause is from the way in which our own active power is exercised.[2] Every man is naturally led to attribute free will to himself, and to regard voluntary acts as in his own power. Human power can be exerted only by will. We cannot conceive of any power to be exerted without will. We impute our actions to ourselves, and consider ourselves to be the causes of our own actions.

III. *Definition of the Will.*

Every man is conscious of a power to determine, in things which he conceives to depend upon his determination. To this power we give the name of *will;* and as it is usual, in the operations of the mind, to give the same name to the power and to the act of that power, the term will is often

---

[1] Reid, Active Powers, I. 1.
[2] Id., ib. I. 5.

put to signify the act of determining, which more properly is called *volition*.

Volition, therefore, signifies the act of willing and determining; and will is put indifferently to signify either the power of willing or the act.[1]

It may be more briefly defined as the determination of the mind to do or not to do something which we conceive to be in our power.

Reid further explains the term, "to distinguish it from other acts of mind, which from the ambiguity of words are apt to be confounded with it."[2] And the following characteristics are enumerated:

1. Every act of the will must have an object.

2. The immediate object of the will must be some action of our own. Desire and will are alike in that there is an object before both. But they differ in that the object of the will must be an action, while desire may be directed towards the object of appetite or affection or passion.

3. The object of the will must be something within our power.

4. When we will to do anything immediately, the volition is accompanied with an effort to execute.

If a man wills to raise a great weight from the ground by the strength of his arm, he makes an effort for that purpose proportioned to the weight he determines to raise. A great weight requires a great effort; a small weight a less effort. Great efforts, whether of body or mind, are attended with difficulty, and when long continued produce lassitude, which requires that they should be intermitted. This leads us to

<hr>

[1] Reid, Active Powers, II. 1.
[2] Id., ib. II. 1.

reflect upon them, and to give them a name. The name *effort* is commonly appropriated to them; and those that are made with ease, and leave no sensible effect, pass without observation and without a name, though they be of the same kind, and differ only in degree from those to which the name is given. This effort we are conscious of, if we will but give attention to it; and there is nothing in which we are in a more strict sense active.[1]

This view of effort which is here so plainly expressed was for a long time prevalent in psychology, but of late years has been vigorously opposed.

Acts may be excited by instinct which do not involve either understanding or will, as when a man recovers his balance after stumbling, or plays a tune without there being a special volition for each particular note. Appetites, passions, and desires without judgment may direct actions, and such actions are not properly voluntary. While passion may influence or control the will, there may be involuntary passionate actions.[2]

Although the faculties of understanding and will are easily distinguished in thought, they are rarely, if ever, disjoined in operation. When understanding and will are combined, there are three species of volition,—attention, deliberation, and resolution.[3] Attention may be given to objects either of sense or of intellect, in order to form a distinct notion of such objects. Deliberation consists in the forming of some judgment as to what ought to

[1] Reid, Active Powers, II. 1.
[2] Id., ib. II. 2.   [3] Id., ib. II. 3.

be willed, and the general rules of deliberation are the axioms of morals. Resolution does not imply immediate action, but is used both for present and future actions and volitions.[1]

IV. *Motives.* There are two parts in the human constitution that may have influence upon our voluntary actions: these are passion and reason. They are described by Reid as motives, or as principles of action, or as incitements to action. Reason influences the voluntary acts which man regards as his own, while actions done through passion are thought of as being alien to a man's true self.[2] Thus we find him following the ancient view already noticed which puts passion in opposition to reason, and regards the former as taking possession of the soul, and so enslaving it. Reid says: "What a man does coolly and deliberately without passion is imputed solely to the man, whether it have merit or demerit; whereas what he does from passion, is imputed in part to passion. The demerit is removed in proportion to the excess of the passion. It is judgment which compares the principles of action, and decides which is worthiest to be pursued." It is not necessary that the incitement to action should be effective in order to be a motive, and so, as will be seen, motives do not determine the will. Reid classifies principles of action as follows: (1) mechanical principles; (2) animal principles; (3) rational principles.[3] Mechanical principles are such as require no attention, no deliberation, and no

---

[1] Reid, Active Powers, II. 3. [2] Id., ib. III. 1.
[3] Id., ib. III. 1.

will. They are of two kinds: instincts and habits. An instinct is a natural blind impulse to certain actions, without any end being in view, without deliberation therefore, and very often without any clear conception.[1] A habit is the facility of doing a thing, acquired by having done it frequently.[2] Animal principles of action are such as operate upon will and intention, but do not involve any exercise of judgment or reason.[3] Among these are the appetites, which are distinguished from other desires in that they are accompanied by sensations of uneasiness proper to them, and are not constant, but periodical. Another kind of animal principles of action, Reid calls desires. These are without the marks or properties which have just been described as belonging to animal appetites. Other animal principles of action are benevolent and malevolent affections, passions, disposition, and opinion. In speaking of disposition, Reid gives a very superficial treatment of that important principle, and does not refer to it later in his discussion of freedom.[4]

Rational principles of action are so called because they can have no existence in beings not endowed with reason. They involve the exercise of intention, will, and reason. Reid makes a distinction between two kinds of rational function: it is one function of the reason to regulate our belief, and another to regulate our actions and conduct.[5] Whatever is rational commands our assent, and assent

---

[1] Reid, Active Powers, III. 2.
[2] Id., ib. III. 3. [4] Id., ib. III. 2–8.
[3] Id., ib. III. 1. [5] Id., ib. III. 1.

influences our will. The notions of the good in general, of duty, moral obligation, and rectitude, are among the rational principles of action.[1]

V. *Freedom.* Reid's discussion of the freedom of the will is elaborate, although somewhat diffuse. He defines the liberty of a moral agent as "a power over the determination of his own will."[2] If the determination of the will be the necessary consequence of something involuntary in the state of the mind, or of something external to the mind, then the agent is not free, and not moral. He is controlled by necessity. Such freedom presupposes understanding as well as will; and in free actions, practical judgment is involved. Necessity is defined, negatively, as the want of this moral liberty.[3] Reid objects to defining liberty as a power to act as we will, which implies that we will to will, and so on to infinity. He distinguishes three kinds of liberty : (1) liberty as opposed to physical restraint; (2) liberty as opposed to obligation by law; (3) liberty as opposed to necessity.[4]

It is liberty of the third kind that is properly predicated of will.[5] Necessity is not a philosophical notion only, but is a principle which the vulgar have appealed to in every age to exculpate themselves and avoid being held responsible for their acts. According to Reid the advocate of necessity lays stress chiefly upon motives. The strongest motive prevails, and determines the will. And the

---

[1] Reid, Active Powers, III. 2–7.
[2] Id., ib., IV. 1.   [4] Id., ib.
[3] Id., ib.   [5] Id., ib.

advocate of necessity affirms that if man be free it is impossible that he should be governed by regard for rewards or punishments. To this objection Reid replies that all rational beings are influenced by motives, but these are not sufficient to determine the will. They are not causes nor agents, they persuade or inform, but acts of will are not necessary effects of them. Motives suppose liberty in the agent, otherwise they could have no influence at all. Reid ridicules the idea of the *Asinus Buridani*, and holds that the conditions of the problem are contrary to experience. It is possible for men to choose in an entire absence of motives, and it can never be proved that the motive determines the will. To hold such a deterministic opinion is to affirm that men never act from wilfulness, caprice, or obstinacy. There is no way of telling what the strongest motive is, except by volition itself: —

How shall we know whether the strongest motive always prevails, if we know not which is the strongest? There must be some test by which their strength is to be tried, some balance in which they may be weighed, otherwise, to say that the strongest motive always prevails, is to speak without any meaning.[1]

The relation of opposing motives to the act of will may be explained as follows: —

Contrary motives may very properly be compared to advocates pleading the opposite sides of a cause at the bar. It would be very weak reasoning to say, that such an advocate is the most powerful pleader, because sentence was given on his side. The sentence is in the power of the judge,

[1] Reid, Active Powers, IV. 4.

P

not of the advocate. It is equally weak reasoning in proof of necessity, to say such a motive prevailed, therefore it was the strongest ; since the defenders of liberty maintained that the determination was made by the man, and not by the motive.[1]

The strength of the motives is apparent very often by the effort which the mind makes and makes successfully to resist them. So far the defence of freedom is negative. Positively Reid argues in the following manner: —

1. The will is free, because there is a natural conviction of its freedom. This is an appeal to the common sense of mankind. And this mode of argument is quite in harmony with Reid's philosophical method in general. This natural conviction is manifest, from the exertions which we make by the power of our will, from the deliberations which presuppose a power to act freely in accordance with the result of them, from our resolutions to act, which imply a belief in our liberty, and from our making promises which imply belief in our ability to keep them. Blame and praise also show the existence of this natural conviction.[2]

2. The will is free, because man is morally accountable for his actions. In fact, Reid affirms that the distinction between just and unjust implies the freedom of the will.[3]

3. The will is free because man has the power of "carrying on, wisely and prudently, a system of conduct, which he has before conceived in his mind,

---

[1] Reid, Active Powers, IV. 4.
[2] Id., ib. IV. 6.   [3] Id., ib. IV. 7.

and resolved to prosecute." This proposition, Reid defends, strange to say, by an appeal to the principle of causality.

"Every indication of wisdom, taken from the effect, is equally an indication of power to execute what wisdom planned. And if we have any evidence that the wisdom which formed the plan is in the man, we have the very same evidence, that the power which executed it is in him also."[1]

And yet Reid was seeking to prove, not the power of the agent, but his liberty. His argument is more *ad rem* in his criticism of Leibnitz. He objects to the principle of sufficient reason as stated by the German philosopher. For, according to Reid, two or more means may be equally fit for the same end; "in such a case there may be a sufficient reason for taking one of the number, though there be no reason for preferring one to another, of means equally fit."[2]

He asserts that to apply the principle of sufficient reason to man's voluntary acts is to make man a machine. If we suppose the principle to be applied to a given action, we shall ask whether there was a sufficient reason for this action or not. Reid admits that there was a motive, but not necessarily a motive sufficient to justify the action. He admits also that there was a cause, but that if the action was the man's, the man himself was the cause. But he denies that it was necessarily produced. When, therefore, it is affirmed that vol-

---

[1] Reid, Active Powers, IV. 8.
[2] Id., ib. IV. 9.

untary acts are effects necessarily produced, it should be answered that the cause of the volition is the man who wills, and that the volition itself is the necessary effect of nothing else. This argument Reid follows up with a general attack upon Hume for insisting that the will is an effect, while denying the efficiency of causation.[1]

Reid attaches more importance, however, to the argument against freedom founded on the foreknowledge of God. "The most formidable argument of this class, . . . is taken from the prescience of the Deity."[2]

He analyzes the inference that because God foresees every determination of the human mind, that which he foresees must happen necessarily. He distinguishes certainty from necessity. That what will certainly be, will certainly be, he does not dispute; but this differs from the assertion that because an event will certainly be, therefore its production must be necessary. He denies also that prescience involves predestination, or that there is a causal relation between God's foreknowledge that an event will happen, and the necessity that such an event must happen. If it be denied that any free action can be foreseen, Reid would say that such a denial involves the denial of God's free agency, since God's future actions can be foreseen by men; also that while the Deity foresees his own free actions, this does not determine those actions necessarily. Lastly, he criticises Dr. Priestley's doctrine of necessity and contingency.

[1] Reid, Active Powers, IV. 9.   [2] Id., ib. IV. 10.

Priestley had denied that a contingent event could be an object of knowledge. His argument had been as follows: —

As certainly as nothing can be known to exist but what does exist, so certainly can nothing be known to arise from what does exist, but what does arise from it, or depend upon it. But according to the definition of the terms, a contingent event does not depend upon any previous known circumstances, since some other event might have arisen in the same circumstances. [1]

Reid replies that a thing may arise from what does exist, either freely or necessarily. A contingent event arises from its cause, not necessarily, but freely. But another event might have arisen from the same cause. Besides this, Priestley's argument simply proves that a contingent event cannot be known to arise necessarily from what does exist, which, however, was not disputed. The whole reasoning is, according to Reid, based on an assumption, that nothing can be known to arise from what does exist, but what arises necessarily from it. The major premise, in which this assumption is contained, is not proved, and so Reid discards Priestley's conclusion.

Any one who is familiar with the psychology since the time of Reid may be disposed to criticise his doctrine of the will. But whatever estimate be made of it, it should be remembered that he published his essays on the *Active Powers* at a time when British philosophy had been disturbed

---

[1] Quoted by Reid, Active Powers, IV. 10.

by the scepticism of Hume, and indirectly by the
determinism of Spinoza and Leibnitz. Reid's arguments with respect to freedom are instructive, particularly when compared with the theories of the
Post-Kantian metaphysicians. In his philosophy
of common sense, he attempted.to reply to Hume's
theory of knowledge; and it is evident that the
same defects which made this reply insufficient,
are more or less manifest in his empirical treatment of the will. While maintaining the objective
validity of the principle of causality, he at the same
time regards the subject which wills as practically
a first cause. By recognizing only the faculties of
the understanding and the will, he did not, like the
Germans, resort to the reason as a superior power
through which he might transcend the causal principle, and so justify a belief in freedom. Just as
Butler's *Analogy* determined for many years the
method and principle of Christian apologetics, so
the philosophy of Reid was for many years the
foundation of all indeterministic theories in Great
Britain and America. Like most Englishmen of
his time, he shows no sign of having been particularly impressed with the force of Spinoza's philosophy; and it may be doubted whether the latter
awakened much interest or found intelligent appre-
ciation during the eighteenth century, except on the
continent of Europe. It is probable, however, that
in Reid's clear statements, and able reasoning, the
indeterminists may find their most adequate empirical defence.

CHAPTER FIFTH

THE metaphysical doctrines of the philosophers
on the continent during the seventeenth century
are in striking contrast to the more psychological
discussions of the writers in England and Scotland.
In the construction of their systems, the Cartesians,
and those more or less directly related to them, set
out from the idea of substance. There is little
uniformity, however, in their conclusions with respect to either knowledge or will. The thought
of Great Britain, during this period, was almost
altogether emancipated from the traditions of the
mediæval schools. But on the continent the departure from the older methods is not so marked.
It is, of course, easy to observe the antagonism between the philosophy of Descartes and that of even
the most advanced schoolman, but his extensive use
of a deductive method, and the formal presentation
of his doctrine, remind one of the older writers.
Malebranche, in spite of his attacks on Aristotle,
is only a belated schoolman; the method of Spinoza
is scholastic; and in Leibnitz especially are to be
found few signs that any very radical change has
passed over the methods of philosophy.

DESCARTES

The philosophy of Descartes is theistic and dualistic. While the English philosophers of the seventeenth and eighteenth centuries were concerned primarily with the theory of knowledge, and especially the nature and origin of ideas, those on the continent set out from the ontological doctrine of substance. The effects of the latter method are apparent in the conclusions of the leading writers of France, Germany, and Holland, especially in the systems of Spinoza and of Leibnitz.

According to Descartes, substance is either uncreated or created. The former is that which depends on nothing else for its subsistence; the latter is that which depends only on God for its subsistence. There is one uncreated substance, which is God. Created substances are mind and matter. The essence of the former is thought; that of the latter is extension. While the soul of man is closely united to his body, it is distinct in essence; for it is of the essence of the soul to think. The soul as extended substance resides in every part of the body: l'âme est véritablement jointe à tout le corps.[1] For it is not only unextended, but indivisible; it cannot be separated, nor can it separate itself when different parts of the body are moved or affected. Besides this general connection of the soul with the body, there is a particular point of union between the two in the brain. By many

---

[1] Descartes, Les Passions, I. 30.

preceding philosophers, it had been taught that the centre of the soul's life in the body was the brain, or the heart. Sometimes both organs were associated with the functions of knowledge and feeling. According to Descartes, the point of union is the pineal gland situated in the interior of the cerebrum. The central situation of this part of the brain, together with its mobility, led him to suppose that it was the point where the affections of the body were transmitted to the soul, and where the volitions were transmitted to the members of the body: toute l'action de l'âme consiste en ce que la petite glande à qui elle est étroitement jointe se meut en la façon qui est requise pour produire l'effet qui se rapporte à cette volonté.[1] The animal spirits or nerves serve to connect this physiological centre with the extended world beyond the body. The will acting on the gland can produce movements in various parts of the body.

The explanation given of this crude physiological psychology need not be given in any detail; it is sufficient to observe that Descartes regards the volitions as finding expression through the animal spirits, either inwardly through the pores of the cerebrum, or outwardly to the muscles: cette volonté fait que la glande pousse les esprits vers les muscles qui servent à cet effet.[2]

The soul has no direct knowledge of what takes place in the gland. Will has simply the power to move the gland in such a way as will propel.tho

---

[1] Descartes, Les Passions, I. 41.
[2] Id., ib. I. 42.

animal spirits towards the pores of the brain, as in imagination, or in the act of attention; it can also expel the animal spirits to the muscles of the body, as has just been said. It is, however, not always the will to excite some motion within us, or some other effect, which can make us excite it. Such excitation takes place in accordance with changes which nature or habit have diversely joined with each thought. For example, in looking at a distant object, there will be a particular will to enlarge the pupil, and at a near object, to contract the pupil. The will to enlarge or contract is useless; that which effects the enlargement or contraction is the movement of the pineal gland. The effect is indirectly produced when the soul wills to look at a distant or near object.[1]

This physiological hypothesis of Descartes was afterwards severely criticised by Spinoza;[2] yet however obscure and extravagant it may now seem, it is a sign of interest in that aspect of voluntary action which has led to the most considerable results.

Thought in the Cartesian philosophy has a general denotation. It includes various kinds of knowledge, — sensations, phantasms, and ideas; it includes also the passions and the will. These varieties of thought are attributed to several faculties. The faculties do not constitute the essence of the soul. The latter can be conceived as existing even in the absence of the faculties; while

---

[1] Descartes, Les Passions, I. 44.
[2] Spinoza, Eth. V. Præfat.

they cannot be conceived as existing without the soul. They appertain, or are attached, to a thinking substance : pour me servir des termes de l'école, dans leur concept formel, elles enferment, quelque sorte d'intellection : d'où je conçois qu'elles sont distinctes de moi comme les modes le sont des choses.[1] There is a passive faculty which receives ideas, and an active faculty which produces ideas. Among thoughts, some are images of realities, and others are only ideas. As examples of the former are the images of those things which have been perceived through the senses ; as examples of the latter are those of which the self is the subject, such as fear, desire, and conceptions. The latter class may be divided into volitions or affections, and judgments.

This brief account of certain general principles in the Cartesian system will perhaps be of assistance in the interpretation of the special theory of volition.

I. *Definition of the Will.* The account given by Descartes of the nature of the will is so ambiguous, that it is difficult to know whether it is to be classified as an action, or as a passion of the soul. In a limited sense, it is that which directs the attention, and which moves and controls the body. But it also comprehends desire, aversion, assurance, denial, and doubt.[2] Yet desire is defined as a passion, which refers to the future. In a letter to Regius, Descartes says : —

---

[1] Descartes, Méditations, VI. 9.
[2] Id., Prin. Phil. I. 32.

Intellectio enim proprie mentis passio est, et volitio ejus actio ; sed quia nihil unquam volumus, quin simul intelligamus, et vix etiam quidquam intelligamus, quin simul aliquid velimus, ideo non facile in iis passionem ab actione distinguimus.[1]

From this and other parts of his philosophy, it would appear that in a limited sense will is considered by Descartes as active, especially as it may control the passions.[2] But he also uses it in the old general sense as equivalent to disposition and its manifestations.

II. *The Will and the Passions.* The passions cannot be directly controlled by an act of the will.[3] They may, however, be excited or controlled indirectly. Things which are associated with such passions as we wish to arouse may be voluntarily represented to the mind, or things which are remote from the passions which we wish to avoid may be voluntarily recalled; the effect will be to excite or allay the feeling. A man, for example, cannot will directly to be angry, but may voluntarily recall the objects which excite his anger. He cannot will not to be angry, but may voluntarily recall considerations which dissipate the feeling. But passions cannot be successfully resisted by direct volition. During their intensity, they have a reality like that of an object present to the senses, which persists whether we will it to be there or not.[4]

1 Descartes, Epistolae, CIII.
2 Id., Les Passions, I. 45, 46.
3 Id., ib. 4 Id., ib.

Descartes alludes to the opinion that a conflict is possible between the inferior and superior parts or principles of the soul,—between the higher and lower passions. Such a conflict, he believes, is unreal. The opinion that it is real is due to a confused idea of soul and body. Passions which have a bodily origin are attributed to the lower principle of the soul; the supposed conflict is not in the soul, but in two contrary impulses of animal spirits meeting in the pineal gland. Some impressions are conveyed to the brain which do not affect the will, but only move the body. The will, having no direct control of the passions, is constrained to use industry in checking the latter, and to apply itself successively to different expedients, which gives rise to the view that there is a conflict between the inferior and superior passions.[1]

A weak will is one in which the volitions are controlled by the passions; and a strong will is one which is controlled by the judgment.

III. *The Understanding and the Will.* The relation of knowledge to volition is important; for that which distinguishes will, as a mere passion, from will as a directing and controlling faculty, is its relation to the understanding. By the understanding alone, however, nothing is either affirmed or denied. Its office is only to conceive the ideas of things which may be either affirmed or denied. The errors into which men fall are thus due partly to the understanding and partly to the will.[2]

---

[1] Descartes, Les Passions, I. 47.
[2] Id., ib. Méditations, IV. 7.

Gassendi criticised Descartes for maintaining that the sphere of the will was wider than that of the understanding. The former maintained that the two powers were of equal extent, puisque la volonté ne peut se porter vers aucune chose que l'entendement n'ait auparavant prévue. Descartes insists, however, that the two powers have an unequal extension. We can will several things about one and the same thing, although we may know very little about the thing. And when our judgment is defective, it is not because we will evil, but only something which may have evil connected with it. There is a will which is not joined with intelligence, which acts on impulse and insufficient knowledge; and the motive for willing, as well as the consequences of willing, may lie beyond our knowledge.[1]

The significance of this discussion can be better appreciated in connection with Descartes's doctrine of freedom. The participation of the will in the errors of the understanding is quite foreign to the conceptions of the earlier philosophy. And yet Descartes, considering the errors of his mind as signs of his imperfections, ascribes them first to the faculty of knowledge, and second to the faculty of choice. There is indeed, he maintains, nothing in the mind which can be called error, provided the word error be taken in a proper sense. On the one hand, will is not the cause of my errors, for it is very ample and perfect in its kind; on the other hand, the understanding is not the cause, for I cannot be deceived by the God who has given me the faculty. The

---

[1] Descartes, Gassendi, Réponses, etc., 71.

cause of error is to be found in the fact that the will is wider than the understanding, and instead of confining volition within the limits of what I understand, I extend it to things which I do not understand. Thus it easily wanders, and leads me into mistakes.[1]

IV. *The Will and Freedom.* Descartes uses the term free will in a peculiar way. He makes a distinction between indifference and freedom. The indifference of the will is due to ignorance. Having maintained that the will has a wider field than the understanding, indifferent volition comes from the exercise of will in the absence of knowledge. When the judgment does not determine it, it is indifferent. Freedom, on the contrary, is in proportion to the knowledge which determines the exercise of the will. The term indifference, says Descartes, has been used in two ways: first, when the mind has no knowledge concerning certain courses of action, as to whether they are bad or good; and second, when the mind wills to follow one course of action in the presence of an alternative. In the latter case there is freedom to choose the good and reject the bad. But the latter use of the term indifference he does not recognize. The latter case he regards as an illustration of true liberty. The extent of our freedom consists in the knowledge which determines our action. The greater the knowledge the greater the freedom. Consequently our liberty is better exhibited when we are commanded to follow a certain course, and decline to obey the com-

<hr>

[1] Descartes, Prin. Phil. I. 6.

mand, than when we are inclined by nothing either
within or without, to do one thing in preference to
another. By freedom, then, Descartes does not
mean freedom from determination, but only freedom from ignorance on the one hand and constraint
on the other. The will is so free in its nature that
it cannot be constrained; but its freedom consists
in its determination by knowledge, *i.e.*, by the intellect. Unless this be the proper interpretation of
the theory of Descartes, he appears to teach that
our freedom is in proportion to our determination;
but this is only to say that when we will according
to knowledge we are free, and it is knowledge which
determines the will.[1]

Descartes is here referring to will in its active
significance. If will be considered only as a passion, then it is absurd to ask whether or not it is
free; nor can we ask whether the mind has control
over aversion, assurance, and doubt, if these be
species of will. This would be to ask whether we
can control the will by the will. But the power
of freedom is not only proportionate to the knowledge we may have of the object of volition; it is
also proportionate to the inclination which we may
have towards a given course of action. The more
settled our inclination, the greater our liberty, just
as the more distinct and the clearer our knowledge,
the greater our liberty. Freedom thus depends on
knowledge and inclination. Freedom consists in
being able to do or not to do a given thing, that

---

[1] Descartes, Réponses aux sixièmes objections par divers
théol. et phil. (II.) VI.

is, to affirm or deny, to pursue or avoid, the objects presented by the understanding. No external force constrains the will; for that to which there is the greatest inclination is that which is willed, and we are enabled by God to will in accordance with our inclinations. Certain Patristic writers had looked upon freedom as determination of a moral kind. Descartes looks upon freedom as determination of an intellectual kind. When the understanding determines the will, the man is master of his own acts; and it is for this reason that he is worthy of praise or blame. That the inclinations are not altogether voluntary is proved by Descartes's statement that it is nature which teaches the avoidance of things which give pain, and the pursuit of those which give pleasure. There is thus such a harmony between our knowledge and our action, that we are able to refer sensations to that part of the body from which they produce their first effects, and we take voluntary measures to avoid or encourage the continuance of the feeling. If we had sufficiently clear and distinct ideas of good and evil, we should always pursue the former and avoid the latter.

The doctrine of freedom is still further enforced by an appeal to internal experience[1] after the manner of the Scottish psychologists. While indifference and freedom may be incomprehensible, we are conscious that they are real. Although we do not will to deceive ourselves, it often happens that our judgments are precipitate. When our knowledge

---

[1] Réponses aux cinq. objections de M. Gassendi (50), III.

Q

is insufficient, that which is untrue is considered as true, and ignorance determines the will.

The essence of the freedom of the will of God differs from that of the human will. The will of God is absolute, not only over all events, but over all truth. God wills what is good or true; and truth and goodness depend for their being on the will of God. Thus an entire indifference in God is looked upon as a proof of his power. He wills absolutely, without any external reasons for his will.[1]

The indifference of God arises from his omnipotence and omniscience; that of man from his impotence and ignorance. The actions of men are simply second causes which operate in order that what God has willed may be carried out. God is not the author of sin; for (a) sin is nothing, and (b) whatever God wills is right, because He wills it.[2] Yet in a letter to the Princess Elizabeth, Descartes hesitates to apply his theory too rigorously to the action of God. When we think of the infinite power of God, we are obliged to believe that all things, even our own wills, depend on his. For it is a contradiction, he says, to hold that God has created men with wills independent of His own, and so has limited his infinite power. And yet we have experience of our own freedom, and we should not let this make us doubt the existence of God, but only

---

[1] Réponses aux sixièmes objections par divers théol. et. phil. (II.) VI.

[2] Descartes, Prin. Phil. I. 6, 23.

recognize that our actions are on this account worthy of praise or blame, and that all men are subject to God. This position of Descartes has been taken since his day, by almost all those who believe in predestination.

While Descartes added nothing of any great importance to the science of volition, he raised some questions which have a distinct bearing on some of the more important problems of the present. His statement that there are acts of the soul without knowledge, in response to affections of the body, is an anticipation of the principle of reflex action.[1] Still more suggestive are his denial that the lower animals have any principle of intelligence or will, and his explanation of all animal movement upon mechanical grounds. It remained for our own century to find in the motions of animals one of the most valuable aids to the explanation of the phenomena of will in man.

MALEBRANCHE

The philosophy of Malebranche may be regarded as a link in the chain of development from the dualism of Descartes to the monism of Spinoza. It is, however, not this alone which makes a notice of his theory desirable. His doctrine of the will has a peculiar interest from its relation to the theory of occasional causes. Together with principles derived more or less directly from Descartes, Malebranche adopts elements of Augustine's philosophy,

[1] Descartes, Les Passions, I. 47.

and modifies them to suit his own conclusions. His system is at once a natural theology and an ontology. While he deals psychologically with the will, his special interest in it is connected with predestination and grace. Instead of the extreme dualism of Descartes he sets forth a peculiar species of idealism, resembling in some points that of his contemporary Berkeley, who was thought to have borrowed from the French philosopher.

Malebranche divides the operations of the soul into sense, imagination, understanding, inclinations, and passions. The object of his principal work, *Recherche de la Vérité*, is to show how these several operations give rise to errors, and to provide a remedy. In his account of the passions he is greatly indebted to Descartes. The following points in his philosophy are comprehensive of his treatment of will.

I. *Faculties.* The mind has two general faculties, understanding and will. There is an analogy between the properties of mind and those of matter. The properties of matter are that of receiving impressions or figures, and that of being moved. These correspond respectively to understanding, which receives impressions, and will, which produces motion. He speaks of the capacity of the will to receive inclinations, by which he means apparently the power to will certain things.[1]

II. *Definition of the Will.* Will is that impression or natural motion which carries us towards universal and indeterminate good. Freedom is

---

[1] Malebranche, Recherche de la Vérité, I. i.

considered as a power, as in the system of Locke. It is the power which the mind has of turning towards agreeable objects, and terminating our natural inclinations upon some particular object, which was previously indeterminate with reference to will. Even the natural inclinations are voluntary. They are not free, however, in the sense of having liberty of indifference. The liberty of indifference is simply the power of willing or not willing; that is, willing the contrary of natural inclination. The love of the good is voluntary, for love proceeds from the will. Yet it is impossible to force the inclination of love freely, just as it is impossible to govern the will by force or constraint.[1]

III. *Will and Understanding.* Will is a blind power, unless it is guided by the understanding. In order that it may have some content, it must be applied to the understanding. For the latter is subject to the control of the will. The power that the will has to determine its inclinations is involved in the ability to apply the understanding to objects at will. In order to illustrate this relationship, Malebranche supposes the case of a man who represents to himself an honor or preferment, under the conception of the good, which he may hope for. He wills the good directly. The impression which is continually carrying his soul towards universal good inclines it towards the honor which he represents to himself. This propensity towards indeterminate good is fixed and natural; so far

---

[1] Malebranche, Recherche de la Vérité, I. i.

there is no voluntary action or free action. But
the soul has choice as to whether it will or will
not identify this particular honor with any species
of the universal and indeterminate good. In this
consists its voluntary power. The soul may further
suspend both its judgment and affection with respect
to this particular object — this honor. It may do
this from a want of conviction that the particular
object desired comprehends all the good which the
soul is capable of loving. Malebranche adds that
the soul may compare all good things with each
other, may love them according to their order, and
in proportion to their excellence. It may consider
them with reference to that universal good which
contains all, and which alone is adapted to satisfy
the affections of the soul.[1]

It is a peculiar doctrine of Malebranche that the
understanding has no power of judging. The function of the understanding is to perceive. To judge
is a function of the will. All errors are therefore
voluntary.[2] The understanding perceives only simple things and their relations, and the relations of
these relations. It is the will which judges and
reasons. In this confused use of terms, Malebranche has fortunately had few imitators. We
are said to attribute judgments to the understanding, when the consent seems so evident that the
voluntary element remains unnoticed; but, as a
matter of fact, all judgments are voluntary. It is
only that the will in such cases seems to follow,

---

[1] Malebranche, Recherche de la Vérité, I. i.
[2] Id., ib. I. ii.

not to guide the understanding. . The latter makes the representation to the former, and when there is easy acquiescence, the judgment is thought to be involuntary. Yet the will may decline to consent to what is represented by the understanding, and in such cases the voluntary nature of judgment is more easily recognized. Malebranche criticises those who distinguish between assent to the action of the understanding and consent to the good. He holds, on the contrary, that the data of the understanding command our assent without awakening doubt. The good may therefore be freely recognized, and yet the will may not be fixed as to whether the particular good represented is to be loved. Consent of the will to truth is therefore to be distinguished from consent of the will to following the good. The reason why man consents so readily to truth is that his interests are less nearly involved. Truth which does not affect the passions and inclinations of men is more readily recognized than when man's selfish interests are involved.

IV. *Freedom.* Man wills and determines his own actions. It is God who causes him to will, not directly, but indirectly. This view of the will is a part of Malebranche's theory of occasionalism. The efficiency of causes comes not from the action of these causes alone. That which makes any cause efficient is the concurrent action of God. According to Malebranche's epistemology, the soul sees all things in God. And in like manner the soul performs all actions by the concourse of God. I

know that I will and that I will freely; and this
volition is the true cause of the movement of the
body. But there is 'no actual relation between
soul and body. Consequently, that the former may
have any effect on the latter, there must be, as it
were, a supernatural interposition through the
agency of God. There is no analogy between volition and motion. There is a physiological change
when the soul wills, and the animal spirits proceed
to the muscle which is to be moved; but I have no
share in this process. That the effort of the soul
becomes effective is due to the will of God, which
never fails of its effect.[1] It is singular to find
here a *rapprochement* to the view afterwards taken
by Hume. Like Hume, Malebranche fails to find
any efficiency in the mind acting as cause to produce the effect. No relation between the two
phenomena can be discovered which can be called
efficiency, or even necessary connection. There
are no efficient second causes. Malebranche admits
that there is a feeling of effort or endeavor which
is a concomitant of the volition, but, like Hume,
he denies that this is the efficient cause of the
movement. The motion of the arm, for example,
is performed at the very moment that the effort is
felt; but the soul has no knowledge of what nerves
must be excited in order that the movement may
be produced. The efficiency of the will in such a
case is owing to the efficiency of the will of God.
Volitions, like cognitions, are thus miraculous
events.

[1] Malebranche, Recherche de la Vérité, II. Liv. VI. 3.

What is true of the willing of movements, is true also of the willing of ideas. It is only a prejudice which leads to the belief that man originates his own ideas. We overlook the action of God, because he is an invisible spirit, and so we attribute our ideas to our own desires.[1] This general view is further enforced by the argument that a contradiction is implied in saying that men are the authors of their own movements or ideas. For a true cause is that between which and its effect the mind perceives a necessary connection. But there is none except the most perfect being between whose will and its effects the mind can perceive such a connection. The application of this to the theory of knowledge is that the understanding is receptive, not active; and particular volitions are only occasional causes of ideas in the understanding.

Spinoza

In the philosophy of Hume volition was interpreted in terms of feeling; in that of Spinoza it is interpreted in terms of intellect. In the systems of these two philosophers the result is shown of that gradual exclusion from the conception of will of those elements which are not immediately related to action. From his theory of knowledge Hume was led to exclude the idea of abiding character, to notice the result only of a process which the earlier philosophy had identified with will. With him, feeling as the effect of action is all that may be

[1] Malebranche, Ill. II.; Liv. VI. 3.

called will.　Will is not judgment, nor choice, nor decision, nor an efferent impulse.　It is an impression.　By a totally different method, and upon totally different principles, Spinoza likewise excludes from will any originative power and all emotional elements.　With him it is simply affirmation and denial, for the will and the intellect are one.

The principle from which he sets out is that of substance.　It is not the dualism of Descartes. His theory is not theistic, but pantheistic.　Substance is that, the conception of which requires the conception of nothing else for its subsistence: per subtantiam intelligo id, quod in se est, et per se concipitur: hoc est id, cujus conceptus non indiget conceptu alterius rei, a quo formari debeat.[1]

An attribute is that which the intellect perceives concerning substance as constituting the essence of substance: per attributum intelligo id quod intellectus de substantia percipit, tamquam ejusdem essentiam constituens.[2]　God is the only substance.　Instead of the created substances of Descartes, we have here thought and extension defined as attributes of this one substance.　Neither of these attributes is cause of the other.　God is the efficient cause of all things.[3]　As free cause, he is called *natura naturans*.　He is an immanent and proximate cause of those things which are determined by him.[4]　They are determined to exist by him in such a way that without him they cannot be conceived of.　They are related to him as

---

[1] Spinoza, Eth. I. Def. 3.　　　[3] Id., ib. I. xvi. Coroll. 1..
[2] Id., ib. I. Def. 4.　　[4] Id., ib. I. xvii. et Coroll. 2; xxviii. Schol.

the properties of a triangle are related to the triangle. All that proceeds necessarily from God. is called *natura naturata*. The attributes have a unity in God, but there is no reciprocal action between them. There is, however, a correspondence between these two attributes. The order of extended things, and the order of ideas, that is of unextended things, is one and the same. This is because *potentia cogitandi* in God is the same with *potentia agendi;* [1] one is considered under the attribute of thought, the other under the attribute of extension. A mode is an affection of substance, or that which is in another by means of which it is conceived : per modum intelligo substantiae affectiones, sive id, quod in alio est, per quod etiam concipitur.[2] Particular things (*res particulares*) are *affectus* of the attributes of God. They are modes which express the attributes of God in a certain and determinate manner. A mode is either a body or a thinking thing (*corpus* or *res cogitans*). The term *affectus*[3] in Spinoza's philosophy is almost equivalent to passion in the philosophy of Descartes. He himself makes it the same with the Greek ὁρμή, and he speaks also of *affectum* seu *passionem*. Passions are affections of bodies; in relation to thought, or viewed under the attribute of thought, they are ideas of affections. But the order of things and the order of ideas is the same. By means of the affections, the power of the body for acting is increased or dimin-

---

[1] Spinoza, Eth. II. VII. et Coroll.   [2] Id., ib. I. Def. 5.
[3] Id., ib. III. explic. ad fin.; III. Def. 3.

ished.[1] The mind of a man is *res particularis*, or more specifically *res cogitans*. The mind is united with the body, and the idea of the body is in the mind. The two constitute one individual mode, considered under the attribute of thought and under the attribute of extension. When we are the cause of our affections, they are called actions, otherwise they are called passions. The former arise from adequate, the latter from inadequate, ideas. The essence of the mind consists in thought: *mentis essentia in cogitatione constitit.*[2]

I have recalled these fundamental definitions and principles to the reader in order to prepare the way for the special consideration of Spinoza's theory of the will.

I. *The Theory of Faculties.* Spinoza's criticism of this theory, which suggests some of the problems left unsolved by Aristotle, has had a very extensive influence upon modern psychology, and is of importance especially in relation to the science of volition. In the mind there is no absolute faculty of knowing, desiring, loving, or willing. The so-called faculties are either convenient pretences (*fictitias*) or metaphysical abstractions, or are universals such as we are accustomed to form from particulars.[3] Intellect and will have the same relation to this or that idea of the mind, that *lapideitas* has to *lapis*, or *homo* to Peter or Paul. They are not called mere names, by Spinoza, but universal notions (*notiones universales*). The only

---

[1] Spinoza, Eth. III. 1–3. [2] Id., ib. V. xxxviii.
[3] Id., ib. I. Appendix; II. xlviii. Schol.

faculty of intellect, then, is the idea or the ideas which the mind has as the objects of thought, and there is no faculty called the will, but only this or that volition. In mente nulla datur absoluta facultas volendi et nolendi, sed tantum singulares volitiones, nempe haec et illa affirmatio, et haec et illa negatio.[1] Thus in Spinoza's philosophy one faculty is not set over against another, nor is one faculty determined by another. The soul is *res cogitans*, and its *cogitationes* are individual ideas, which are modes of the attribute of thought, which in turn expresses the essence of God in a certain and determinate manner.

II. *The Nature of the Will.* As has just been shown, no absolute faculty is recognized. Both intellect and will are modes belonging only to *natura naturata*. *Voluntas* is only a certain mode of thinking; and individual volitions are related to the mind as the properties of the triangle are related to the triangle. Concipiamus itaque singularem aliquam volitionem nempe modum cogitandi, quo mens affirmat, tres angulos trianguli aequales esse duobus rectis.[2] For the sake of making his meaning clear, however, Spinoza often speaks of will and intellect as faculties; and so he defines the will as a faculty of affirming and denying, by which the mind affirms what is true, and denies what is false.[3] It is not a desire by means of which the mind pursues or avoids: facultatem, inquam, intelligo, qua mens, quid verum

---

[1] Spinoza, Eth. II. xlix.   [2] Id., ib.
[3] Id., ib. II. xlviii. Schol.

quidve falsum sit, affirmat vel negat, et non cupi-
datem, qua mens res appetit vel aversatur.[1] Volitions are individually nothing but the ideas of
things; they are concepts of thought, *cogitationis
conceptus*.[2] To this radical view of volition, the
first natural criticism which might arise is that in
this case there is no difference between intellect and
will.   But this conclusion is accepted by Spinoza,
who says: voluntas et intellectus unum et idem
sunt.[3] Descartes had held that, while will is infinite,
intellect is finite; and Spinoza considers that this
might be urged as an objection to his affirmation of
their identity.[4] He replies that if by intellect is
meant a knowledge of clear and distinct ideas, then
the will is wider than the intellect; but if reference
is had to perceptions of all kinds, then the field of
the will is not more extended than that of the
intellect; for the will acts only in so far as there
is knowledge.   According to the definition, it simply affirms or denies, and so is one with the intellect.   A second criticism which he supposes may
be made to his theory is, that the mind can suspend
judgment as to affirmation or denial; while intellect in knowing, must affirm or deny.   But Spinoza
denies that we can suspend judgment.   When it
is said that we suspend judgment, the meaning is
that we do not adequately perceive the object.   A
third supposed objection is that we do not seem to

---

[1] Spinoza, Eth. II. xlviii. Schol.   [2] Id., ib.
[3] Id., ib. II. xlix. Coroll; Korte Verhandeling, II. 16; Cog.
Met. II. 12.
[4] Id., ib. II. xlix. Schol.

need a greater power for affirming a thing to be
true which is true, than for affirming a thing to be
true which is false; but we perceive one idea to
have more truth and reality than another, which
proves that will and intellect are not the same.
Spinoza replies that the affirmation of truth is
related to the affirmation of falsehood as being is
related to nothing. Lastly, the objection is made
that if will be only affirmation or denial, a man
who is in a state of equilibrium, like the famous
Asinus Buridani, will die of hunger or thirst.
Spinoza replies, with some vivacity, that, under the
conditions assumed, death by starvation or thirst
will follow; but that it might be asked whether
such a man would be an ass or a man. He would,
for his part, say that he did not know what value
should be put on a man who suspended himself in
this way, nor did he know what value should be
put on the judgments of children, fools, and madmen: dico me nescire, ut etiam nescio, quanti
aestimandus sit ille, qui se pensilem facit, et
quanti aestimandi sint pueri, stulti, vesani, etc.[1]

Many critics have called attention to the use of
the term *conatus* by Spinoza, and have objected
that he should have spoken of effort or endeavor,
if the will is only affirmation or negation. Considering his care in defining the terms of his philosophy, it is *prima facie* improbable that Spinoza
should have fallen into an inconsistency in this
respect. The term *conatus* in his *Ethics* is
applied to body as well as to mind. It is either

---

[1] Spinoza, Eth. II. XLIX. Schol.; Cog. Met. II. 12.

an affection or the idea of an affection of the body.
He says: Unaquaeque res, quantum in se est, in
suo esse perseverare conatur.[1] It has been said
already that singular things are modes which
express the essence of God in a certain and
determinate manner. It follows from this that
nothing has in itself anything by which it could
be destroyed, but on the contrary is opposed
(*opponitur*) to everything which could deprive it
of existence. The *conatus* is simply the persistence of modes of God, whether extended or non-
extended. It is therefore perfectly evident that
Spinoza does not use *conatus* as meaning a mere
phenomenon of consciousness, but as an objective
property of all modes of thought and extension.
The *conatus* of a stone is its persistence in being
a stone; the *conatus* of the mind is its persistence
in being as a mode of thought. In the volition,
conatus is only the mind by affirmation, persisting
in its existence as *res cogitans*.[2]

Because the *conatus* is such persistence in the
existence of *res cogitans*, it stands for its actual
essence.[3] That this interpretation of Spinoza's
doctrines is correct is evident from the statement
that the mind is conscious of *conatus*, in so far as
it has ideas, and endeavors to persevere in its own
being in a certain indefinite duration: mens tam
quatenus claras et distinctas, quam quatenus con-
fusas habet ideas, conatur in suo esse perseverare

---

[1] Spinoza, Eth. III. vi, in Part III., prop. 6.

[2] Id., ib. III. vi.–viii. and xxx.   Compare Prin. Phil. Cart. III.
Def. 3.   [3] Id., ib. III. vi. vii.

indefinita quadam duratione, et hujus sui conatus est conscia.[1] The *conatus* of mind alone is will; the *conatus* of mind and body together is appetite: hic conatus, cum ad mentem solam refertur, Voluntas appellatur, sed cum ad mentem et corpus simul refertur, vocatur Appetitus. Men follow their appetites, which tend to their conservation as men. *Cupiditas*, or desire, relates to men in so far as they are conscious of their appetites. In one place, *conatus* and *cupiditas* are used synonymously.

That there is no effective effort in the ordinary meaning of the term is further proven by the argument that the mind does not determine the body, nor the body the mind. As has been said already, Spinoza regards God as the efficient cause of all things, and as determining all things, as well as all events. The ideas of the mind are thus not caused by body, nor do the volitions of the mind determine the acts and affections of the body. Their relationship is in God, and not in reciprocal action.[2]

And inasmuch as both mind and body are one and the same mode, one being perceived under the attribute of thought, and the other under that of extension, it would be absurd to say that either of them determines the other. Nor are the passions determined by the will. In so far as they are related to the mind, they can neither be coerced nor removed, except by the idea of a contrary affection of body, and by the affection of a stronger body. But both mind and body are determined necessarily

---

[1] Spinoza, Eth. III. IX.   [2] Id., ib. II. XXI. XXII.

R

by nature.   Descartes is criticised for saying that the mind has any power over its acts.   Spinoza gives some attention to the reasons which lead to the belief that the body is moved by the mind, especially by the will.   No one has yet had experience as to what his body might do without his mind; no one understands the structure of the body well enough to explain its action; yet the instinct of the lower animals is in many respects superior to the intelligence of man.   To assert that the mind is the only thing that can move the body is to speak ignorantly.   Spinoza asks what becomes of the mind when the body is inert, as in sleep; he shows the interdependence of mind and body, and he affirms that so far from speech, appetites, memory, and forgetting, being controlled by the will, all these are beyond a man's control. What has been called *decretum mentis* is not to be distinguished from imagination or memory.   It is nothing except that affirmation which the idea *quatenus idea* necessarily involves.[1]

III.   *The Will and Freedom.*   Spinoza denies that there are any contingent events.   All things are determined from the necessity of the divine nature, so that they exist and act in a certain way.   It is of the nature of the reason to perceive things not as contingent but as necessary; and this is the very necessity of the eternal nature of God.   The term contingent has only a relative meaning.[2]   Things are regarded as contingent in so far as we find

---

[1] Spinoza, Eth. III. II. Schol.
[2] Id., ib. IV. Def. III. and I. xxix.

nothing pertaining to their essence which necessarily supposes their existence, or which prevents their existence. Real contingency cannot be predicated of volitions. As has been already seen, they are determined, not by the will of God, for God has no will in the sense that man uses the term, but by the nature of God.[1] A man can therefore no more will freely, than a triangle can have its three angles equal to more than two right angles. God himself acts according to the necessity of his nature, and has no free will. Still less can man be called a free cause. His will acts necessarily. Nothing which proceeds from God could have been differently produced, and all is necessarily determined. The mind is determined to will this or that by a cause, and this cause is determined by another, and so on *ad infinitum*.[2] Belief in freedom comes from the consciousness that men have of their own actions, and their ignorance of the causes by which they are determined: ratio doceat, quod homines ea sola de causa liberos se esse credant, quia suarum actionum sunt conscii, et causarum, a quibus determinantur, ignari.[3] The decrees of the mind (*decreta mentis*) are only the appetites, which vary with the disposition of the body. The only case in which man can be said to be free is when his will is determined wholly by reason; and to act from reason is to do those things which follow from the necessity of our nature considered in itself alone.

<hr>

[1] Spinoza, Eth. I. xxix. Schol.; xxxii.
[2] Id., ib. II. xlviii. and Epist. XX.
[3] Id., ib. III. ii. Schol.; Korte Verhandeling, II., xvii.

It is interesting to find repeated in Spinoza's *Ethics* the same expressions of doubt concerning the power of the soul to affect the body which have been already noticed in connection with the theories of Descartes and Malebranche. However unsatisfactory one may think the supposition of Descartes as to the supposed function of the pineal gland, or the miraculous theory of causation taught by Malebranche, or the assertion of Spinoza that will does not move the body, it will be found that in all of these systems of philosophy there is an anticipation of the problem of the will as it has appeared in the psychology of our own day. Here are the questions about feeling of effort, and innervation-feeling in the germ.

LEIBNITZ

I. *The Theory of Monads.* — The first principles of the philosophy of Leibnitz are contained in his *Monadologie.* Like Spinoza, he proceeds from a doctrine of substance; but his conception of substance differs in important particulars from that of his predecessors. Substance is not one, but many; its essence is not in extension, nor in thought, but in force. The plurality of substances which compose the world are called monads. Of these there is an infinite number, of which God is the highest. A monad is a simple substance which enters into all compounds.[1] It is unextended and without parts. It is therefore indivisible. Each monad has entele-

---

[1] Leibnitz, La Monadologie, 1.

chy, — a term which is not to be taken in the Aristotelian sense. By it Leibnitz means a primitive or substantial tendency. Monads differ in proportion to the clearness and distinctness of the perceptions which they possess. For the nature of the monad is spiritual, not material. Each is free from subjection to any external influence. Changes occur within the monad, but it is not altered from without. The principle of change is internal, — the inner activity of each monad. Yet while each is a unit, it may have a plurality of affections; although the substance remains one and undivided. The action of a monad consists in the changes of its perceptions.[1] Perception is a term which is used by Leibnitz in the most general way, denoting thoughts of every kind. The principle of inner change is designated by the term appetition.[2] The soul may be defined as that which has perceptions and appetitions of this general kind. It is not necessary that the soul should be conscious of these perceptions and appetitions; there are many changes of the soul which are not the objects of consciousness. The tendency of the soul in appetition becomes action when it is not interfered with. *Du vouloir et du pouvoir joints ensemble, sont l'action.*[3] The distinction between appetition and volition is that the former is the result of unconscious perceptions, while the latter is the result of conscious perceptions.

II. *The Will and the Faculties.* Leibnitz regards the doctrine of independent faculties in the soul as

---

[1] Leibnitz, La Monadologie, 15.　　　[2] Id., ib. 15.

[3] Id., Nouveaux Essais, II. xxi. 5.

a logical deduction from realism; and quotes approvingly from Episcopius to show that such a logical theory forbids a doctrine of freedom.[1] It is not correct to say that the will is a superior faculty of the soul, that it rules and orders all things, that it is free or that it is not free, that it determines the inferior faculties, that it follows the dictates of the understanding. For the faculties are not agents with distinct actions. It is not the qualities or the faculties which act, but the substances by means of the faculties. In the *Nouveaux Essais*, Leibnitz follows closely the teaching of Locke with respect to the will and freedom. Power (*puissance*) is the possibility of change.[2] It is of two kinds, active and passive. Active power is faculty; passive power is receptivity. Will may be defined as the power to change the actions of body and mind. This was the definition of Locke; and Leibnitz would modify it, and say that the will is the effort (*conatus*) or tendency to attain the good and avoid the bad: pour parler plus rondement et pour aller peut-être plus avant, je dirai que la volition est l'effort ou la tendance (*conatus*) d'aller vers ce qu'on trouve bon et loin de ce qu'on trouve mauvais, en sorte que cette tendance résulte immédiatement de l'apperception qu'on en a.[3] The close connection between Leibnitz's conceptions of substance, of power, and of will, is shown in his view of the spontaneity of substance. If all changes within the monad consist of

<hr>

[1] Leibnitz, Nouveaux Essais, II. xxi. 6.

[2] Id., ib. II. xxi. 4.

[3] Id., ib. II. xxi. 5.

the alternation of perceptions, and if the tendency of the monad is towards action, there is no definite line dividing knowledge from volition. Spontaneity is of the very inner nature of the soul; it belongs to the soul because the principle of our actions is not external to us, but is an inward principle.[1] External things have, strictly speaking, no effect upon the soul whatever. This spontaneity is common to all substances, and in the substance which is free and intelligent, it governs all actions.

Volition must, however, not be confounded with desire. While it rarely happens that an action of the will is produced in us, unaccompanied by some desire, will and desire should not be confounded: il arrive rarement qu'aucune action volontaire soit produite en nous, sans que quelque désir l'accompagne; c'est pourquoi la volonté et le désir sont si souvent confondus ensemble.[2] There is an uneasiness which excites desire, and there is an uneasiness which moves the will. Wherever there is desire, there is uneasiness; but one cannot say that wherever there is uneasiness, there is desire. In an act of volition, in the true sense of the word, there is a concurrence of several perceptions and inclinations. And volition cannot subsist without desire or avoidance. Yet sometimes a violent passion can act upon the mind, without knowledge, and without intervening volition: comme le vent le plus furieux agit sur nos corps.[3]

<hr>

[1] Leibnitz, Théodicée, 59.
[2] Id., Nouveaux Essais, II. XXI. 39.
[3] Id., ib. II. XXI. 12.

III. *The Doctrine of Preëstablished Harmony.*
The freedom of the monad from all external affections, and the reflection in its consciousness more
or less perfectly of the entire universe, raise the
question of the possibility of such knowledge.[1]
External objects are not known by their effects
upon the soul; nor does the soul see all things
in God, as Malebranche had supposed. Leibnitz
teaches that there is a correspondence between the
ideas in the consciousness of the monad, and the
ideas or events in the world without. The theory
resembles that implied in the statement of Spinoza,
that the order of ideas and that of things are
the same. This, according to Leibnitz, does not
arise from the unity of substance, but from the
harmony preëstablished by God, between the world
beyond the soul, and the world within the soul: et
par son moyen l'univers entier, suivant le point de
vue propre à cette substance simple; sans qu'elle
ait besoin de recevoir aucune influence physique du
corps: comme le corps aussi de son côté s'accom-
mode aux volontés de l'âme par ses propres lois, et
par conséquent ne lui obéit qu'autant que ces lois le
portent.[2] The soul is thus so spontaneous that it
depends only on God and itself in its actions.

IV. *The Principle of Sufficient Reason.* This
forms an important element in Leibnitz's theory of
the determination of the will. Two principles lie
at the foundation of all our reasoning: that of
contradiction, and that of sufficient reason. The
following is the definition of the principle of suffi-

[1] Leibnitz, La Monadol. 51 f.   [2] Id., Théodicée, III. 291.

cient reason: there is nothing true or existent, no real statement (*enunciation*), without there being a sufficient reason why it should be so and not otherwise, although the reasons cannot generally be known to us. This principle does not exclude contingency, because of the immense variety of things in nature, and the division of bodies *ad infinitum.*[1] Specifically, there is an infinity of imperceptible inclinations in the soul which enter into the final cause of action. But this view of nature is not mechanical, although each body is a kind of divine machine or natural automaton. The machines of nature differ from those of art, in that they are related, not to a particular end, but to infinity: les machines de la nature, c'est à dire les corps vivants, sont encore machines dans leurs moîndres parties jusqu'à l'infini.[2] The principle of sufficient reason implies that there is nothing dead, or sterile, or useless in nature.

V. *The Will and the Idea of Freedom.* The term liberty, or freedom, is ambiguous. It does not refer to liberty from external restraint. With relation to the will, it is of two kinds: (*a*) when the will is not constrained by the passions, *i.e.*, by the affections of the mind itself; (*b*) when the will is not constrained by necessity.[3] The first of these is freedom in the sense of the Stoic philosophy. But the relation of the will to necessity is of more importance. Voluntary is not opposed to necessary, but to involuntary. And volitions are not

---

[1] Leibnitz, La Monadol. 32 f.   [2] Id., ib. 64.

[3] Id., Nouveaux Essais, II. xxi. b.

necessary, but contingent. By the necessary Leibnitz means that of which the contrary is impossible, or that which implies contradiction. Acts of the will are only hypothetically necessary, which is the same as saying that it is contingent, whether a certain action of the will is about to take place. If we accept the above definition of the necessary, it will follow that volitions, although they are determined, are not necessary.[1] If it be asked then what determines the will, the answer given is that the mind determines the will; but the mind is determined by some uneasiness, and the latter is the motive of volition. It is internal, not external. Leibnitz follows Descartes in holding that freedom of the will is dependent on knowledge. When there are several desires before the mind, the mind may consider them in succession previous to the final volition. This is called deliberation, and in it consists *liberum arbitrium* in its true sense. And this deliberation is not a defect, but rather a perfection of our nature: vouloir et agir conformément au dernier résultat d'un sincère examen, c'est plutôt une perfection qu'un défaut de notre nature.[2] Our choice is not compelled by our judgment, or by any antecedent cause. It is said to be inclined, and not necessitated: la prévalence des biens aperçus incline sans nécessiter, quoique tout considéré cette inclination soit déterminante et ne manque jamais de faire son effet.[3] The desire, as has been said above, must

---

[1] Leibnitz, Nouveaux Essais, II. xxi. 11–13.
[2] Id., ib. II. xxi. 48.   [3] Id., ib. II. xxi. 49.

not be confounded with the will. The former is a
kind of incomplete volition; it is excited by happiness, and inclines the will.[1] There is no power of
contrary choice. This is not inconsistent with the
contingency of acts of the will, for objectively the
certainty of these actions is assured. It is sometimes said that we can will not only what we please,
but what we do not please to will. This Leibnitz
declares to be absurd : le choix est toujours déter-
miné par la perception. The perception is not
always before consciousness. There are impulses,
accompanied by pleasure and pain, and all perceptions are either new sensations or imaginations
remaining from some past sensations, which renew
the inducements which these sensations have presented at former times. This renewal may be
either accompanied by memory or not, and is in
proportion to the vivacity of the imagination. The
prevailing effort (*l'effort prévalant*) is the result of
all these impulses, which realizes the action of the
will. It is possible that the most pressing uneasiness may not determine the will. This failure
occurs when the other impulses taken together prevent the decisive volition in accordance with the
otherwise strongest motive. Up to the time of the
volition, there is, as it were, a balancing of motives.
The order of determination will appear from what
has been said: it is happiness which excites the
uneasiness, and it is uneasiness which, in union
with the judgment, determines the will in accordance with the inclination of the mind. Leibnitz

---

[1] Leibnitz, Nouveaux Essais, II. xxi. 30.

differs from Hobbes in that he does not regard the motives as efficient causes of volition. The volition is determined, not by an efficient, but by a final cause. Efficient causes operate only in the corporeal world, while the soul is governed by final causes: les âmes agissent selon les lois des causes finales par appétitions, fins et moyens. Les corps agissent selon les lois des causes efficientes ou des mouvements. Et les deux règnes, celui des causes efficientes et celui des causes finales, sont harmoniques entre eux.[1] But from a more general point of view, it is the principle of sufficient reason which requires the affirmation that the will is determined. The freedom of indifference is an impossibility, if the principle of sufficient reason be admitted. As for freedom, it consists only in the power of deliberation which precedes the final volition. In this Leibnitz is in agreement with Locke. Considering the polemic which is carried on in parts of the *Nouveaux Essais*, against the principles of Locke's philosophy, it is singular that the chapter on power and the will contains no important criticism of the English philosopher's doctrine. Like Spinoza and other preceding writers, Leibnitz considers the problem of the *Asinus Buridani*.[2] Bayle had maintained that under such circumstances, which were quite possible, the animal would starve to death. Leibnitz denies that such a case is possible; but admits that if it were, that result would follow. He is careful to explain

---

[1] Leibnitz, La Monadol. 79.
[2] Id., Théodicée, I. 49.

that the determination of the will does not conflict with the spontaneity of the soul. He objects that Hobbes and Spinoza have defended a doctrine of absolute necessity which makes the will inactive (*la volonté paresseux*).[1] The soul, he concludes, is a kind of spiritual automaton; although contingent actions in general, and free actions in particular, are not on this account necessary, with an absolute necessity, which would be incompatible with contingence. Samuel Clarke, who was engaged in active controversy with Leibnitz, criticised the doctrine of the latter, holding that it conducted to necessitarianism and fatalism. The activity which Leibnitz admitted in the soul was urged by Clarke as a proof of its freedom. The motive may be external; it impresses the mind, which. so far is passive; but when the mind is thus impressed, it is aroused to action, and freely wills. The motive is not " the principle of action ; " for the spring of action is the free will. Clarke also raises the rather formidable objection that absolute necessity is the only true necessity, and that the hypothetical or moral necessity of which Leibnitz speaks is a mere figure. The question is whether the motives are causes of volition or not. It may be added that the death of Leibnitz prevented his replying to Clarke's last criticism.[2]

In the *Théodicée*, the will is considered in relation to God; and most of the questions which engaged

---

[1] Leibnitz, Théodicée, I. 67.

[2] Recueil de Lettres entre Leibnitz et Clarke. 4me Écrit de M. L. 5me Écrit de M. L. 5me Réplique de M. C.

the attention of the theologians of the seventeenth
and eighteenth centuries, with respect to grace and
original sin, were discussed by Leibnitz. God is
said to foreknow the future, because the future has
been predetermined. But Leibnitz declares that
there are two famous labyrinths in which our reason
wanders : one relates to the question of necessity
and freedom, including the problem of the origin
of evil; the other has reference to the constitution
of matter. There is, he says, a good and a bad
kind of fatalism. The first is the imperfect fatalism of the Mahometans; the second is the philosophical fatalism of the Stoic philosophy and the
Christian religion. The good doctrine teaches that
man should do his duty, and leave the result to an
overruling power. God permits evil, but is not
the positive cause. It is admitted, however, that
the permissive will of God has efficaciousness in
bringing on evil. God's will is either antecedent
or consequent. The antecedent will of God is the
general willing of the best result among infinite
possibilities. The consequent will of God is a
single volition embracing the final effect of the
diverse evil and good willing in the contingent
world.[1]

Down to the time of Kant, the theory of Leibnitz
prevailed in Germany. His determinism was
emphasized by Wolff, who gave the dogmatic philosophy its German form. According to Wolff, the
soul of man has the power to present or to represent the universe to itself; and from this representa-

1 Leibnitz, Théodicée, Preface.

tion (*Vorstellung*) arises an effort on the part of the subject to change these presentations. This effort may assume one of two forms: impulse or will. There is in man a tendency to follow the good, and avoid its opposite. If the idea of the good be obscure, the effect is merely appetite; if it be clear, the effect is *will*. If a greater and a lesser good be contemplated by the mind, the greater good, or what seems to be the greater good, will inevitably determine the will.[1]

[1] Wolff, Vernünftige Gedanken, etc., passim.

CHAPTER SIXTH

THEORIES OF THE WILL IN GERMAN PHILOSOPHY FROM KANT TO LOTZE

PHILOSOPHY on the continent of Europe until the time of Kant has no national peculiarity. The development of doctrine from Descartes to Wolff leads us from France to Holland, and from Holland to Germany, and shows many traces of the influence exercised by Hobbes and Locke. While the development of the German philosophy, beginning with Kant, was more or less due to the stimulating effects of Hume's scepticism, the German systems of the nineteenth century are distinctively national; although of late years there has been a free exchange of philosophical ideas between the several European nations. Lotze forms a connecting link between the old and the new. His predecessors had deduced their theories of the will from their metaphysical doctrines. Lotze, while eminent as a metaphysician, was among the first to take the theory of the will out of the metaphysical domain, and consider it in the light of positive science. Whatever estimate may be made of the value of his conclusions, it can hardly be denied that, since the appearance of his first psychological treatise, no German philosopher of importance has been able to overlook the questions raised by his method and inquiry.

KANT

In the system of Kant the psychological aspects of volition are for the most part unnoticed, while the metaphysical and moral aspects appear prominently. Not the nature of the will as a psychical act or process, but the freedom of the will as a metaphysical or moral principle, is the prevailing conception. And whereas the philosophy before Kant had at length reached a point of specialization in which the extent of the will had been limited to an act of the mind as a result of deliberation, or to the act of deliberation itself, Kant returned in a measure to the older view of the will. He uses it in its most liberal significance. It is more than an act of affirmation or denial; it is more than a feeling of effort or an executive faculty. In the absence of any doctrine of an Ego, other than the synthetic unity of apperception, and of any definite theory of personality, he identifies the practical reason with the will, and apparently with the autonomous and spontaneous soul itself. Practically the will acts in obedience to certain laws, but it is its own lawgiver. It is not only a faculty, but a fundamental faculty, the existence of which does not have to be demonstrated, and the freedom of which has to be postulated, in spite of the limitations of speculative philosophy.

s

In the philosophy of Kant there is both a theoretical and a practical doctrine of the will, in accordance with the general Kantian method. The first of these is contained in the *Critique of Pure Reason*. The second is already anticipated in that theoretical work, and is explicitly presented in the *Critique of Practical Reason* and in the *Metaphysics of Ethics*.

I. *Theoretical Doctrine of the Will.* This is formally set forth in the Third Antinomy of the Transcendental Dialectic. In order that it may be the better understood, certain fundamental principles of the *Critique of Pure Reason* must be recalled.

1. *Matter and Form.* The matter of knowledge must be distinguished from the form. The first of these comes from experience, and is *a posteriori;* the second is that which makes experience possible, but is not given by experience. It is *a priori*. The matter of knowledge comes from the outer and from the inner sense, in the sensible intuition (*Anschauung*). The forms of sensibility are space and time. They are *a priori*, not *a posteriori*, forms. In sensibility the mind is receptive. Space is the form of external, and time of internal, phenomena. A higher faculty than sensibility is the understanding. This is not receptive, but spontaneous. It is the faculty by which the knowledge of the intuition is thought in concepts or categories. It is a formal faculty, and its *a priori* concepts or categories are deduced from the forms of the logical judgment, with respect to quantity, quality, relation, and modality.

The problem of the *Critique of Pure Reason* is stated thus: how are synthetic judgments *a priori* possible? This, in less technical language, means: how do we reach a knowledge of necessary truth? and the solution of the problem is to be found in Kant's doctrine of *a priori* forms. The necessary truths of science, whether mathematical or physical, cannot be derived from experience. The failure of empiricism had been proved by Hume. "Experience teaches us, indeed, that anything is created in such and such a way, but not that it cannot be otherwise." It does not give necessity:

Erfahrung lehrt uns zwar dass etwas so oder so beschaffen sei, aber nicht dass es nicht anders sein könne. Findet sich also erstlich ein Satz, der zugleich mit seiner Nothwendigkeit gedacht wird, so ist er ein Urtheil *a priori*.[1] Nothwendigkeit und strenge Allgemeinheit sind also sichere Kennzeichen einer Erkenntniss *a priori*, und gehören auch unzertrennlich zu einander.[2]

It is the *a priori* forms which make the *a priori* or necessary judgments possible. That is absolutely necessary the opposite of which is in itself impossible. All our conceptions of inner necessity in the qualities of possible things, of whatever kind, proceed from this, that the opposite involves a contradiction.[3] Thus the doctrine of Hume is denied, that the empirical cognition through the force of custom or habit becomes necessary.

2. *The Phenomenon and the Thing in itself.* This

---

[1] Kant, Werke [Hartenstein], III. 35.
[2] Id., II. 125.   [3] Id., III. 34.

is the most important distinction in the Kantian philosophy, and is at the foundation of the whole system, both theoretically and practically. It is said that we know only phenomena, and not things in themselves: was die Gegenstände an sich selbst sein mögen, wurde uns durch die aufgeklärteste Erkenntniss der Erscheinung derselben, die uns allein gegeben ist, doch niemals bekannt werden.[1] The phenomena themselves are not things, because space and time are not given by experience, but are *a priori* forms. We have, therefore, no assurance that the forms of our intuition are forms of the real world. To go beyond this is dogmatism. That there are things in themselves (*Dinge an sich*) is not denied; it is only affirmed that they are unknown. This ignorance of the *Ding an sich* has reference to the world in time as well as to the world in space. The Ego, or self, according to this doctrine, is unknown as thing in itself. Just as we know only the phenomena of matter, and not matter as thing in itself, so in like manner is our knowledge of mind limited. In the *Critique of Pure Reason*, instead of self, or Ego, there is the formal principle which Kant calls the synthetic unity of apperception (*die synthetische Einheit der Apperception.*) In the proposition "I think" is by implication contained an act of spontaneity. This Kant calls "pure apperception" (*reine Apperception*). While I am conscious of myself as identical with respect to the manifold content of consciousness, because I can call them my ideas, yet the manifold

[1] Kant, III. 72.

is not given by means of the Ego. But the highest principle of the possibility of all intuition in relation to the understanding is that all the manifold of the intuition stands under the conditions of the original synthetic unity of apperception. The Ego as *Ding an sich* cannot be an object of knowledge; and so, to account for the unity of the manifold, and the identity of the subject in experience, Kant presents the principle of synthetic unity of apperception. This has a merely theoretical significance, so that it is not a principle of volition, but only of knowledge. In the *Critique of Pure Reason*, there is likewise no definite doctrine of personality, and one must go to the practical philosophy for an explanation. The doctrine of the unity of apperception is not put forward as an explanation of the moral personality, but in order to establish the important principle of the *Ego cogito*, for the sake of the unity of thought: durch den allgemeinen Ausdruck, ich denke, zusammenfassen kann.[1]

Corresponding to this distinction between the phenomenon and the noumenon, (*Ding an sich*) is that between the sensible and intelligible world. The value of the intelligible in relation to the doctrine of the will is first apparent in connection with the Third Antinomy.

Kant's insufficient explanation of the Ego in his

---

[1] Kant, III. 19. See, also: Ich bin mir also des identischen Selbst bewusst, in Ansehung des Mannigfaltigen der mir in einer Anschauung gegeben Vorstellungen, weil ich sie ingesammt meine Vorstellungen nenne, die eine ausmachen, III. 117, 118.

Critique of Pure Reason has been justly criticised, and undoubtedly leads to great confusion.
From the fact that we know only phenomena, it
is obvious that our knowledge of self can be only
phenomenal, and consequently it is difficult to
interpret the assertion that "I am conscious of
myself," however the term self be explained.   In
Kant's theoretical philosophy, the Ego is identified
with none of the faculties of knowledge, and the
relation of the faculties to that which has or exercises the faculties is quite obscure.   I simply refer
to this in passing, as Kant's discussion of the will
in the first *Critique* is not essentially related to
any particular doctrine of the Ego.   In another
work, he attributes autonomy not only to the practical reason, but also to the understanding and to
the faculty of judgment (*Urtheilskraft*).

3. *Causality.*   Causality is a category of relation
which is deduced from the hypothetical judgment.
It is not derived empirically, but is a condition
which makes experience of natural phenomena possible.   Cause and effect form a sequence in time,
and a necessary sequence.   The necessity of the
causal judgment comes from the *a priori* nature of
the category.   Cause and effect are necessarily
connected, not because they are associated in experience as invariable antecedent and consequent, but
because they are thought in the understanding in
the category of causality, which is *a priori*, and
therefore necessary.[1]

Like all other formal elements in our knowledge,

---

[1] Kant. III. 174 ff.

the category of causality is applicable only to phenomena. Whether things in themselves are thus causally connected we do not know, for we know only phenomena, and not things in themselves. In the observation of phenomena it is observed that a certain condition of things prevails at one time, and another condition just before. The two observations are combined in time. The combination or conjunction is not effected through the sensibility or through intuition, but is the product of thought. The conception of their necessary union is due to the understanding. The conception is that of the causal relation. Effects are thus observed as changes, and for every change a cause is thought necessarily. Often the cause and effect are simultaneously observed, but this does not contradict the law of succession. The temporal sequence of effects is required because the cause cannot exercise its whole effect in one moment: hier muss man wohl bemerken, dass es auf die Ordnung der Zeit, und nicht den Ablauf derselben angesehen sei; das Verhältniss bleibt, wenn gleich keine Zeit verlaufen ist. Causality suggests action, and action suggests force, and force suggests substance. But it may be added that substance, like cause, is not given in experience, but is itself an *a priori* concept or category.[1]

4. *Freedom and Causality.* The *Critique of Pure Reason* has to do with knowledge, not with will. It deals with judgments, not volitions. The latter are phenomena like other phenomena, are

[1] Kant, III. 183, and cf. 144.

known in the same way, and are subject to the same laws. The volition is known, not as the Ego choosing or deliberating or acting, but each volition is a change, is known as an effect, and is conceived as necessarily determined by an antecedent cause. The difficulties which this conclusion suggests are discussed in the Transcendental Dialectic.

The Transcendental Æsthetic, which is the first part of the *Critique* has to do with the *a priori* forms of intuition; the Transcendental Analytic, which is the first subdivision of the Transcendental Logic, is the science of the *a priori* forms of the understanding. The Æsthetic shows how mathematics as a science is possible; the Analytic shows how a science of nature is possible. The Transcendental Dialectic, which is the second part of the Logic, deals with the question whether metaphysics as a science is possible. According to Kant, metaphysics is the science of the ideas of pure reason. An idea is a conception of the totality of experience.[1] The conceptions or concepts of the understanding have no significance unless their form is filled by the content which comes from the intuition, which in turn comes from experience, being known in the forms of space and time. But the ideas of pure reason have no corresponding empirical content. The being of these ideas cannot be denied, and even if they are illusions, they must be examined.[2] The totality of experience is the content of the idea, and we have

<hr>

[1] Kant, III. 261, 262.   [2] Id. III. 247.

no intuition of such a totality. In this respect especially, the concept of the reason, that is, the idea, differs from the concept of the understanding. The reason is the faculty of reasoning. In this process we are led from conclusion to premises, and from these premises to other premises, from which the former are conclusions. This process may either proceed *ad infinitum*, or else a premise may be reached which depends on no antecedent premises. In either case the result is the unconditioned. In one case, the series is unconditioned, because unlimited; in the other case, the principle is the unconditioned. In the Æsthetic and Analytic the unconditioned, or *Ding an sich*, was simply a negative limit to knowledge. It was that which is unknown. In the Dialectic, it has a positive significance, for it is the idea of the reason. Whether it is a valid conception or not, metaphysics exists, and the validity of the science has to be examined.

There are three ideas of the reason, which are deduced from three forms of the syllogism,— the categorical, the hypothetical, and the disjunctive. From the first of these, by a *regressus* from predicate to subject, and from this subject to another subject, we arrive at last either at an infinite series, or at a subject which is the predicate of no other proposition.[1]

The idea of the unconditioned subject is the idea of the soul, which is the object of rational psychology. The hypothetical syllogism leads us to

[1] Kant, III. 262.

the idea of a proposition which is conditioned by no antecedent. This is the idea of the world which is the object of rational cosmology. The disjunctive syllogism leads us to the idea of an aggregate of members of a unity in the unconditioned, which is the idea of God, the idea of rational theology.

It is only the second of these ideas of the reason which need here be considered.

The idea of rational cosmology, as has just been suggested, is derived from a *regressus* from each antecedent to a preceding consequent, until a proposition is reached which does not depend on any other antecedent; or else the *regressus* is *ad infinitum*. The meaning of this, if we drop the language of logic, is that either there is an infinite *regressus* in the series of causes and effects, or else a first cause is reached which is an effect of no preceding cause.[1] Either of these alternatives is capable of demonstration, and the result is the Third Antinomy.

The Third Antinomy

Thesis

Causality according to the Laws of Nature is not the only [causality] from which the totality of the phenomena of the world can be derived. There is another causality through freedom, to be accepted as necessary for explaining these [phenomena].

(Die Causalität nach Gesetzen der Natur ist nicht die einzige aus welcher die Erscheinungen der Welt ingesammt

---

[1] Kant, III. 297.

abgeleitet werden können. Es ist noch eine Causalität durch Freiheit zu Erklärung derselben anzunehmen nothwendig.)

Antithesis

There is no Freedom, but everything in the world happens altogether according to the Laws of Nature.

(Es ist keine Freiheit, sondern alles in der Welt geschieht lediglich nach Gesetzen der Natur.[1])

It will be at once observed that the thesis is a statement of the possibility of free will, and the plain assertion that there is a causality through freedom. The antithesis insists that all events happen in the causal series, and that freedom is impossible. Judged by the principles of the Analytic, the thesis has no scientific value; and the problem raised in the Dialectic is: can there be an exception to the laws of nature which have been deduced in the Analytic? It is further to be noticed that the law of cause and effect as deduced from the hypothetical judgment is a necessary law, and to suppose that an effect can occur without a cause implies a contradiction. Nevertheless, here the necessary law is contradicted in the thesis.

In the presence of these two alternative conclusions, one might be justified in holding that there was no possibility of demonstrating the truth of either freedom or its opposite, and the result would be scepticism. This is not the attitude taken by Kant. In the discussion of the Antinomy, we find him seeking a reconciliation of these two contradictory conclusions. If the conclusion of the thesis is valid, however, then the results of the

---

[1] Kant, III. 316, 317.

critical method in the Analytic are not final.   For
if there is freedom from the necessity of causality, then either freedom is not a phenomenon, or
else the law of causality is not necessary.   Kant
takes the former alternative.   Freedom is not phenomenal.   But, according to him, the freedom
affirmed in the thesis is not empirical, but transcendental freedom.   It refers to a spontaneous
beginning of a causal series, but not to a temporal
or chronological beginning.   It is a noumenal, not
a phenomenal freedom, and is thus independent of
the form of time, which is a form of phenomena,
not of things in themselves.[1]   It is independent
also of the category of causality, which is a form
of phenomena as well.   To posit a free cause is to
supply a need of the reason.   Kant admits that
the thesis is dogmatic,[2] because freedom is predicated of the *Ding an sich*, which according to the
critical method cannot be known.   To believe in a
free cause, and to believe that I am free, are the
two foundation stones of religion and morality.   It
is not a matter of mere speculative interest whether
the thesis or the antithesis be accepted as true.
There is a practical interest as well.   The antithesis fails to answer the question how the series of

---

[1] Es wird aber immer merkwürdig bleiben, dass Kant, nach-
dem er zuerst Dinge an sich von Erscheinungen nur negativ,
durch die Unabhängigkeit von der Zeit, unterschieden, nachher
in den metaphysischen Eröterungen seiner Kritik der prakti-
schen Vernunft Unabhängigkeit von der Zeit und Freiheit wirklich als correlate Begriffe behandelt hatte, etc.   Schelling, W.
I. vii. 351, 352.

[2] Kant, III. 332.

causes has begun, or whether it has had a beginning. The thesis has popularity on its side; for the ordinary understanding has no difficulty in imagining a beginning of the series, or the freedom of the will. Nor can the antithesis be denied by the empiricist, for that would be empirical dogmatism.[1] The antithesis requires an infinite *regressus*, which is a conception too great for a synthesis of the properties of the universe. The thesis is, moreover, the foundation of the conception of practical freedom. Freedom in the practical sphere is the independence of the will of necessity, especially of the necessity of sensible causes.[2] The fact that a man does not have to obey the senses and the sensible impulses, but can will in opposition to them, shows that he has a free faculty which determines the act independent of these impulses. The knowledge of freedom does not conflict with a knowledge of natural causality; for the former is "intelligible,"[3] the latter is phenomenal. The freedom of the *Ding an sich* is intelligible, that is, it is not derived from experience, nor is it conditioned by the forms of experience. Kant's contention is that the reason, which exists in neither space nor time,[4] and which is itself transcendental, is unconditioned, and can be conceived as a free cause. Causality, while it is a category of phenomena, is not a category of noumena. And causality through freedom, while it cannot be proved, cannot be disproved.

<hr>

1 Kant, III. 332 ff. 343 f.   3 Id. III. 374.
2 Id. III. 371.   4 Id. III. 382.

In holding that the freedom of the will is not known empirically, Kant differs radically from the majority of indeterminists.   Their contention is that consciousness informs us empirically that we are free, while Kant holds that experience teaches us that the will is determined.   This is to be explained partly from the influence of Hume on Kant, but more particularly from Kant's doctrine of causality in relation to the phenomenal world.   While apparently desirous of vindicating the validity of the thesis of the Antinomy, he admits that it is as easy to think of an infinite number of successive changes, as to think of eternally existing substances.   But the practical interest in the thesis is that which triumphs in weighing the alternative conclusions.   The ideas of the pure reason are not scientifically necessary, but they are indispensable to practice.   Indeed, Kant defines practical as all that is possible by means of freedom: praktisch ist alles, was durch Freiheit möglich ist.[1]   But freedom can be established, not as a constitutive principle, but only as a regulative principle.   It is related to action, not to theory.   From this point of view, we have no longer to ask whether freedom is possible.   For practically we are brought to recognize it as a canon of moral action.[2]   What this freedom implies is left in some obscurity by Kant.   Transcendental freedom must mean, of course, freedom from causes which determine the will; and it means also freedom from sensual impulses.   For we have a faculty which can postpone

----

[1] Kant. III. 529.   [2] Id. III. 529 f.

the reaction against the impulse, and can resist the inclinations of sense.[1]

It need hardly be said that this Antinomy has been a favorite point of attack for the critics of Kant. Whether a defence of the thesis is consistent with the validity of the results reached by the critical method may be fairly open to doubt. At all events Kant's practical philosophy awakens in the reader a suspicion that the doctrine of regulative principles introduced at the close of the first *Critique* is advanced in order to admit practically what had been excluded theoretically, and to save ethics after the foundation of ontology had been undermined. That the thesis is regarded as even possibly true, opens the way for the practical discussion of volition as contained in the *Critique of Practical Reason* and in the *Metaphysics of Ethics*.

It is part of the irony of fate that Kant's practical philosophy should have been accepted by many who have denied the validity of the *Critique of Pure Reason*. He has often received high praise as a defender of the rights of the moral law, of conscience, and of free will, by those who found their belief in freedom on an appeal to consciousness, and who dissent altogether from the great critical distinction between the phenomenon and the *Ding an sich*. Such philosophers apparently overlook two facts with respect to the Kantian philosophy. The first of these is that Kant maintained that the empirical method leads inevitably and logically to determinism; and the second is that

<hr>

[1] Kant, III. 531.

according to Kant, unless the distinction between phenomenon and *Ding an sich* be made, there is no ground upon which the freedom of the will can be defended.

II. *Practical Doctrine of the Will*. Certain affirmations made in the *Critique of Pure Reason* introduce Kant's practical doctrine of the will. His statements that there may be a causality through freedom in the intelligible world, that freedom is essential to morality, and that it is empirical dogmatism to deny the existence of transcendental freedom, introduce the principles of his practical philosophy.

It is admitted that free will is not given empirically, and is therefore not subject to the principle of causality. Everything in nature acts according to laws, but the will is not subject to the laws of nature. It gives its own laws; it is autonomous.[1] The introduction to the Kantian ethics is the treatise on the *Metaphysics of Ethics*, in which an attempt is made to discover the principles or laws of a pure will. These laws are necessary; they do not depend on empirical conditions. They carry with them absolute necessity. They exclude all contingency. Only a rational being has the faculty to act according to the idea of certain principles. That faculty is will. The will is defined as a faculty of choosing only that which reason, independent of inclination, recognizes as practically necessary. That which is practically necessary is identical with the good.[2] That which

---

[1] Kant, IV. 281, 284; V. 30, 35.   [2] Id. IV. 260.

in all the world deserves to be called good, without limit or qualification, is a good will. Its peculiar characteristic or property is a good character. For a good will is good *per se,* and not because of its volitions or results.[1] The nature of a good will is made still plainer by the definition of duty. Duty is the necessity of an action, out of respect for law.[2] If the will is determined by external necessity, it cannot be called good. The good will is determined by its own laws, that is, by subjective laws. Hence it is both rational and free. Kant identifies these three conceptions, freedom, the will, and the practical reason. Die Freiheit ist demnach, ein Vermögen, welches zugleich praktisch und vernünftig ist: sie ist Wille und praktische Vernunft.[3] The will is a fundamental faculty (Grundvermögen), it is therefore incapable of more exact definition and explanation: nun ist aber alle menschliche Einsicht zu Ende, sobald wir zu Grundkraften oder Grundvermögen gelangt sind.[4] This fundamental character of the will, or, to adopt a later term, this primacy of the will, implies that it is a faculty which controls all subjective moving causes. It is Kant's doctrine, not only that the will is free from external co-action, and free from the determination of external motives, but is free from any causality of subjective states or processes. It is subject to its own laws, and by virtue of this autonomy it is free. It is not determined by another, but is self-determined. The determinists of the seventeenth

---

[1] Kant, IV. 242.
[2] Id. IV. 248.
[3] Cf. Id. IV., 260; V. 16.
[4] Id. V. 50.

T

and eighteenth centuries, had taught that the motive is the efficient cause of the volition. Kant holds that the will controls the motives, and determines whether or not the volition shall be in accordance with them. Thus the principle of every human will is the unconditional law which it imposes upon itself. This law, which is none other than the moral law, is *a priori*, and therefore universal and necessary. The principle of autonomy of the will is distinguished from that of heteronomy. In the heteronomy of the will there is no element of morality. In such a case the will is under an alien law, and is neither good nor free: Autonomie ist also der Grund der Würde der menschlichen und jeder vernünftigen Natur.[1] The Scottish moralists of the sentimental school, and the French sensualists of the eighteenth century had regarded morality as obedience to certain feelings of different degrees of worth. Kant excludes the feelings from his ethical principles, and regards volitions as absolute when they are moral. We are free because we are autonomous, and we are autonomous because we are free.[2] The only proof of this freedom is to be found in the demands of morality. The reason why we believe that we are free, is that we believe in the imperative obligation to be moral. And conversely, the reason why we believe that the obligation is imperative, is because we believe in the freedom of the will. Yet freedom must be postulated as ultimate, and cannot be proved. It is incapable of any theoretical demonstration. It is

[1] Kant, IV. 284.   [2] Id. IV. 297, 298.

the only idea of the reason, the possibility *a priori*
of which is known without comprehending how it
is the condition of the moral law. Freedom is
ratio essendi of the moral law; and the moral law,
ratio cognoscendi of freedom.[1]

Kant says:—

Freiheit ist aber die einzige unter allen Ideen der specula-
tiven Vernunft wovon wir die Möglichkeit *a priori* wissen,
ohne sie doch einzusehen, weil sie Bedingung des moralischen Gesetzes ist, welches wir wissen.[2]

Kant thus defends the freedom of the will in an
entirely novel manner. Former philosophers did
not so distinguish the phenomenal and noumenal
world, as to limit the application of the principle
of causation to the former. They were unable to
explain how the will as phenomenon or as noumenon or as both together in a world of causes and
effects, could be free from the law of causality.
Kant claims, and justly claims, that he has discovered
a way of avoiding the difficulty. For by insisting
that the will as *Ding. an-sich* is not subject to the
principle of causality, he virtually asserts its freedom. At least, he asserts that its freedom is not
unthinkable. He is able then to open the practical
consideration of the doctrine with a *prima facie*
case. It is, however, not empirical, but transcendental freedom. It is the practical reason willing
as *Ding an sich*, in obedience to a moral law. It
wills, not according to desire or inclination, but be-

---

[1] Kant, V. 4, note.   [2] Id. V. 4.

cause of an imperative maxim.[1] While duty and
desire may coincide, the will does not conform to
duty because of desire, but because of the principle
of " ought " (*sollen*). Whereas in the natural order
of things, the reason is determined by objects, and
has no freedom ; in the moral order the will determines the objects.[2] If we cannot prove consciousness of freedom directly, still less can we show how
it is possible : wie nun dieses Bewusstsein der
moralischen Gesetze, oder welches einerlei ist, das
der Freiheit, möglich sei, lässt sich nicht weiter
erklären, nur die Zulässigkeit derselben in der theo-
retischen Kritik wohl vertheidigen.[3] The moral
law, which is absolute, is a law of causality through
freedom. It has a standing equal to the causal
necessity of the phenomenal world. Causality is
contained in the idea of will ; and in the conception
of pure will (*reinen Wille*), that is, of pure practical
reason, is included the idea of causality with freedom. From this idea of freedom is derived that
of personality. Personality consists in the freedom of the whole soul from the mechanism of nature. Man is peculiar in this respect that he is an
end to himself in moral action : nur der Mensch
und mit ihm jedes vernünftiges Geschöpf, ist Zweck
an sichselbst. The requirement for personality is
susceptibility to respect for the moral law, as a
sufficient motive for the will.[4]

Kant's extreme conception of autonomy is espe-

[1] Kant V. 93.   [2] Id. V. 48.

[3] Id. V. 49.

[4] Id. V. 91 ; VI. 121. Compare Rosmini, Sistema. 206.

cially apparent in his scornful treatment of the determinism of Leibnitz.

He denies that the determinism of Leibnitz is consistent with freedom in any true sense; for causality, whether it be that of mind or of material objects, is inconsistent with freedom. The determination of the will by psychological causes takes the volition out of the power of the agent, as much as material causes would do. This *Verkettung der Vorstellungen der Seele* gives what Kant calls "psychological freedom," which differs *toto coelo* from transcendental freedom: und wenn die Freiheit unseres Willens keine andere als die letztere (etwa die psychologische und comparative, nicht transcendentale, d. i. absolute zugleich) wäre, so würde sie im Grunde nichts besser, als die Freiheit eines Bratenwenders sein, der auch wenn er einmal aufgezogen worden, von selbst seine Bewegung verrichtet.[1]

The reality of transcendental freedom, according to Kant, depends on the validity of the distinction between phenomena and things in themselves. Rational freedom is a quality of the causality of living beings, in so far as they are rational. As free, the will is independent of every kind of causality except its own spontaneous and autonomous determination. Therefore, as a rational being, Man can never think of his own will except as a free cause.[2]

With respect to the liberty of indifference, it would appear that Kant accepted the doctrine, and was moreover disposed to lay very little emphasis

[1] Kaut, V. 101, 102.　　　　[2] Id. V. 300.

upon the original badness or goodness of men. His theory is Pelagian rather than Augustinian.[1]

THE ABSOLUTE PHILOSOPHY

In general there have been two interpretations of the Kantian philosophy. In one case, the *Critique of Pure Reason* has been interpreted in the light of the practical philosophy, and an attempt has been made to avoid the destructive results of the first *Critique* by reconstructing a system on the foundations of Kant's practical treatises. In the other case, the conclusions of the second Critique have been thought inconsistent with those of the first; and attempts have been made to overthrow the practical doctrines by an appeal to the speculative conclusions of Kant. In this way a difference has arisen between two schools of thought, both of which claim a Kantian justification. The so-called philosophers of the Absolute, Fichte, Schelling, and Hegel, represent the first of these interpretations; and the critical sceptics, like Schulze and Maimon, represent the second. At the present time these two classes still exist, and the watchword of both is "Back to Kant." There are those who maintain that to go back to Kant is to go back also to the successors of Kant, who are thought to be the philosophers of the Absolute. But there are also those who recommend a return to Kant, because they believe that the philosophers of the Absolute do not exhibit a faithful develop-

[1] Kant, VI. 114.

ment of the Kantian principles. In few cases is it urged that there should be a return to the results of both the speculative and the practical philosophy of Kant, and that his philosophy should be adopted as he left it. Indeed if the critical method were applied to Kant's practical philosophy, it might be shown that there is a dogmatism in the latter, equal to the dogmatism against which Kant primarily rebelled. And if Kant himself could know the results of his revolution in philosophy, as these appear in the systems of the Absolute, he would no doubt conclude that much of his labor had been in vain.

There has, perhaps, been undue emphasis laid, especially in England and America, upon the relation between the Critical and the Absolute philosophy, and a tendency to regard the latter as an inevitable and logical result of the former. This misapprehension has not been shared, and has been partially corrected by some of the leading historians of philosophy in Germany. It has been demonstrated, for example, that Lessing, Herder, and Jacobi were not without considerable influence on Post-Kantian thought. It will be admitted that there is as much of Plato as of Kant in the speculations of Hegel. But almost as conspicuous as the effect of Kant has been that of Spinoza on all later German philosophy. This is evident, not only in the unity of principles from which these systems set out, but also in many points of method, and in the prominence of the ethical element. Much of this may be the result of tradition, descending through Kant or apart from Kant, from the earlier German dogmatism. But in spite of the fact that Fichte is looked upon as an able opponent of Spinoza's philosophy, it is not too much to say that the influence of the latter is as evident in *Die Wissenschaftslehre*, as is that of Hume in the *Critique of Pure Reason*. The indebtedness of Schelling to Spinoza,[1] especially in the late period of the former's career, is well known; and it is not without reason that Hegel regarded acquaintance with Spinoza as requisite for the pursuit of philosophy at all. That which differentiates these later systems from the system of Spinoza is, however, the emphasis laid upon the principle of evolution; and this, it must be admitted, is altogether foreign to the latter's conception of the universe. Instead of a statical system founded on the doctrine of substance, attributes, and modes, we find now a dynamic philosophy, developed from a principle which is active and essentially changing. It is a process, not a mere subsistence. The *Ding an sich*, which Kant had declared to be unknown, becomes the first principle of philosophy in the systems of his successors. It is this which is the principle of principles in the systems of Fichte, Schelling, and Hegel.

FICHTE.

The first principle of the philosophy of Fichte is a postulate or requirement; it is not a hypothesis,

---

[1] On the contrast between Schelling and Spinoza, see Schelling, Werke, I. VII. 348, 349.

nor an assumption, nor a datum of experience. It is not the result of observation or of proof. It is the affirmation or position of the active Ego; and to affirm or posit the Ego is to become conscious of myself. The first principle of the *Wissenschafts-lehre* is not objective, but subjective, and as subjective principle it is known not by sensible, but by intellectual intuition. This is the Kantian *Ding an sich*. It belongs, not to the sensible, but to the intelligible world, and so the intuition by means of which it is known is intellectual.

I. *The Ego and the Non-Ego.* Through the positing or affirmation of the Ego, self-consciousness arises; the activity of the Ego is self-consciousness. The activity and the self-consciousness go together, and the cause of both is the will. Will is therefore logically antecedent to knowledge. The activity of the Ego, by which it is required to be self-conscious, is voluntary activity. The beginning, middle, and end of Fichte's system is the free activity of the Ego. This activity is called *Thathandlung*, which means, literally, an activity which performs a deed.[1] In the philosophy of Kant, a world of things (*Dinge an sich*) was affirmed as the limit of the phenomenal universe, and in these was found the reason (*Grund*) of all phenomena. In the philosophy of Fichte, the world of self-consciousness is the only world; it is the world of experience, and as experience it proceeds from the *Thathandlung* of the Ego. The Ego corresponds to the practical reason in the philosophy of Kant. The Ego is a

1 Fichte, I. 91.

practical principle, and is theoretical only in so far as it is practical. As subject, the Ego may be regarded either as knowing or as active; as that which knows, it is active intelligence, and as that which does, it is active will. But both theory and practice are the objects, not of two sciences, but of one.

The Ego not only posits or affirms itself, it also posits or affirms a Non-Ego, which is simply its opposite. Without the Ego, there would be no Non-Ego. The Non-Ego is, because the Ego is. The Non-Ego is not *Ding an sich*, but has the ground and origin of its being in the Ego. Daher ist der Satz; ohne Ich kein Nicht-Ich, gleich dem Satze; das Ich setzt ein Nicht-Ich. The position or affirmation of the Non-Ego is the affirmation of the objective world, through the *Thathandlung* of the Ego.[1]

The Ego not only posits itself, and posits the Non-Ego, but it also posits the reciprocal limitation of Ego and Non-Ego. These are not to be conceived of as two opposing principles, for there is no dualism in Fichte's philosophy. The limitation of the Ego by the Non-Ego to a certain extent cancels or removes the activity of Ego, and this is knowledge of the objective world. The limitation of the Non-Ego by the Ego is an overcoming of this limitation, and corresponds to free action. This distinction corresponds also to that between theoretical and practical philosophy. Neither of these processes takes place alone. There is no activity of the Ego

---

[1] Cf. Fichte, Werke, I. 276.

without passivity (*Leiden*), and no passivity without
activity. The objective activity results in passion
or affection, and this is known intuitively. It is
an intuition of the impossibility of the opposing
activity. It is a feeling of compulsion which is
represented to the imagination as compulsion, and
this is necessity: wird im Verstande fixirt als
Nothwendigkeit. In contrast to this activity which
is conditioned by passive affection, is free activity,
which may be presented to the imagination as an
alternation or hesitation (*Schweben*) between the
performance of one and the same action; and in
the understanding, this is possibility. Both species
of activity are joined in one synthesis; free activity
determines itself to self-affection, and freedom arises
from compulsion. Freedom in this sense is not
mere activity *in vacuo*, but is activity as a consequence or concomitant of the compulsion exercised
by the Non-Ego upon the Ego in the process of
limitation.[1] The Ego, however, is independent,
and everything else depends upon it. The essence
of the Ego is in its activity, and this activity is
constitutive, not regulative.[2] Just as the source of
the influence of the Non-Ego on the Ego is to be
found in the latter, so there would be no activity
manifested in the latter without the former.[3] Thus
the causality of the Non-Ego does not consist in action (*Wirkung*) but in interaction (*Wechselwirkung*).
The original activity of the Ego is not determined
from without, nor are its inclinations and impulses
determined by the Non-Ego. In all its activity it

<hr>

[1] Fichte, I. 238 f. 276.   [2] Id. I. 272.   [3] Id. I. 239.

is spontaneous, and all the objects of its feelings and inclinations are posited by itself. But freedom and spontaneity are not the same. Before there can be freedom there must be limitation; and the process is endless—the limitation of the Ego by the Non-Ego, and the ceaseless endeavor of the Ego towards freedom, which is its ethical goal.

The force of the Ego is an object of feeling. The feeling of force (*Kraftgefühl*) is the principle of all life. It is the transition from death to life. Force is felt as impulsive (*treibendes*), but this impulse is without causality upon the Ego; it may furnish an object for the exercise of free activity, but does not itself originate any activity. This is a sufficient statement of Fichte's general theory of the motive. It is deduced from his doctrine of the relation between the Ego and the Non-Ego. The motive does not determine the free activity of the Ego; it is only feeling without self-consciousness. And just as the Non-Ego is necessary to the exercise of the free activity of the Ego, so, in order to volition, there must be a presentation of the object of volition. The two are in necessary reciprocity.[1]

II. *The Will and Freedom.* While Fichte sometimes refers to several faculties in the soul, he regards it as unphilosophical to hold that the Ego differs from its act and its product (*seine That und sein Product*). It is not a substratum in which activity as a mere faculty resides. The Ego is not something which has a faculty; it is itself not a faculty, but an active, acting being: Das Ich ist

---

[1] **Fichte, I. 296, 372.**

nicht etwas das Vermögen hat, es ist überhaupt kein Vermögen, sondern es ist handelnd; es ist was es handelt, und wenn es nicht handelt, so ist es nichts.[1] The will is, therefore, not a faculty of the Ego, but is the Ego itself exercising its free activity; it is not in the Ego, but is a way in which the Ego acts. In another way this relation is expressed by Fichte, when he says that there are two manifestations of substance: thought and will. "I find myself as myself, only willing" (Ich finde mich selbst als mich selbst, nur wollend).[2] This means that I consider myself as one with the object known; it is assumed that it is known what volition means, and the volition is known through the intellectual intuition. I am conscious of willing, and this consciousness is immediately and simultaneously related to a substance, which substance I am. The manifestation which alone I originally ascribe to myself is volition. It is only under the condition that I become conscious to myself of it as such, that I am conscious of myself. The volition is not an ideal activity; it is a real self-determination of one's self through one's self. Thus the expression "find myself" is equivalent to "find myself willing." While in philosophical abstraction, we may speak of will or volition in general, in observation it is always singular and determinate; it is the willing of some particular object. An object of the Non-Ego is always postulated in all volition. But will in general, as this abstraction, must be distinguished from the individ-

<hr>

1 Fichte, III. 22.   2 Id. IV. 19.

ual will, which is called *Wollen*.[1] In general it is characteristic of Fichte's teaching to emphasize the supremacy of the will. It alone is said to be the original expression of the reason. It is that which effects the representation of the infinite in the finite Ego. In positing myself as active, I posit a determinate activity. More specifically it is the will which has immediate causality in reference to the body ; not that it directly creates the body, but that it uses the body as an instrument.[2] But the relation of knowledge to volition is of such a kind, that the former is necessary to the latter; for the volition is not volition in general, but, as has been said already, volition (*Wollen*) and presentation (*Vorstellung*) go together.[3]

From Fichte's teaching concerning the act of will, it is easy to anticipate his theory of freedom. Objectively considered, all being is necessary being, and is not *thought* as the product of freedom. But being must itself have proceeded from thought; and thought is the product of free activity. Fichte refers with approval to Kant's statement, that freedom is the power absolutely to begin a new condition of things. But the doctrine of the *Wissenschaftslehre* is necessary to explain this beginning. For this shows how the Ego posits itself as free activity. In positing myself as active, I posit myself as rational, and in positing myself as rational, I posit myself as free. The conception of freedom involves before all, only the faculty of

---

[1] Fichte, IV. 23–25.   [3] Id. III. 21.
[2] Id. IV. Vorrede, x. and 11.

projecting conceptions of our possible activity, through absolute spontaneity : —

Im Begriffe der Freiheit liegt zuvorderst nur das Vermögen durch absolute Spontaneität Begriffe von unserer möglicher Wirksamkeit zu entwerfen ; und nur dieses blosse Vermögen schreiben vernünftige Wesen einander mit Nothwendigkeit zu.[1]

The Ego thinks itself as free, and thinks this necessarily. Freedom is the only true being, and is the basis of all other being. Belief in the subjective validity of the phenomenon of Freedom is derived from the *Thathandlung* of the Ego. Belief in the objective validity of the phenomenon of Freedom is deduced from the consciousness of the moral law.

I am really free, is said to be the first article of belief which makes a transition to the intelligible world possible, and offers a firm place to stand. Doing is not the second idea, and being the first; but doing is the first, and being the second.[2] For I am conscious of myself as an independent free being. This is not an inference from effects, but is immediate. This fact is established in spite of the subjection of nature to determining causes. Indecision is the war of opposing forces; while it is of the essence of freedom, not to *be* decided, but to decide. I am therefore the author of my own thought, and am free.[3] The difference between freedom and the general spontaneity of the mind is carefully drawn by Fichte when he says: Ein Act des Geistes,

---

[1] Fichte, III. 8.   [2] Id. IV. 54 f.   [3] Id. II. 187.

dessen wir uns als eines solchen bewusst werden, heisst Freiheit. Ein Act ohne Bewusstsein des Handelns, blosse Spontaneität. The freedom of the will is freedom from mechanical necessity of any kind; and it is limited only by the content of the volition.[1]

While Fichte reiterates the doctrine of indeterminism in a great variety of forms, he does not find it necessary to argue at length in opposition to the contrary theory. This is because his doctrine is deduced from the principles of his philosophy; and if the latter be accepted, the possibility of a denial of freedom is eliminated. If the universe is the result of a *Thathandlung* of the Ego, there is nothing which can limit the Ego unless it be the Ego itself; and so determinism extrinsically considered is excluded, and the only determinism is the determination of the Ego by itself, which is freedom. On the contrary, the self-dependence and freedom of the Ego are not given empirically; they are abstractions independent of the conflict between inclinations, desires, and impulses.

Considered practically, the conception of freedom determines the moral imperative. And because other men are free like myself, I should treat them as if they were free, while my own body should be used as a means to freedom. However the motives may conflict, in the free act the opposition ceases because they are united in the same thought. In the free act one does not feel his own will, but feels the limitation of activity and its successful

1 Fichte, II. 217.

removal.> In the series of natural phenomena, every member can be explained by some antecedent member; but in the volitional series no such explanation is possible: *Jedes ist ein erstes und absolutes.*[1] In the one case there is the principle of cause and effect; in the other, that of substance. The last member of the natural series is impulse (*Trieb*), but this is not a cause. The impulse or inclination does not cause the particular volition. The volition is effected by my force: *meine Kraft.* Belief in determinism is ascribed to defective intuition; and its advocates are only discursive thinkers: *man muss gegen sie nicht disputiren, sondern man sollte sie cultiviren, wenn man könnte.*[2] In short, the will is absolutely free; and to deny this is an absurdity> Kurz der Wille ist schlechtin frei; und ein unfreier Wille ist ein Unding.[3]

SCHELLING

It is customary to distinguish three stages in the development of Schelling's philosophy. These are a manifestation partly of an inner process of evolution, and partly of external influences. He did not teach three systems of philosophy, but in each period the same system is exhibited with different modifications. <In the philosophy of Fichte, the conception of the will was transferred from the narrower psychological and ethical territory which it had occupied in some of the theories of an earlier time; it was no longer regarded merely as a

---

[1] Fichte, IV. 134.   [2] Id. IV. 136.   [3] Id. IV. 159.

U

faculty or as a phenomenon. In the philosophy of Fichte, and in that of Schelling and Hegel, the will is a first principle. The Ego of the *Wissenschaftslehre* is the equivalent of Kant's practical reason; it is formal will. And there is some justice in Schopenhauer's claim to have been the most faithful interpreter of the Kantian philosophy, in so far as he identified the *Ding an sich* with will. In the first period of his philosophical career, Schelling takes his departure from the principles of Fichte, but differs from Fichte in his view of the development of intelligence out of nature. In the second period, he identifies subject with object, and finds their unity in the absolute, which is higher than both. In the third period his philosophy is modified in accordance with ideas taken from Plato, Böhme the German mystic, and Aristotle. There is a greater difference between the philosophy of the second and that of the third period, than there is between the philosophy of the first and that of the second period. The doctrines of the absolute and the identity of subject and object are contained implicitly in the writings of the earliest part of his literary activity. Up to the time of his excursion into mysticism, the gradual composition of his system illustrates in many ways the development of German philosophy from the point where Kant left it to the more elaborate discipline of Hegel.

In considering Schelling's theory of the will, it is more convenient to disregard the above threefold division, and to notice his teaching as it is contained in the writings of the first period and of the third: on the one hand, in his *Philosophy of Nature* and *Transcendental Idealism;* on the other, in his treatise on human freedom.

I

According to Schelling there are two fundamental sciences. One sets out from the idea of nature, and seeks to explain the development of consciousness or intelligence; the other sets out from the idea of intelligence, and seeks to explain nature. The first of these sciences is the *Philosophy of Nature;* the second is the *Transcendental Idealism.* It is chiefly in the second that his earlier view of the will is presented.

Nature, according to Schelling, is not dead, but only unconscious. It is not being, but becoming. It is a process, the end of which is intelligence. According to Fichte, the objective world was the Non-Ego which was affirmed or posited by the Ego; according to Schelling nature is unconscious spirit. In distinguishing conscious and unconscious spirit, Schelling shows the influence of Leibnitz, and prepares the way for von Hartmann. Nature is an activity, and has the potentiality of consciousness within it. The realization of consciousness is the goal of its evolution. While the lower processes in this evolution are mechanical, the unity of nature is to be found in a world-soul. There are two principles of force in nature, one positive, the other negative; one progressive, the other limitative. The unity of both is a formative and organizing principle which is called the world-soul:—

Diese belden streitenden Kräfte zugleich in der Einheit und im Conflikt vorgestellt, führen auf die Idee eines organi-sirenden, die Welt zum System bildenden Princips. Ein solches wollten vielleicht die Alten durch die Weltseele andeuten.[1]

When the natural process is manifested in life, individuation is the result, and individual beings or organisms are determined according to a *telos*, and are not merely mechanical. The highest stage in this evolution is reached with man; but it cannot be explained, or is not explained, how intelligence is evolved from the unconscious. The individuality of man as Ego is superior to the stream of causes and effects in nature.[2]

The beginning of all philosophy, according to Schelling, is the postulate that there is a produc-tive Ego which is both subject and object of an intellectual intuition. The Ego is the identity of being and production; it is both process and prod-uct. By free activity, Schelling does not here mean free choice, but only the active process by which the Ego comes to a knowledge of itself. As productive of being, it is not a conscious, but a blind, unconscious activity; and so we are theo-retically coerced in appearance, by knowledge which limits the Ego's activity. In the objective world we see our free activity conditioned by objects; but it is the same activity which limits itself, and yet is unlimited. The active Ego, then, is not deter-mined except by itself; it is both *bestimmbar* and *bestimmt*. The distinction implied here may be

---

[1] Schelling, I. ii. 381.   [2] Id. I. ii. 17.

otherwise expressed by saying that, as activity, the Ego is undetermined, but as being, it is determined: —

Aber ein Werden lässt sich nicht denken als unter Bedingung einer Begrenzung. Man denke eine unendlich producirende Thätigkeit als sich ausbreitend ohne Widerstand, so wird sie mit unendlicher Schnelligkeit produciren, ihr Produkt ist ein Sein, nicht ein Werden. Die Bedingung alles Werdens also ist die Begrenzung oder die Schranke. Aber das Ich soll nicht nur ein Werden, es soll ein unendliches Werden sein.[1]

The productive activity and the activity of the product imply one another; and so idealism and realism imply one another. Theoretical philosophy is idealistic; practical philosophy is realistic.

Ideas or presentations (*Vorstellungen*) arise within us, proceeding from the world of thought into the world of reality. The productive source of these is the active Ego, and its activity is manifested in acts of will. All free activity is productive; and the objective world is product of free activity.[2] For the proper understanding of the conceptions of philosophy two things are necessary: first, that we should be the productive causes of presentations (*Vorstellungen*); and, second, that we should be both the subject and the object of the intuition (*Anschauung*). Nothing can be predicated of the Ego *per se*, excepting activity, which is manifested as self-consciousness. And it is only through a particular act of freedom that the Ego

---

[1] Schelling, I. iii. 383.　　[2] Id. I. iii. 318.

becomes the object of consciousness. An original underived knowledge of the Ego is impossible, — it is not an inference, nor demonstration, but an intuition. It is an intellectual intuition, because the Ego is at once the subject and the object of the intuition: —

Die intellektuelle Anschauung ist das Organ alles transcendentalen Denkens. Denn das transcendentale Denken geht eben darauf, sich durch Freiheit zum Objekt zu machen, was sonst nicht Objekt ist.[1]

The intellectual intuition presents the Ego to us as productive of itself as object, and is a free act. The Ego, as both subject and object of an intellectual intuition, is the principle from which one must proceed in the transcendental philosophy.

In the *Transcendental Idealism* this process is reversed, and the problem is to explain the production of the object by the subject. In the *Philosophy of Nature*, the first principle was the Non-Ego, out of which the self-conscious Ego was supposed to proceed; in the *Transcendental Idealism*, the first principle, as in Fichte's philosophy, is the Ego, the productive activity of which is manifested in the objective world. In the *Philosophy of Nature*, certain problems were suggested, but were not solved: whence is man, what is he, and what is his meaning? If, on the one hand, man is a product of nature, on the other hand he is himself the beginning of a series of causes, and this is not the effect of natural causes. It is this view which

---

[1] Schelling, I. III. 369. See Fichte, II. 33, 38.

makes the *Transcendental Idealism* necessary as a complement of the *Philosophy of Nature.*

Like Fichte, Schelling makes a distinction between matter and form, which has a bearing on his theory of will. Matter is determined, but form is free. But both matter and form are so related, that, if one be taken away, the other is also removed (*aufgehoben*). That is, the free process of the Ego's activity goes on, and its product is the matter of knowledge. The world of the productivity of the Ego is free, but the product, the world produced, is determined.[1]

The Ego is not to be understood as being a thing (*Ding*); it is productive activity. The product of this activity is a thing; but the latter is the negation of free activity. Knowledge depends on the agreement between the objective and the subjective; that which is objectively a product of the evolution of nature is subjectively the result of the productive activity of the Ego. The productive activity of the Ego begins outside of all space and time, and so is not thought in the category of causality; it is absolutely free. The principle of causality is only a principle of the succession of ideas; for there is no arbitrary succession : —

Alle Kategorien sind Handlungsweisen, durch welche uns erst die Objekte selbst entstehen. Es gibt für die Intelligenz kein Objekt, wenn es kein Causalitätsverhältniss gibt, und dieses Verhältniss ist eben desswegen von den Objekten unzertrennlich.[2]

<hr>

[1] Schelling, I. i. 347, 348.
[2] Id. I. iii. 471.

This shows that the activity of the Ego is prior to the principle of causality; and while this activity is limited by the production of the object, and while the object has a causal effect upon the activity of the Ego, and limits it, the source of the causality, like the source of the free activity, lies in the Ego itself, and so there is no determination of the transcendental will.

The beginning of consciousness can only be explained as self-determination, that is, as an act of the intelligence upon itself. This self-determination is called volition, in the most general meaning of the term: —

. . . eine Handlung, wodurch die Intelligenz sich selbst bestimmt, ist ein Handeln auf sich selbst . . . Jenes Selbstbestimmen der Intelligenz heisst Wollen in der allgemeinsten Bedeutung des Worts.[1]

In this act there is a combination of will as such, in its free activity, and the will to effect a possible object. It is the free Ego which determines the object and the will towards the object. In productive activity there was opposition between that process and its product; in volition there is harmony, in that there is idealizing intelligence on the one hand through freedom, and realizing intelligence on the other hand through the product.[2] The free act of the productive Ego is not itself volition, but simply furnishes the object of volition. Mere activity is not the willing of anything; and in order to free volition, an object must be presented

1 Schelling, I. III. 533.   2 Id. I. III. 546.

as an occasion of volition. There is an object, and an impulse towards an object, and the realization of the impulse is volition. The activity of the Ego is infinite, but a finite object is presented, which serves as a point of departure for the voluntary act. There is a harmony preëstablished between the ideal and the real, for this is not the effect of interaction: —

indem jenes von diesem und dieses von jenem so getrennt ist, dass gar kein wechselseitiger Einfluss beider aufeinander möglich wäre, wenn nicht durch etwas ausser beiden Leigendes eine Uebereinstimmung zwischen beiden gestiftet wäre.[1]

Thus, as in the philosophy of Fichte, objects are eternally presented to the free activity of the Ego, which is so far limited by them; yet by virtue of its freedom it conditions these objects by which it is itself only relatively conditioned. Free will in the individual is only a phenomenon of the absolute will: —

also ist die Willkür die von uns gesuchte Erscheinung des absoluten Willens, nicht das ursprüngliche Wollen selbst, sondern der zum Objekt gewordene absolute Freiheitsakt, mit welchem alles Bewusstein beginnt.[2]

It is evident that in Schelling's earlier philosophy there is very little if any advance upon the position occupied by Fichte. While the *Philosophy of Nature* contains some elements which did not enter into Fichte's purely subjective idealism, the position of Schelling seems less logi-

[1] Schelling, I. III. 579, 580.   [2] Id. I. III. 576.

cal and satisfactory than that of his predecessor. Even assuming that the *Philosophy of Nature* has successfully explained the evolution of consciousness, and that the activity of the Ego has successfully accounted for the presentation of an object, the relation between the two points of view is left in some obscurity. If the question be raised, what is the ultimate relation between the unconscious nature, from which we set out, and the unconscious Ego which freely produces the objective world, only two answers seem possible: either subject must be derived from object and object from subject, in an endless circle, or else their unity must lie in some principle above them both. The latter answer seems to be implied in the writings of Schelling's first period, in which nature has its unity in a *Weltseele*, and is productive of a conscious Ego. But in the writings of the second period, the problem of the relation of the two principles is solved by finding the identity of subject and object in the absolute. This part of Schelling's system has great significance in the general history of philosophy. In so far as the theory of the will is concerned, it raises for consideration some questions which did not occur to Fichte, but which are discussed by Schelling in the writings of his latest period. Just as Kant left insufficiently explained the relation between his theoretical and practical philosophy, so the writings of Schelling's first period leave unexplained the relation of the *Philosophy of Nature* to the *Transcendental Idealism*. But he does not commit this explanation to his successors, and so enters himself a region where it is difficult to follow him.

II

Without discussing specially the doctrines of the second period of Schelling's philosophical development, I shall pass directly to the consideration of the doctrine of the will contained in his treatise on the Essence of Human Freedom (*Philosophische Untersuchungen über das Wesen der menschlichen Freiheit*), which belongs to what has been sometimes called the mystical period in the development of his system. In his identity-philosophy he had reached the unity of subject and object in a principle which is the identity of both. Setting out from this pantheism, his aim is to avoid the conclusion that God, the Absolute, is the cause of evil ; and so he is led to explain the nature of freedom and necessity, and the relation of the human will to God. In the philosophy of identity, he showed that the first principle of the universe is one ; in the treatise just mentioned, he seeks to show that the first principle of the universe is free. He is more polemical in manner in this very interesting work than in any of his other formal treatises. While he adopts much from the philosophy of Spinoza, he opposes many of his doctrines. He finds fault with the doctrine of evil in the *Théodicée* of Leibnitz ; he criticises the subjective idealism of Fichte.

According to Schelling, the opposition between

necessity and freedom raises the inmost central question of philosophy. Just as it had been shown that the opposition between subject and object is removed by the absolute identity of intelligence and nature, so the opposition between freedom and necessity is to be removed by showing their identity in the absolute. When it is said that God is nature, or that freedom is necessity, the relation between subject and predicate is that of antecedent and consequent, of *implicitum* and *explicitum;* and Schelling speaks severely of those who misunderstand the significance of such propositions, and draw absurd conclusions, as if subject and predicate were exchangeable terms. He finds fault also with those who maintain that the idea of freedom is incompatible with any systematic view of the universe, and holds that it is only by defining the term *systematic* incorrectly that freedom can be excluded from such a consideration of philosophy.[1]

But he holds also that the will must be considered from a point of view far wider than that of subjective idealism. The principle of the universe is not the Ego nor the Non-Ego, but the absolute. He would prefer to deny the existence of freedom to affirming that only the Ego has will: —

Kürzer oder entscheidender wäre, das System auch im Wille oder Verstande des Urwesens zu leugnen; zu sagen, dass es überhaupt nur einzelne Willen gebe, deren jeder einen Mittelpunkt für sich ausmache, und nach Fichte's Ausdruck eines jeden Ich die Absolut Substanz sei.[2]

[1] Schelling, I. vii. 336 ff.   [2] Id. I. vii. 337.

To solve the problem of the relation of freedom to the system of the universe is the problem of problems, and its solution is necessary if philosophy is to have any value. But an opposition between freedom and necessity is necessary : —

ohne den Widerspruch von Nothwendigkeit und Freiheit würde nicht Philosophie allein, sondern jedes höhere Wollen des Geistes in den Tod versinken, der jenen Wissenschaften eigen ist, in welchen er keine Anwendung hat.[1]

The problem is one from which Schelling does not shrink; and he finds it as absurd to deny necessity as to deny freedom. If it be said that pantheism is necessarily fatalistic, Schelling is ready with a denial. Yet by freedom we do not mean an absolute power which in man is equal to that of God. Infinite power extinguishes all lesser powers, as the sun puts out the light of the stars. If absolute causality be predicated of any one being, then all other beings must be passive. It is here that it is difficult to prove the reality of freedom. But the difficulty may be avoided if it be affirmed that man exists, not outside of God, but in God: dass der Mensch nicht ausser Gott, sondern in Gott sei, und dass seine Thätigkeit selbst mit zum Leben Gottes gehöre.[2]

If it can be shown that such a view of man's relation to God is in harmony with the possibility of freedom, and if most men have a firm belief in the reality of freedom, it may, Schelling thinks, be said that such a solution is probably true. God

---

[1] Schelling, I. vii. 338. [2] Id. I. vii. 339.

according to his nature is eternal, and the individual things exist only in so far as he exists, as a consequence of his being. But things proceed out of God, as the result of his self-revelation; they thus have a life and character of their own. And man, as a manifestation of God, is God's representative. The pantheism of Schelling differs from that of Spinoza. The latter was realistic, while that of Schelling is idealistic. The absolute of Schelling is the God of Spinoza endowed with life and energy: der Spinozische Grundbegriff, durch das Princip des Idealismus vergeistert.[1] The relation of things to God is of such a kind that their very relationship involves their endowment with life and freedom; for God is not the God of the dead, but of the living. Individual freedom is related to universal necessity as the eye is to the rest of the organism. While the eye would not exist without the rest of the organism, yet it has a certain function and mobility of its own. The relation of the human will to that of God is not mechanical: wobei das Bewirkte nichts fur sich selbst ist.[2] God reveals himself in man, and man must therefore resemble God. The individual man is a derived absolute; and this brings out an essential point in Schelling's theory. Immanence in God and freedom are not contradictory. Only that which is free, and in so far as it is free, is in God; and that which is not free, in so far as it is not free, is necessarily outside of God:—

<hr>

[1] Schelling, I. vii. 350.
[2] Id. I. vii. 347.

So wenig widerspricht sich Immanenz in Gott und Freiheit, dass gerade nur das Freie, und soweit es frei ist, in Gott ist, das Unfreie, und soweit es unfrei ist, nothwendig ausser Gott.[1]

The mechanical law of causality has no application to that which exists in God. By his idealistic pantheism, Schelling seeks to avoid the determinism of Spinoza. The first principle of Spinoza is a *Ding,* and all things in his system are governed mechanically; but his pantheism is not held responsible for this: —

Dieses System ist nicht Fatalismus, weil es die Dinge in Gott begriffen sein lässt; denn, wie wir gezeigt haben, der Pantheismus macht wenigstens die formelle Freiheit nicht unmöglich; Spinoza muss also aus einem ganz andern und von jenem unabhängigen Grund Fatalist sein.[2]

The reality of freedom is an ultimate reality; for ultimate being is nothing else than will: es gibt in der letzten und höchsten Instanz gar kein anderes Sein als Wollen.[3]

Schelling proceeds to consider freedom in a more special sense. According to him there is no liberty of indifference. To suppose that freedom consists in an equilibrium between two alternate courses of action, so that there is equal inclination towards either, and a possibility of free decision in favor of one, is absurd. The problem of the *Asinus Buridani* presupposes an impossible condition of things. There is no exercise of volition without

<hr>

[1] Schelling, I. vii. 347.　　[2] Id. I. vii. 349.　　[3] Id. I. vii. 350.

some reason; and to suppose that there is liberty
of indifference is to suppose that the will in order
to be free must be irrational. It makes free volition equivalent to chance volition:—

Zufall aber ist unmöglich, widerstreitet der Vernunft wie
der nothwendigen Einheit des Ganzen; und wenn Freiheit
nicht anders als mit der gänzlichen Zufälligkeit der Handlungen zu retten ist, so ist sie überhaupt nicht zu retten.[1]

But if freedom in such a sense is to be rejected,
so also, according to Schelling, is determinism to
be rejected, which regards all volitions as the
product of necessary causes. The mistake which
men have made is in supposing that only one of
these alternatives can be true, and in neglecting
that higher unity of necessity and freedom with
which Schelling's treatise is concerned. If the
will be determined at all, it must be necessarily
determined, and the modification of the theory of
necessity in the philosophy of Leibnitz is not justifiable. It is idealism which saves us from either
of these extreme conclusions. According to transcendental and absolute idealism, the *intelligible*
essence of man is outside of time and beyond the
series of causes and effects :—

Das intelligibile Wesen jedes Dings, und vorzüglich des
Menschen, ist diesem zufolge ausser allem Causalzusam-
menhang, wie ausser oder über aller Zeit.[2]

Man's volition is determined by nothing which
goes before, and it makes all that follows it possible.

[1] Schelling, I. vii. 383.   [2] Id., ib. 383.

The act of the will is free, because it has its origin in the intelligible being of man, and proceeds from it. It is determined only in so far as the nature of the subject which wills determines it. This determination is not effected by external causes, nor through the inclination of the will by causes, but by the essence or being (*Wesen*) to which the will belongs. If it be said, however, that it is determined by the nature from which it proceeds, and yet that this nature is undetermined, it is difficult to see wherein we have avoided the absurdity of the liberty of indifference to which Schelling has called attention. If it be held that the free will of the intelligible essence acts without a motive, then the free will must be indifferent, which has been denied. Schelling replies that the reconciliation of the determination and indetermination of the will lies in the fact that it is the very nature of the being which determines the will to be itself indetermined. The result is determined, but the cause is not determined: —

Es ist ja kein bestimmtes Allgemeines sondern bestimmt das intelligibile Wesen dieses Menschen; von einer solchen Bestimmtheit gilt der Spruch *determinatio est negatio*.[1]

No matter how freely the intelligible nature may act, it must act in accordance with its own nature; and so such action, although absolutely necessary, is a manifestation of the highest freedom.

In this way, then, Schelling seeks to avoid the absurdities of chance, and yet to save the freedom

[1] Schelling, I. VII. 384.

X

of the will. It may be asked, wherein lies this inner necessity? If the intelligible essence were lifeless being (*todtes Sein*), and the action were mechanically produced, there would be an end of freedom; for the cause of the act would be external. But the inner necessity is itself freedom. Necessity and freedom are thus two aspects of one and the same thing. As Fichte said:—

Das Ich ist seine eigne That. Bewusstsein ist Selbstsetzen aber das Ich ist nichts von diesem verschiedenes, sondern eben das Selbstsetzen selber.[1]

Intelligible being, then, is primitive volition. The will is *Ursein;* and intelligible being is *Ur-und Grundwollen.* Man determines himself, and the determination happens before time, and not in time; for man, although born in time, was created from the beginning. As a product of nature, and as existing in God, the life of man reaches back to eternity; and man is from the beginning indetermined.[2] The conclusion from this is that when a man is good, he is good not arbitrarily, but from the necessity of his nature; and when he is bad, he is bad not arbitrarily, or by chance, but from the necessity of his nature. This does not mean that he is good or bad against his will, but that he wills the good or the bad because he is either good or bad. Judas Iscariot betrayed his Master, but no creature could have prevented him from willing this act of treason. And yet he was not coerced, but acted according to his inclination. The good

---

[1] Schelling, I. VII. 386.   [2] Id., ib.

man is not forced to be good, but even the gates of hell cannot prevail to make him bad. The voluntary act does not perform itself; it is performed by the man, and if performed by him, he is to blame, or he has the merit of the act. He knows also that he is accountable. Schelling supports this conclusion by calling attention to the early manifestation of character, so that even in infancy a certain bias in a bad direction may be observed, without any deliberate volition.

Schelling therefore agrees with Fichte in holding that the will is not determined, but self-determined. As to the origin of the character which determines the will, he is scarcely less mystical or mythical in his treatment than Plato. As has been already shown, Plato accounted for character by supposing that man had freely chosen his own destiny in a preëxistent state. Schelling holds that the fault of those who have taught the doctrine of predestination has been that they attributed the evil in the world and in man to a decree of God in time, and did not perceive that before time there was no succession, but that man was born from all eternity, and that his character had no beginning in time. The determination of the wills of men is not the effect of a special decree or act of God; but this determination is the effect of their eternally predestinated characters. As man acts here, so he has acted from all eternity. For these reasons, no choice more free could be demanded than that which now belongs to man.

If it be further asked why some men necessarily

determine themselves to will what is bad, and some to will what is good, we have one of the riddles of the universe suggested. Not content with the bold attempt to harmonize necessity and freedom, Schelling proceeds to grapple with the question of the origin of evil. It would carry this exposition too far away from the subject were I to enter into any detailed consideration of this doctrine of Schelling's philosophy, which is a remarkable speculative achievement. Schelling himself regarded the problem of evil as the most difficult problem connected with the doctrine of freedom. Having shown that all things exist in God, he must now show that God is not the cause of evil. He rejects the optimism of Leibnitz, and draws a distinction between existence and the ground of existence. It is evident that God cannot be altogether viewed in this twofold way; for, as has already been shown, all things exist in God, and the existence and the ground of existence must therefore be included in God. The ground (*Grund*) of the existence of God is in absolute nature. Nature and God are inseparable, but are distinguishable. There is a circle in the principle of God and nature; that which is produced produces the producer. The ground of God's existence is not God as God, but is in that which exists eternally with him. The ground of God's existence is in the desire (*Sehnsucht*) which the Absolute has to beget himself. And this *Sehnsucht* is to be interpreted as will. Will is therefore the eternal principle of the universe and of God:—

Der erste Anfang der Schöpfung ist die Sehnsucht des Einen, sich selbst zu gebären, oder der Wille des Grundes.[1]

Following the longing of the One to beget itself, is the second beginning of creation, which is the will of love, by means of which God makes himself a person. The first kind of will is not free in the same sense in which the second is free. For the first will (*Der Wille des Grundes*) is unconscious and blind, and proceeds according to natural necessity. The revelation of the second will is act and deed (*Handlung und That*). In God is the union of all living forces, and man is a part of this union in so far as he remains good; but so soon as he falls from this equilibrium of forces in the divine being, and makes his own will the principle of his action, then he becomes bad, and is in darkness. Where God is, there is light.

This theory of the origin of evil was the occasion of a letter written by Eschenmayer (1810), in which he opposed Schelling's idea of God, to which Schelling wrote a reply. Some years later he found that in the development of his philosophy he had made the idea of freedom less prominent than he had at first desired, and he published his treatise *Ueber die Natur der Philosophie als Wissenschaft*. In this he seeks to remove the contradiction between freedom and necessity by a species of mysticism. The apparent contradiction between the two is said to be removed by the soul rising in ecstasy to a view of the union and harmony of the two conceptions.

[1] Schelling, I. vii. 395.

Hegel

The connection is very close between the general principles of Hegel's philosophy and his doctrine of the will. The will is explained in a statement at — the beginning of the *Philosophie des Rechts;* but the principles from which this statement proceeds, and on which it depends, are found in the theoretical part of his system.   For this reason I shall notice, first, his idea of the Absolute; second, his theory of subjective and objective spirit, including his view of the will in relation to the principles of freedom and necessity.

I. *The Absolute.* Philosophy is defined as the science of the absolute. The absolute is not subject alone, as in the philosophy of Fichte; it is not nature alone, nor God as distinguished from the world. It is not the mere identity of subject and object. It is best defined as spirit; it is also absolute subject, an all-embracing principle, the first principle of all thought and of all philosophy : —

diejenige Region, worin alle Räthsel der Welt gelöst, alle Widersprüche des tiefer sinnenden Gedankens enthüllt sind, alle Schmerzen des Gefühls verstummen, die Region der ewigen Wahrheit, der ewigen Ruhe.[1]

On the one hand, the absolute is the negation of — all predicates; on the other hand, it is the position or affirmation of all. It is therefore the most formal contradiction (*der formellste Widerspruch*).[2] The absolute of Hegel differs radically from the

[1] Hegel, XI. 3.   [2] Id. XI. 179.

God of Spinoza in that it is *becoming* as well as being; it differs from the Ego of Fichte in that it is the identity and unity of subject and object; it differs from the absolute of Schelling in that it is not transcendent, but only immanent. Although it is known by reflection, it is not known as a being here and now, but as a becoming, a process, so that the complete being of the absolute is a process and a result (*Resultat*). It is an evolution or development, not in an infinite succession, but as a cycle of self-movement (*Selbstbewegung*). The development starts from the absolute *an und für sich*; this is the first moment; the absolute as such is an implicit and explicit principle. The second moment in the evolution is the externalization of the absolute as nature (*im Anderssein*). The third moment is the return of the absolute out of nature to itself, completing the cycle, and attaining to self-consciousness. Logic treats of the first of these stages, the philosophy of nature of the second, and the philosophy of spirit of the third. The process which begins with the absolute ends with the absolute.

The absolute cannot be adequately manifested in nature; its real manifestation is in the world of finite spirits. The consciousness of finite spirits is only a stage in the life of the absolute, in the process towards that *Resultat* which the absolute is. The end or last stage in the evolution of the absolute is spirit, which is a return of the absolute out of nature. Nature is bound by a necessary chain of causes and effects; but the essence of spirit is freedom. Every system is a system of freedom and

necessity. Freedom and necessity are ideal factors.[1]
They are not really in opposition. The absolute
does not posit itself exclusively as free ; nor exclusively as governed by necessity. As an inner principle, freedom is characteristic of the absolute; in
so far as the absolute is externalized or manifested
as objective totality, necessity is characteristic of
it. Yet necessity belongs to intelligence in a certain sense, just as freedom in a certain sense belongs
to nature. Every form (*Gestalt*) of the intelligence is conditioned by means of its opposite ;
while the freedom of nature consists in the fact
that as becoming, it is posited by itself, and is not
produced by any extrinsic principle. The causes
of evolution are inner and free. In the possibility
of spirit manifesting itself, lies the possibility of
its return to freedom. Freedom and spirit are inseparable conceptions : —

**Das Wesen des Geistes ist deswegen formell die Freiheit,
die absolute Negativität des Begriffes als Identität mit sich.[2]**

The absolute as the infinite and universal abides
as becoming; but it is actualized in the finite and
individual spirits which come and go.

The three moments in the life of the absolute
correspond with the three parts of Hegel's dialectical method. In this method, the concept is first
apprehended immediately (*unmittelbar*) as *an und
für sich*. A second stage of the method is the cognition of the concept as that which is not immediate and stable, but as mediate and fleeting, as the

---

[1] Hegel, I. 265.   [2] Id. VII₂, 24, 25.

negation or opposite of the first. The third stage is the apprehension of the truth of the first in the second, the union of the two moments, and the cancellation (*Aufhebung*) of the opposition between them.[1]

II. *Subjective and Objective Spirit, in Relation to Will.* As was said just now, the absolute is best defined as spirit; and the adequate manifestation of the absolute is not in nature, but in the succession of finite spirits. In this process is the actuality of spirit. In subjective spirit, the actuality of the absolute is manifested in knowledge and will; in objective spirit, in right (*Recht*), the state and history. The unity of these is absolute spirit, with which we are here not immediately concerned.

Hegel uses the term psychology in a wider and in a narrower sense. In a wide sense it is the whole science of subjective spirit, and includes anthropology, the science of the natural soul (*Seele oder Naturgeist*), phenomenology, the science of consciousness, and psychology in the narrower sense. In this sense, psychology is the science of the self-determining spirit as explicit subject (*Subject für sich*). Anthropology treats not only of the natural soul (*die natürliche Seele*), but of feeling and the actual soul. Phenomenology treats of consciousness, self-consciousness, and reason, as the three stages in the development of the subjective spirit. Psychology in the narrower sense treats of the theoretical, the practical, and the free

<hr>

[1] Hegel, VI 2, 33, 40 ff.

spirit. The science of the natural, feeling, and actual soul, which is discussed in the anthropology of Hegel, is conversant with soul in relation to body, and includes a consideration of the influence of various external influences, such as climate, race, and magnetic forces. The phenomenology, which is a name given also to Hegel's first important treatise, deals with the stages of development in the subjective life, particularly with the cognitive process.[1] In the phenomenology, the soul, through the negation of its corporeality, rises to ideal identity with itself, and becomes an Ego. But the Ego of the phenomenology is still implicit (*an sich*), since its being is only in relation to something else, that is, to something which is given (*ein Gegebenes*). The freedom of the Ego is here only an abstract, conditioned, and relative freedom, just as the Ego in the theoretical science of Fichte was conditioned relatively by a Non-Ego. That which conditions the Ego is the externalization of the absolute, and so far the Ego does not reach actuality and freedom. The activity of the Ego consists in its filling up the vacuum of its abstract subjectively, and in so doing it creates the objective within itself, and makes the subjective objective : —

Die Thätigkeit des ich besteht hier darin, die Leere seiner abstracten Subjectivität zu erfüllen, das Objective in sich hinein zu bilden, das Subjective dagegen objectiv zu machen.[2]

[1] Hegel, VII₂, 40 ff.
[2] Id. VII₂ 44.

In consciousness the content of spirit becomes objective, and in self-consciousness it becomes subjective. This general self-consciousness is in itself and for us (*an sich und für uns*) reason; but in the third part of the science of subjective spirit, reason becomes an object to itself. That part of the science of subjective spirit which is especially related to the will is psychology in the narrower sense. Spirit and reason are related as body and gravity, or as will and freedom, are related. The reason forms the substantial nature of spirit. Spirit, as including both the subjective and the objective, posits itself subjectively as theoretical and practical, that is, as knowledge and will.[1] That which the intelligence knows is the objective concept, while the object loses the form of a content which belongs to the spirit itself. Psychology treats of the forms of the theoretical and practical spirit. The soul is a unity, and cannot be properly split up into a number of faculties, or distinct forces, or activities. It is a self-conscious, real idea. It acts necessarily, but overcomes this necessity, and attains to freedom. In the expression Ego=Ego, the principle of the absolute reason and freedom is pronounced. Freedom and reason consist in this, that I raise myself to the form of Ego=Ego : —

kurz darin, dass ich in Einem und demselben Bewusstsein Ich und die Welt habe, in der Welt mich selber Wiederfinde, und umgekehrt in meinem Bewusstsein Das habe, was ist, was Objectivität hat.[2]

<hr>

[1] Hegel, VII₂, 43–45.   [2] Id. VII₂, 267.

This again resembles the doctrine of Fichte, the affirmation or positing of the Ego by the Ego. The Ego is known as such, not alone, but as a member of a system: dass ich jedes Object als ein Glied in einem Systeme Desjenigen fasse, was ich selbst bin.

There are several steps or stages in the development of knowledge. There is sense, which gives a knowledge that objects exist; perception, which gives a knowledge of their qualities; understanding, which gives a knowledge of the essence, and laws of phenomena.[1]

When, in the process of cognition, the theoretical intelligence has reached thought, it attains to a kind of freedom. The relation between the thought and the object of thought is free. The intelligence knows itself as determining the content, which is determined as being, as well as being its own. And this intelligence is will: Die Intelligenz sich wissend als das Bestimmende des Inhaltes der ebenso der ihrige, wie als seiend bestimmt ist, ist Wille.[2] Spirit as will knows itself as determining itself in itself, and realizing itself out of itself: Der Geist als Wille weiss sich als sich in sich beschliessend, und sich aus sich erfüllend.[3] The inward determinateness of the will is in its bringing freedom into existence. The determinate concept of the will is in its giving its own content (*Inhalt*); and true freedom in the moral sense consists in the will making the content not selfish, nor subjective, but universal. In this Hegel's

[1] Hegel, VII₂, 261 ff.   [2] Id. VII₂, 358.   [3] Id. VII₂, 359.

doctrine is derived from the Kantian imperative.

Thought which forms the point of departure, as it were, for freedom, is the last stage in the process of the knowledge of theoretical reason. The first stage is intuition or perception of an external world in space, and of an inner world in time, after the manner of the Kantian *Æsthetic*. The second is the presentation (*Vorstellung*) consisting of memory, phantasy, and the reproduction of ideas. The third is thought, in which the knowledge of the two former processes is appropriated and made object.[1]

Practical spirit is developed, in general, in three stages, in practical feeling, inclination or impulse (*Trieb*), and happiness. In the first of these psychological stages, the will is in the form of immediateness (*Unmittelbarkeit*). It has not yet posited itself as free, as objectively determining intelligence. It only finds itself as objective determination : —

Zunächst erscheint der Wille in der Form der Unmittelbarkeit ; er hat sich noch nicht als frei und objectiv bestimmende Intelligenz gesetzt, sondern findet sich nur als solches objectives Bestimmen.[2]

Inclinations or impulses, and voluntary decision between them, is the second stage. Whether the desire agrees with the inner determination of the will is only contingent. When such an opposition between desire and will exists, the will cannot

---

[1] Hegel, VII₂, 308.   [2] Id. VII₂, 360.

remain satisfied, but asserts itself. Inclination or
impulse (*Trieb*), is more than desire. Desire is a
mere fact of self-consciousness, while impulse
requires satisfaction, and is a form of will. Yet
in so far as man is governed by impulse he is not
free. In relation to impulses, the will must be distinguished as thinking, and as free ; as a unity, it
reflects in the presence of a manifold of inclinations. It decides between them; this is *Willkür*.
Er ist auf dem Standpunkt, zwischen Neigungen
zu wählen, und ist Willkür.

In this sense it is explicitly (*für sich*) free. But
it must be observed that such a will is merely the
realization of one inclination to the exclusion of
another. It is choice between inclinations, and not
necessarily a free, that is, a moral choice. As Kant
expressed it, the will is in this case *heteronomous*,
not autonomous.

Happiness is the representation of an abstract
universal of content, which ought to be, but is not.
The content becomes particularized, and is willed.
In such a determination of content, in which the
concept and the object are identical, and in which
the will determines itself, consists the freedom of
the will : — .

Die Glückseligkeit ist die mir vorgestellte, abstracte Allgemeinheit des Inhalts, welche nur sein soll. Die Wahrheit
aber der besondern Bestimmtheit, welche eben so sehr ist,
als aufgehoben ist, und der abstracten Einzelnheit, der
Willkür, welche sich in der Glückseligkeit eben so sehr einen
Zweck giebt als nicht giebt, ist die allgemeine Bestimmtheit
des Willens an ihm selbst, d. i. sein Selbstbestimmen selbst,

die Freiheit. . . . In dieser Wahrheit seiner Selbstbestimmung, worin Begriff und Gegenstand identisch ist, ist der Wille, — wirklich freier Wille.[1]

Hegel is far from agreeing with Kant, however, that the freedom of the will is simply a practical postulate, which cannot be demonstrated theoretically. In his criticism of the Third Antinomy, his chief objection is that Kant regarded the contradiction of thesis and antithesis as absolute; whereas it is only a contradiction which manifests the two first stages in the dialectical method. The contradiction is cancelled in the absolute.[2]

The most difficult point of interpretation in the Hegelian theory of the will is that in which it is asserted that the will when free has freedom as its content and object and end. In the interpretation of Hegel's philosophy, it is always possible to misapprehend his meaning, because of his peculiar use of terms; but if I have correctly stated his doctrine, it is difficult to say in what sense the individual will can be free. The evolution of the absolute is a process of the free activity of the absolute, and inasmuch as spirit and freedom are as inseparable as body and gravity, the finite spirit as well as the absolute spirit must be free. It is admitted by Hegel that spirit is limited by the content of the will, but as in the systems of Fichte and Schelling, that which is limited is also that which limits, and the contradiction is cancelled. Moreover, when spirit reaches self-con-

---

[1] Hegel, VII₂, 371, 372.   [2] Id. VI. 105, 115, 116.

sciousness, it knows itself as free. The ultimate
result of the development of the absolute is to
know itself as free spirit theoretically; and practically to will its freedom. Whether such a doctrine
should be called deterministic or not, is a mere
matter of definition.

Der Geist, der sich als frei weiss und sich als diesen seinen
Gegenstand will, d. i. sein Wesen zur Bestimmung und zum
Zwecke hat ist zunächst überhaupt der vernünftige Wille,
oder an sich die Idee, darum nur der Begriff des absoluten
Geistes.[1]

According to Hegel, the willing of freedom in a
moral sense seems to be the willing on a basis of
character, not of inclination. But if freedom is
realized through the will to be free, the inference
is that such volition is not yet free; if freedom is
already possessed, it is a work of supererogation to
will to have it. The ever ready dialectic is at hand
to remove this contradiction, which disappears in
the higher unity:—

Die Freiheit, zur Wirklichkeit einer Welt gestaltet, erhält
die Form von Nothwendigkeit, deren substantiellerer Zusammenhang das System der Freiheits-Bestimmungen, und
deren erscheinender Zusammenhang als die Macht, das
Anerkanntsein, d. i. ihr Gelten im Bewusstsein ist.[1]

At the same time, it is doubtful whether Hegel
intended to affirm that the subjective spirit was
actually free, for he speaks of its freedom as a
Schein, or false appearance of freedom, and attrib-

[1] Hegel, VII₂, 359.　　　[2] Id. VII₂, 376.

utes true freedom to the objective spirit only, in which personality is actualized.

In any case the practical freedom of the will is unambiguously asserted. In the *Philosophie des Rechts*, it is said that will without freedom is an empty word; and there is no freedom except that of the willing subject. Will is not antithetical to thought. Man does not have will in one pocket, and thought in the other. The difference between them is only the difference between practical and theoretical conduct. Will is only a particular mode of thought. It is thought translating itself into existence. It is the impulse to give existence to itself.[1] When I think of an object, I make it a thought, it becomes essentially and directly mine. It is no longer something beyond me, but it is my own. To think is to make a thing universal. The Ego is thought; not a special thought, but a general thought, empty, a metaphysical point, and simple (*leer, punktuell, einfach*). The image of the world is before me; I make its content mine. So much for the theoretical side. The practical side is that the Ego posits itself as opposed to the world, and determines an opposition between the world and itself. This opposition and distinction are again my own. I myself have made these determinations and differences. Thus the theoretical is contained in the practical. For there is no will without intelligence. The theoretical intelligence is included in the will. That which is willed is an object for me (*für mich*).[2] The will determines itself.

<hr>

[1] Hegel, VIII. 33.   [2] Id. VIII. 41–46.

Freedom is given as a fact of consciousness, and must be believed.   It is possible to prove the reality of freedom; but it is more convenient to appeal directly to inner experience.   The will contains (1) the element of pure indeterminateness.   There is a will in general, expressed in needs and desires immediately without any content.   There is an absolute possibility of any determination which I may find in myself.   This, however, is mere empty freedom.   It is negative, not positive.   It is one-sided.   The will contains (2) the transition from this negative condition to the determining of a particular content and object.   This content may either be given by nature, or may be created and generated by the concept of the mind.   By affirming itself as determined, the Ego attains to existence in general.   This second moment, like the first, is negative; it is the negation of the first negation.   It is one-sided, for the will is posited or affirmed as determined.   This second moment is a part of freedom, but does not constitute freedom in the true sense.   In the first moment, the will is purely will, without the willing of anything in particular.   In the second moment, the will is a will of something, but this something is limited, and so the will is limited by its content.   The will is (3) the unity of these two moments.   Neither the first nor the second moment is the will in the true sense.   In the third, it is the Ego, not the object nor the possible object, which determines the will.   This self-determination is freedom of the will:—

Ich bestimmt sich, insofern es die Beziehung der Negativität auf sich selbst ist; als diese Beziehung auf sich ist es ebenso gleichgültig gegen diese Bestimmtheit, weiss sie als die seinige und ideelle als blosse Möglichkeit, durch die es nicht gebunden ist, sondern in der es nur ist, weil es sich in derselben setzt. — Diess ist die Freiheit des Willens.[1]

Thus we have on the one hand an abstraction from all determinateness, which is the universality of the will, and on the other hand a determinate object and content, which is the particular will. They are both moments of the understanding. The true and speculative moment is reached, when the concrete conception of freedom is attained, without the universality on the one hand, and the particularity on the other. The will is at first pure activity; it then determines itself, and from being universal becomes particular, because it has posited a content. In the third moment, it does not cease to retain the universal, although it is determined. In this determinateness, man does not feel determined, for in the recognition of another, as another, he attains to real self-feeling.

From the standpoint of the understanding, the will is determined, not only as to matter or content, but also as to form. As to form, the will is determined by the final cause. The final cause, which is first an inner conception, is objectified, and made the external object of the will. The content determines the will, but the will is free, in that the possibility exists of the content being different from what it is. At first the will is a natural will, and is affected by

<hr>

[1] Hegel, VIII. 41.

the various inclinations and impulses; but it has
the power to make one object its content, to the
exclusion of other objects. It is not like the lower
animal will, subject wholly to the desires or appetites. It is above these, and decides between
the desires. As was shown in the doctrine of subjective spirit, true freedom of the will is not in
following one inclination to the exclusion of another.[1] In such volitions, there is an alien content.
True freedom consists in the willing of the will's
own realization. From the point of view of arbitrary volition between inclinations, freedom is an
illusion; for the will is really determined. It is
the self-realizing will which is free. In the will
between inclinations, the content is determined, not
by the nature of my will, but by contingency or
chance (*Zufälligkeit*). The will which follows an
inclination may be called free, but it is really determined by its content. In the true act of free
will, the desire, that is, the finite content, is destroyed or set aside, and the content is the product
of the will itself. The willing of itself is the willing of the right,[2] and so we reach in the end a point
in Hegel's theory where he is in substantial agreement with Kant. What Kant lays down as a
postulate of morality, that Hegel reaches by the
application of his method to the evolution of the
absolute. Free will according to such a view as
Hegel's must be viewed rather as an ideal than as
a reality. The natural will is the finite will which
is governed by inclinations. So we have also in

<hr>

[1] Hegel, VIII. 43 ff.   [2] Id. VIII. 48-60.

Hegel's philosophy a return to the Patristic doctrine, that the finite will is evil rather than good. Freedom is an ideal which the natural or finite will has not reached.

SCHOPENHAUER

(In the philosophy of Schopenhauer the will is both an universal principle and a faculty of man. These two are ultimately the same. The world is will, but it is my will. The *thing in itself (Ding an sich*) of the Kantian philosophy is not a mere negative limit, but the sufficient reason of being and knowledge. The thing in itself is will.)

By many writers Schopenhauer is described as a reactionist against the post-Kantian systems which preceded him. This is partially true. (His is a philosophy of the understanding, not of the reason. The idea of the absolute as spirit or nature, or as the identity of both, is absent from his thought.) His interpretation of Kant is radically different from that of the absolute philosophers. He is a pessimist, while the German philosophy before him was optimistic. And yet, in spite of these and other differences, there is a strong resemblance between the system of Schopenhauer and those which he attacks with so much spirit. (While he criticises the theory of the Ego in Fichte's philosophy, as being a merely formal principle, his own doctrine that the world is my will is not essentially different from Fichte's conception of the *Thathandlung* of the Ego as the first principle of philosophy. Schopenhauer's modification of the Platonic theory of ideas is not out of harmony with certain phases of Schelling's thought. The analogy between Schelling and Schopenhauer is well illustrated in the philosophy of von Hartmann, who is indebted to them both.

In a system which begins and ends with the will, it is difficult to separate the special from the more general teaching. The philosophy of Schopenhauer is preëminently a theory of the will. But I shall here consider it, first, as one of the fundamental principles of his philosophy; secondly, as a human faculty or phenomenon of the soul of man; and, thirdly, in relation to the principle of sufficient reason.

I. *The World as Will and Presentation.* According to Schopenhauer, the world is my presentation, and the world is my will. One side of the world is knowledge; the other side is will. To say that there is anything which is neither presentation nor will is absurd. Neither idealism alone nor materialism alone can explain the universe. The explanatory principle is neither matter nor knowledge. It is will.[1]

The will is not the cause of the universe; it is the universe. As it exists in neither space nor time, it is not a cause, and it is not known in causal relation with anything else.[2] It is, however, the sufficient reason of the world, and is objectified in the presentation (*Vorstellung*). The will as thing in itself cannot be defined. The term

[1] Schopenhauer, II. 3–5.   [2] Id. II. 166.

indicates the inner essence of the nature of everything. We know it better than we know anything else.[1] Every cognition or conception is presentation, but will is not presentation, but an inner principle. It lies beyond the principle of sufficient reason, and needs no explanation. The objectified will is body. The latter is a presentation like other presentations. It is an object among objects. The subject, as distinguished from the object, finds itself in the world as an individual. That is the subject of knowledge. That to which the presentation is made appears as an individual. It is the will which determines the changes of the body; and body is immediately known as will. Every movement of the body is an act of will; they are not two different acts, but they are one. These acts are given in two ways, — first, by immediate knowledge; and second, by the intuition (*Anschauung*) of the understanding. The act of the body is only objectified will.

Die Aktion des Leibes ist nichts Anderes, als der objektivirte d. h. in die Anschauung getretene Akt des Willens.[2]

The will is the cognition *a priori* of the body; and the body is the cognition *a posteriori* of the will. Deliberations about the future and resolutions are rational acts, and not acts of will. Willing and doing are the same. We may separate them in reflection, but they are not actually separable. Every act of will is an act of body; and every effect upon body is an act of will. In so far as the body is known, the will is known.

<hr>

[1] Schopenhauer, II. 131, 132.　　　　[2] Id. II. 119.

Ich erkenne meinen Willen nicht im Ganzen, nicht als
Einheit, nicht vollkommen seinem Wesen nach, sondern ich
erkenne ihn allein in seinen einzelnen Akten, also in der
Zeit, welche die Form der Erscheinung meines Leibes,
wie jedes Objektes ist: daher ist der Leib Bedingung der
Erkenntniss meines Willens.[1]

The importance of body in Schopenhauer's philosophy is manifest here.   The corporeal world, in
so far as it is not presentation, is will.   The reality
or actuality of the will is the actuality of the body;
and the movements of the latter are visible acts of
the former.   In like manner the so-called vital
forces, the various bodily functions, the members
and organs of the body, are expressions of the
will.[2]   Will is the active principle in all nature,—
in the movement and changes of organic as well as
inorganic bodies, in gravitation, heat, and light.
It is, however, one, and not manifold; the forces
of nature are its manifold appearance.

There are certain stages in the "objectivation"
of will.   In its lowest stage, it is blind force or
tendency, which is not known immediately as will.
In organic nature it appears as impulse.   In man
it comes to consciousness.   In the objectivation of
will, man is the highest stage.[3]   The nature of this
process of objectivation is difficult to understand.
It is the *Schwerpunkt* of Schopenhauer's otherwise
lucid philosophy.   The will is said not to be the
cause of the phenomena; for as thing in itself, it
lies outside the causal series, and is not subject (as
Ding an sich) to the principle of sufficient reason.

[1] Schopenhauer, II. 121.   [2] Id. I. 127.   [3] Id. II. 178, 179.

Nor is the relation of the objectified will to the intelligible will that of mode to substance, as in the philosophy of Spinoza. The presentation is said to be *gewordene Wille*,[1] and yet the will is not its cause. But while the will as intelligible is not in the causal series, the will as phenomenal is an effect among other effects.) In his criticism of the Kantian philosophy Schopenhauer says:—

Wenn von Ursach und Wirkung geredet wird, darf das Verhältniss des Willens zu seiner Erscheinung (oder des intelligibeln Charakters zum empirischen) nie herbeigezogen werden, wie hier geschiet; denn es ist vom Kausalverhältniss durchaus verschieden.[2]

II. *The Will as Phenomenon.* The will is not only *Ding an sich*. It is likewise phenomenon in space and time. Individual acts of the will are presentations (*Vorstellungen*) and so belong to the empirical or phenomenal world. Man is the most perfect manifestation of the will, and in man the will comes to full self-consciousness. The relation of will to intellect is that of *Ding an sich* to phenomenon, and so Schopenhauer ascribes what he calls primacy to the will over the intellect. Spinoza is criticised by Schopenhauer because he affirmed that will is an act of thought, an intellectual affirmation or denial. Schopenhauer takes an opposite view. It is will which is the original and primitive; knowledge is a phenomenon of will and its instrument. Man does not become what he is by means of knowledge. Will

[1] Schopenhauer, II. 199.   [2] Id. II. 601.   Cf. Id. I. 133–135.

makes him what he is, and knowledge is only the manifestation of will.[1] The intellect is the instrument of the will, just as the hammer is an instrument of the smith.[2]

The subject knows itself as willing, but not as knowing. *I know* is an analytic proposition, while *I will* is synthetic; for it cannot be said, I know that I know. I will is a datum of experience; and there are many gradations of will, from the mildest inclination to the most passionate resolve. The identity of the subject which knows, with the subject which wills, is something which cannot be explained; it is *der Weltknoten.*

Die Identität nun aber des Subjekts des Wollens mit dem erkennenden Subjekt, vermöge welcher (und zwar nothwendig) das Wort " Ich " beide einschliesst und bezeichnet, ist der Weltknoten und daher unerklärlich.

But personal identity is founded on the identical will and its unchangeable character: im Herzen steckt der Mensch, nicht im Kopf.[3]

Will is not peculiar to man. There is blind, impulsive will in the lower animals, but in man it comes to consciousness. It is not connected with any particular part of the body, but is everywhere present. It is not consciousness but will which constitutes the essence of the animal soul. The latter remains after the body perishes; but intellect depends for its existence on the body.

III. *The Will in Relation to the Principle of Sufficient Reason.* As phenomenon, but not as

---

[1] Schopenhauer, III. 224.   [2] Id. III. 253.   [3] Id. I. 143.

noumenon, the will is subject to the principle of sufficient reason. Schopenhauer's treatise on this subject is fundamental to his whole philosophy. The principle is especially related to his doctrine of motive.

As there is a reason for everything, the most important of all scientific questions is expressed in the word *why*. Why, says Schopenhauer, is the mother of all the sciences.[1] In it is implied the principle of sufficient reason. This principle he states in the form adopted by Wolff: *Nihil est sine ratione cur potius sit quam non sit* (Nothing is, without a reason why it is rather than is not).[2] All our knowledge implies a subject which knows and an object which is known. To be object for the subject, and to be presentation (*Vorstellung*), is one and the same. All presentations are objects for the subject; and, conversely, all objects for the subject are presentations. All our presentations stand in relation to one another in a regular determinate union (*Verbindung*), according to *a priori* forms. Nothing in our knowledge is independent and separable. The principle of this union is that of sufficient reason. The expression of this principle varies with different classes of objects. The principle is the same, but its root varies.[3]

.1. *Principle of Sufficient Reason of Becoming* (*principium rationis sufficientis fiendi*). Here it appears as the law of causality. It is applicable exclusively to changes, and to nothing else. Every change is an effect, and every cause is an effect of

[1] Schopenhauer, I. 4.　　[2] Id. I. 5.　　[3] Id. I. 27.

some previous cause.   The series has no beginning.
There has been much sophistry concerning the
definition of cause.   Many difficulties are removed,
according to Schopenhauer, if it be shown that it
is not an antecedent object which constitutes a
cause, but the condition as a whole which precedes
any event or change: —

Bei genauerer Betrachtung hingegen finden wir, dass der
ganze Zustand die Ursache des folgenden ist, wobei es im
Wesentlichen einerlei ist, in welcher Zeitfolge seine Bes-
timmungen zusammengekommen seien.

Ganz falsch hingegen ist es, wenn man nicht den Zustand,
sondern die Objekte Ursache nennt.[1]

Cause brings nothing new into being; it involves
only change in that which has continuous existence.
The law is known *a priori;* it is transcendental and
valid for all possible experience.   Given a first relative condition, a second determinate condition must
follow according to a rule.   The relation is a necessary relation.   There is a succession in time usually
to be observed, with the cause as antecedent, and the
effect, as consequent; but sometimes the sequence
is so rapid that it can hardly be said which is cause
and which effect.   In opposition to Kant and Hegel,
Schopenhauer declares that the category of reciprocity (*Wechselwirkung*) has no meaning.   It rests
on the misconception that the effect is part of the
cause.

Aus dieser wesentlichen Verknüpfung der Kausalität mit
der Succession folgt wieder, dass der Begriff der Wechselwirkung, strenge genommen, nichtig ist.   Er setzt nämlich

<hr>

[1] Schopenhauer, I. 35.

voraus, dass die Wirkung wieder Ursach ihrer Ursach sei, also dass das Nachfolgende zugleich das Vorhergehende gewesen.[1]

It is the previous condition in point of time which constitutes the cause. There are three species of causality: (1) cause in the narrow sense; (2) stimulus (*Reiz*); and (3) motive. In the first of these, the effect seems to be proportionate to the cause. The second is the cause which operates in the organic world, and in this case there is no proportion necessarily between the cause and its effect. The medium of motive, which is the third species, is knowledge, and intellect is implied in its action.[2]

(According to Schopenhauer, Locke entertained two false conceptions with respect to causality. He taught that the action of the will on the body was one type of causality, and that the other type was the resistance offered by the body to objects external to it. Schopenhauer agrees with Hume in denying these propositions, and he holds that there is no causal nexus between the act of the will and the movement of the body. The movement of the body is the actualization of the will. They are immediately one and the same act, which is perceived in a twofold way,— by self-consciousness as an act of will, and by external intuition as an act of body.) Resistance as a sensation is not an objective intuition, but merely a feeling which of itself gives no idea of causality. That the resistance is attributed to an external something implies, but does not originate, the conception of

---

[1] Schopenhauer, I. 41, 42.   [2] Id. I. 46 f.

causality. It is motive which differentiates the will in man from that in the lower animals.

Schopenhauer's whole theoretical discussion of the human will, and its relation to the intelligible will which he regards as the first principle of the world, shows that the Third Antinomy of the Kantian philosophy forms the essential centre of all such discussion. (At the root of Schopenhauer's determinism is his scepticism with respect to the knowledge of the reason. It was an appeal to reason which saved the absolute philosophers from reaching a like deterministic conclusion. But if all our knowledge is in the form of presentation, then every event known must be known as causally determined. Any appeal to an intelligible freedom is an appeal to something which is an illusion. The freedom ascribed by Schopenhauer to the will as *Ding an sich* is simply an activity which has no particular direction and no particular meaning. The only will which is known to us is a determined will.

From this statement of the principle of sufficient reason, it appears that the motive is the necessary cause of the act of the will. The motive is that without which there would be no volition. In what way the effect is produced, we do not know. It is a mystery. But our knowledge of the action of the will is more intimate than our knowledge of the action of external objects, because the motive acts through cognition. Motivation is causation viewed from within. In so far as there is voluntary control and direction of knowledge, it is because of the identity of the knowing with the willing subject. In knowledge which is controlled by will, the sequence is so rapid that we do not distinguish the cognition from the volition: —

Die Thätigkeit des Willens hiebei ist jedoch so unmittelbar, dass sie meistens nicht ins deutliche Bewusstsein fällt; und so schnell dass wir uns bisweilen nicht ein Mal des Anlasses zu einer also hervorgerufenen Vorstellung bewusst werden, wo es uns dann scheint, als sei Etwas ohne allen Zusammenhang mit einem Andern in unser Bewusstsein gekommen.[1]

Thus every image which comes before consciousness is due to an act of will, which act has a motive; although neither motive nor volition may have attracted notice.

Motives do not determine that I shall will, but only what I shall will.[2] The fact that the will as *Ding an sich* is not subject to the principle of sufficient reason, has led to the belief that there is freedom of the will.[8] Every man thinks beforehand that he is free, and that in any given past case he might have willed differently; but *a posteriori* he must admit that his volitions have been determined by motives. Acts of the will in so far as they are known are controlled by causes, and so are necessarily determined. While the principle of sufficient reason does not control my will as intelligible, that is, as *Ding an sich*, it controls necessarily the manifestations of my will.[4] The only freedom is the action of the will in general; the particular direction is absolutely determined. It is not neces-

1 Schopenhauer, I. 143–146. 8 Id. II. 133–135.
2 Id. II. 127. 4 Id. II. 195, 320.

sary that the motive should be clearly before consciousness, but the intelligible will works freely in organic processes, and in the instinct of animals. Freedom is a negative conception; it is a conception of action in the absence of the principle of sufficient reason. It is not only because the will is thing in itself that man is persuaded of his freedom. The conflict of motives within him gives him such an impression; but in reality the strongest motive always triumphs, and is the cause of the volition.[1]

Character is an expression of the will, and when once the will has been expressed in a man's character, the latter cannot be changed.[2] Variations in the will are effected by changes in the motive, and these are effected by various kinds of knowledge and different degrees of certitude. But persuasion does not change the character or the will. It may change the means which are to be willed for a certain end, but the character remains constant. The will cannot be taught, and so virtue is not teachable. It is therefore absurd for a man to will to be other than he is.[3] It is no argument in favor of freedom for a man to assert that he can do what he will. Freedom of the will is not to be confounded with physical or intellectual freedom.[4] An appeal to consciousness is not sufficient to establish the freedom of the will. Self-consciousness is not broad enough to give us the exact truth concerning the relation of the particular volition to the motive

[1] Schopenhauer, II. 336–341.   [2] Id. II. 347.   [3] Id. II. 361.
[4] Id. IV. 3–9 (Die Freiheit des Willens).

and the character upon which it depends. While
the volition itself is given in self-consciousness,
the conditions of the volition are not given. The
act of will is first known as a movement of body.)
There is no possibility of any of man's volitions
being other than it is. The supposed possibility
arises from the conflict of motives and desires.
Which of the conflicting principles is triumphant
can be known only after the fact of volition.
The possibility of alternate courses is a possibility
which is delusive:—

Ich kann thun was ich will: ich kann, wenn ich will,
Alles was ich habe den Armen geben und dadurch selbst,
einer werden,—wenn ich will!—Aber ich vermag nicht, es
zu wollen; weil die entgegen stehenden Motive viel zu viel
Gewalt über mich haben, als dass ich es könnte.[1]

In thus including all conscious volitions in the
same class with natural phenomena, Schopenhauer
rejects definitely the doctrine of freedom, and
leaves no escape to those who would find in
the character a self-determining principle. The
variety of effects which similar motives will produce on different men is ascribed to differences
in character. Yet character is not known beforehand, but only empirically. It is innate, and, as
has been said, cannot be changed.[2] If we say that
character is formed freely through acts of will, we
make all explanation of it impossible. To suppose
that the will is free is to suppose a miracle; for
every uncaused event is a miracle. As for the

---

[1] Schopenhauer, IV. 43 (ib.). [2] Id. II. 357.

z

common consciousness of mankind, its affirmation that we are free has no force with Schopenhauer, who holds that the ordinary understanding is incompetent to grasp the truth of either idealism or determinism.[1]

Schopenhauer's view of necessity need not be extensively considered, for, from what has been said, it is plain that everything and every event which is related to sufficient reason is necessary, and so contingency is a negative idea. Nor need the moral aspects of his doctrine be discussed, except in so far as to say that his pessimism led him to oppose the principles of Kant's *Practical Philosophy*. He finds a contradiction in saying that man is under obligations to will in any particular way; and so far from accepting the fact of freedom as a postulate of morality, he would prefer to deny the possibility of morality, and so find the determinism of the will in harmony with his principles of ethics.

That which moves the will in the lower animals is impulse, and there is no motive in the true sense. In man the motives lie in thought; and thus the will acts according to choice. In human action there may be intention and purpose, with deliberation according to a plan and according to maxims: —

Wenn gleich die Handlungen des Menschen mit nicht minder strenger Nothwendigkeit, als die der Thiere erfolgen; so ist doch durch die Art der Motivation, sofern sie hier aus Gedanken besteht, welche die Wahlentscheidung

---

[1] Schopenhauer, IV. 45-47.

(d. h. den bewussten Konflikt der Motive) möglich machen,
das Handeln mit Vorsatz, mit Ueberlegung, nach Planen,
Maximen, in Uebereinstimmung mit andern u. s. w.[1]

2. *Principle of Sufficient Reason of Knowing*
(*principium rationis sufficientis cognoscendi*). This
refers to the truth that all knowledge implies a
reason from which it is a consequence. The forms
of this root of the principle are the fundamental
laws of identity, contradiction, and excluded middle.[2]

3. *Principle of Sufficient Reason of Being* (*principium rationis sufficientis essendi*). This refers to
the ground or reasons of arithmetical and geometri-
cal propositions. For example, the relation of the
angles in a triangle is a principle of the relation
of the sides of the triangle.[3]

4. *Principle of Sufficient Reason of Acting* (*principium rationis sufficientis agendi*). This refers to
the immediate object of the inner sense. This is
the subject of volition, which is object for the
knowing subject.[4]

IV. *The Denial of the Will.* Near the close of
his principal treatise, Schopenhauer suggests a way
by which the will may be freed from subjection to
the principle of sufficient reason, so that a general
quietive of volition (*ein allgemeines Quietiv*)[5] may
be possible. (Having shown that the will as phenomenon is determined by motives, that the object
of the will, even when attained, does not afford

<hr>

[1] Schopenhauer, I. 97.   [2] Id. I. 105, 106.   [3] Id. I. 131, 133.
[4] Id. I. 140.   [5] Id. II. 477.

satisfaction, and that the character cannot be changed, he teaches that a recognition of the will as *Ding an sich*, apart from the principle of individuation, will free the individual from the control of motives, and that the latter will cease to be active and effective. This is the cancellation of the motive and of the character in so far as their influence on the volitions is concerned. He compares such a result to the effect of regenerative grace in the doctrine of Christian theology. This is, in his opinion, the only true freedom of the will :—

sie tritt erst ein, wenn der Wille, zur Erkenntniss seines Wesens an sich gelangt, aus dieser ein Quietiv erhält und eben dadurch der Wirkung der Motive entzogen wird, welche im Gebiet einer andern Erkenntnissweise liegt, deren Objekte nur Erscheinungen sind.[1]

This is the self-cancellation (*Selbstaufhebung*) of the will. It is not explained, however, under what conditions such a self-cancellation is possible. There is no regenerative grace vouchsafed to effect this change of knowledge, and we are left in doubt as to whether the object of the volition in the will to deny the will may not be as elusive as the phenomenal object after which the will has striven, but which it has failed to attain.

LOTZE

It has been said that Lotze's philosophy cannot be systematically stated; and it must be admitted

[1] Schopenhauer, II. 478.

that his doctrines are suggestive rather than con-vincing.   His indebtedness to Herbart is often evident, especially in the importance which he attaches to psychology.

I. *The Soul and its Faculties.*   Among all people there is a tendency to believe in a psychical unity, as opposed to the mere variety of phenomena. This belief tends also to separate the soul from the ordinary course of nature, and to attribute to it a self-determining energy.   It is an immaterial substance, and from its nature proceed the phenom-ena of knowledge (*Vorstellung*), feeling, and will. These are progressively developed as the result of a reciprocity between the outer world and the soul's inner activity.   It is a mistake to think of the soul under material forms, or to make it a mere background or skeleton of psychical phenomena. It is rather the source of certain known properties. It is a centre of effects or activities, and is a sub-stance.   But whatever view be taken of the soul *per se*, scientific interest is confined to the known properties.   And the plainest way of regarding these properties is from the standpoint of mental faculties, a conception which is antiquated, and capable of being wrongly interpreted.[1]

It is not to be supposed that the faculties exist independent of any occasion of their exercise.   The theory of faculties rightly interpreted holds that the reason for the activity of every manifestation of the soul is the external stimulus.   Upon the

[1] Lotze, Medicinische Psychologie, Leipzig, 1852, 145–150; Mikrokosmus, I. 160.

occasion of such stimulus, the soul may choose between different and equally possible reactions in response. The different expressions of the soul in so responding do not depend on the nature of a given stimulus, but on the soul's original nature and capacities. A certain stimulation takes place, the soul is in a certain state of receptivity, and a third condition is the resultant of the two former conditions. For such an explanation, the theory of faculties is convenient. There are secondary disadvantages in this conception, and the hypothesis of faculties is somewhat barren. They are, however, sources of explanation (*Erklärungsquellen*) of the quality of their products: —

Die Seelenvermögen dagegen sind nicht aus Massverhältnissen psychischer Erscheinungen, sondern lediglich aus ihrer Qualität abstrahirt; sie konnen daher auch nur als Erklärungsquellen der Qualität ihrer Erzeugnisse gelten.[1]

II. *The Will.* Although we seem to have the power of moving our bodies, yet in this we are often deceived. To will is not to perform. The movement of our bodies is a part of the chain of mechanical phenomena of the world. Although our will is closely connected with these, the changes in the organism in connection with an act of will take place without our coöperation. Our own part in the process is to furnish points of departure (*Ausgangspünkte*) for these physical processes.[2] The soul is not like an artisan who has constructed the machine with which he performs his work, and

---

[1] Lotze, Medicinische Psychologie, 151.   [2] Id., ib. 288.

knows the reason and manner of its working. It is rather like one who has been taught by arbitrary rule to manipulate a mechanism, the structure and inner workings of which are unknown to him. The soul is not identical with the body, but is the master of the body: —

Das Verhältniss der Seele zu dem Leibe ist nie das der Identität, sondern stets das einer Herrschaft.[1]

There is a great variety in the responses of the soul to outward stimulus; and even if the latter did not occur, it is not to be supposed that the body would be motionless, as the condition of the nerves in the absence of such stimulus would doubtless give rise to movement. A variety of motions is produced, however, at the first moment of life. The stated repetition of these movements is an occasion for the development of voluntary activity. The co-ordination of motions occurs automatically, without our voluntary interference and without our consciousness. When the stimulus does not reach the soul itself, the action is reflex and mechanical. The reflex-motor actions are not psychical in origin, but purely mechanical. And too much stress must not be laid upon the *telos* which they seem to involve. The reflex movements are the letters of the alphabet, the elements of further teleologic activity. Having observed them in experience, the soul can combine them and imitate them. But it is to the advantage of the organism that they

---

[1] Lotze, Medicinische Psychologie, 289.

should be mechanical, in so far as they tend to the preservation of life and to defence:—

> Nur die Beherrschung eines gegebenen Mechanismus kann für die Seele von Werth sein, ihn selbst hervorzubringen und zu dirigen, würde nur eine lastige und überflüssige Erschwerung ihrer Aufgabe sein. Sind doch jene Bewegungen zum Theil dazu bestimmt, als heilende Reactionen schädliche Reize zu entfernen, oder als nützliche Triebe zur Erhaltung des Körpers mitzuwirken. Aber wie schlecht würde es in der That um unser Leben stehen, sollte die Ueberlegung es vertheidigen, und nicht der Mechanismus.[1]

This passage was written some years before the appearance of von Hartmann's *Philosophy of the Unconscious*, and the question of a non-mechanical but still unconscious activity in reflex phenomena is not raised.

In automatic movements, like playing the piano, the movements follow one another so rapidly that it is inconceivable that they should be directed or controlled by specific independent acts of will. In such automatic processes, the soul exercises an act of will at the beginning, while the succeeding steps take place mechanically. In certain pathological conditions movements take place with apparent purpose, when any psychical control is out of the question.[2]

Many crimes likewise have an automatic genesis, when there is no train of feeling sufficiently strong to oppose them. The act takes place without real deliberation or conscious volition. The transition from idea to act is immediate. This does not free

---

[1] Lotze, Medicinische Psychologie, 291, 292.
[2] Id., ib. 293, 294.

the agent from responsibility, because the idea of the crime should have been resisted at an earlier stage. But this does not apply to the insane. It is only when the state of mind is intense; it is not when it is abnormal.

Wholly different from these elementary reflex phenomena are the voluntary employments of muscular contractility, by which the will accomplishes a purpose. Yet, like those acts already considered, they are only voluntary combinations of involuntary elements. The will's efficiency is limited to a certain self-chosen combination and succession in the production of those inner psychical conditions, as related to the origin of the movement: —

dass auch sie nur willkührliche Combinationen unwillkührlicher Elemente sind, oder selbstgewählten Verbindung und Reihenfolge jene innern psychischen Zustände erzeugen, an welche die Organisation die Entstehung der Bewegung geknüpft hat.[1]

Midway between reflex action and conscious and intentional acts of the will is the blind impulse. Motions which proceed from impulse seem to be neither mechanical nor conscious. Impulse does not reach its goal as the physical cause does, but is an endeavor to reach a given end. The only clear perception of this impulse is furnished in the conscious voluntary endeavor. It may be checked, and this gives rise to the feeling of effort: —

Aber eben dieser Begriff des Strebens hat seine einzige klare Anwendung, wo er identisch mit dem bewussten

---

[1] Lotze, Medicinische Psychologie, 296.

Wollen einer Seele gefasst wird; die übrige Welt der Ereignisse kennt nur ein Geschehen, das sich frei ent-wickelt, oder in solches, das in der Erreichung seines ihm sonst gewöhnlichen Erfolges gehindert wird, Der letztere Fall ist es, wo wir glauben, dass die gehemmte Kraft sich in ein Streben verwandle und gegen das Hinderniss einen Druck ausübe, den wir als eine absichtliche Anstrengung zu seiner Hinwegräumung deuten.[1]

When there are no obstacles, the effect of the will's action is not attended with effort. There is no more effort in the act of will than in the impulse which is actualized. All these feelings of resistance are purely physical in their origin. This serves to make the nature of the impulse more conceivable.

In every impulse there are three moments. The beginning of the impulse as a whole consists of certain bodily or mental occurrences (*Ereignisse*), as, for example, nervous activity, or ideas which may be a reason for motion. . If the soul were conscious of these, it would be conscious of them as disturbances only, but would not be awakened to impulse. A second moment is in the case of these occurrences awakening pleasure or pain; yet in this there is no essential element of impulse. The first excitation to impulse is the consciousness of a peculiar position in which the soul finds itself, like the *uneasiness* described by Locke. Experience has taught us what to do when this occurs. The peculiar feeling is removed by motion from the uneasy position. Inclination and disinclination

---

[1] Lotze, Medicinische Psychologie, 296.

are the result. These are characteristic of grow-
ing impulse (*Triebwerdens*), but are not impulse
itself. Thus impulses arise out of experience, and
ultimately are the result of feelings. Appetites,
such as hunger and thirst, are not impulses, but are
only disagreeable feelings of change in the nerves
which terminate in the intestine, by reason of certain deficiencies. In the lower animals the reaction
produced by these painful feelings is automatic.
This is true of certain higher feelings peculiar to
man. The poetic impulse has an automatic character, for it arises from a feeling which finds no
relief until it is satisfied, and yet its satisfaction
is not deliberate. The poetic impulse cannot be
exercised without experience.[1]

These impulses play a very prominent part in
our life. Impulsive actions are more common than
deliberate voluntary actions.

The act of will cannot be defined or explained.
It has to be experienced: —

Man wird nicht verlangen, dass wir den Act des Wollens
schildern sollen, der so einfach eine Grunderscheinung des
geistigen Lebens ist, dass er nur erlebt nicht erläutert
werden kann.[2]

There are, however, two mistaken views of this
act which must be corrected. One regards the will
as only a clear idea (*klare Vorstellung*); the other
concentrates it in a dense atmosphere of a capacity
to act. The first makes the will do nothing; the
second makes it do everything. I will does not
mean I shall; to will to be happy is different from

[1] Lotze, Medicinische Psychologie, 297–300. [2] Id., ib. 300.

a certain occurrence of happiness. One of these
mistaken conceptions confounds volition with the
thought of volition, while the other confounds volition with the bringing to pass of the thing which
has been willed:—

Wie nun die erwähnte Ansicht Wollen mit Vorstellen
des Gewollten, so verwechselt die andere Wollen und Voll-
bringen des Gewollten.[1]

That which accomplishes the volition is only
bodily organization carrying out the purpose of
the will, and this is a purely mechanical process.
While, on the one hand, the thought of a future
act is different from the actual volition, so, on the
other hand, the will simply removes such psychical
obstacles as stand in the way of setting in motion
the process of the body. We are brought back to
the idea of the will as point of departure (*Ausgang-
spunkt*), as already explained.

In dealing with the important question whether
the feeling of effort is of central or peripheral origin,
Lotze holds that what we feel in a voluntary effort
is the effect of the impulse on the termination of the
nerve in the muscle. And although each muscle
must have its own nerve terminations, yet the muscular feeling is a general one, like the sensation of
heat, and is so localized in the organism. The
feeling of effort, then, is not a feeling of the out-
going impulse, but of an effect of that impulse:—

Wir schliessen daher, dass es nicht der Willensimpuls,
sondern seine Folgen sind, die das Gefühl veranlassen.[2]

---

[1] Lotze, Medicinische Psychologie, 301.   [2] Id., ib. 310.

The will is not a function of the brain, but it is of purely mental origin. The common control of the various motor centres requires something more than a mere physiological unity.

Lotze defends a doctrine of the freedom of the will. There is a general belief that man has the freedom of self-determination,— that there is a free activity independent of the natural necessity which governs natural conditions. All our spiritual existence, all worth of our actions, and the value of our own personality, are connected with the idea of freedom. And yet it must be admitted that empirically we do not gain such a knowledge of freedom as the importance of the fact seems to demand. While many of our voluntary movements seem to be uncaused, yet most of them seem to depend on antecedent states of stimulation and irritation; so that reflection inclines us to the idea that the will must be determined. This is at variance with our moral conceptions with respect to the worth of our actions. But to make moral requirements the ground of an argument in favor of freedom is not sufficient, for there are those who make moral requirements the ground of an argument in favor of necessity. Furthermore, the close connection between states of body and states of mind increases this suspicion that the will is conditioned. Yet these mechanical antecedents do not at all account for the variety of our inner life, and so do not explain the determination of the will. Materialistic determinism is unthinkable. In any event the principle of the plurality of cause forbids

us to suppose that the mental effect is due directly
to a material cause.[1] It must also be considered
that the mind itself has properties. We are prone
to attribute to will many mental phenomena which
are really involuntary, such as the change of ideas
in consciousness from one subject to another. Most
changes in the direction of thought and feeling are
involuntary, and are due to impulse, not to will.
Active volition is comparatively rare; the prevailing principle of action is impulse from the senses,
or from the inner spiritual self. Impulse (*Trieb*)
is not free, but mechanical. Will is not inclination, which is common to man and the lower animals.   It is free choice, and the conception of will
is almost coincident with that of freedom. The
fact of free will cannot be denied. But if we
attempt to defend it, or to reduce it to simpler
terms, this is found to be impossible. Lotze
opposes, on the one hand, the prejudice which
finds the freedom of the will inconsistent with the
order of nature; for freedom of the will does not
mean freedom to accomplish, and God, the author
of nature, is absolutely free. Nor does the invaria-
bility of causality interfere with the truth of free
will. So far from deducing determinism from the
law of causality, we should rather modify our law
of causality in order to reconcile it with the fact
of freedom.[2]

In his *Metaphysics*, Lotze characterizes the doctrine of determinism as an opinion of the scientific school (*Meinung der wissenschaftslichen Schule*),

---

[1] Lotze, Mikrokosmus, I. 162 ff.   [2] Id., ib. I. 286–289.

and holds that the common sense of mankind is a guarantee of the falsity of such a doctrine.[1] The spirituality of the soul implies the freedom of the will. Yet, while taking this position, he adds that too much emphasis must not be laid upon freedom, in case men lose the clew to the general course of ideas in the active consciousness. The course of nature in general determines the sphere of the will's activity. It is seldom that any individual is sufficient for solving the problems which the general feelings and thoughts of the mass present to him. The man of genius is not, however, the child of circumstances, but is one who through freedom overcomes circumstances. Thus, although human progress is slow, it is changed and furthered by the free voluntary acts of individual men.

Fechner, who was partly contemporary with Lotze, made a still bolder defence of freedom, which he sought to reconcile with an explicit pantheism. According to him the universe is composed of unextended atoms, which are simple in their constitution. The substantial being of both soul and body is made up of these atoms. God and the world are not substantially different, but are the inner and outer aspect respectively of the same being (*Wesen*). The world on the one hand is a mass of atoms, and on the other hand is a collection of individual self-conscious beings. But all the latter are comprehended in God, and every soul is immanent in the divine substance.[2] The

---

[1] Lotze, Metaphysik, 473.

[2] Fechner, Ueber die Seelenfrage, 204–210.

harmony between the individual and the divine will is sustained by an appeal to certain facts which Lotze had also noticed. Many of our thoughts and feelings, as well as actions, proceed not only independently of our will, but against our will. If we, as voluntary agents, have so many involuntary thoughts and feelings, *a fortiori* must this be true of God; and just as our involuntary acts are possible, so it is possible for beings which are immanent in God to will without his will, or even in opposition to his will. Freedom is as conceivable upon the supposition that the soul has its being in God, as if it is supposed to have an independent existence. And as our wills are not the same with the will of God, so God is not responsible for our misdeeds. As for the will of God, it accomplishes not what is best for certain men individually, but what is suitable for men collectively. To use the phraseology of Bentham, God wills "for the greatest happiness of the greatest number."

The theory of Lotze brings us virtually to contemporary philosophy. From about the middle of the present century, the activity in subjective psychology, the fruitful researches in the physiology of the brain and other parts of the nervous system, the restatement and new interpretation of the ancient doctrine of natural evolution, have opened new avenues, and have suggested new solutions of many of the older problems. It is not my intention to anticipate in any way conclusions which may hereafter be drawn with respect to the many points which this progress has brought into prominence. It is plain that no man can hope to defend his doctrines without justifying them, not at the bar of reason only, but also at the tribunal of positive science. For this reason, the work done by Kant must not be forgotten, and yet the work done by Kant must be done over again in a new way. So long as there is a distinction drawn between reason and understanding, so that the conclusions of the latter are not valid in the domain of the former; so long as psychologists are willing to regard the soul as a creation and not a development; and so long as the moralist dictates what we shall think about freedom because of presuppositions as to what we ought to think about freedom, — so long must the way of progress lie through destructive criticism to a clearer recognition of the facts and laws of nature. It is to be hoped that the confusion which a speculative philosophy has occasioned in psychological science, having been partly removed, may eventually disappear.

2 A

INDEX OF NAMES